DEAN MARTIN

DEAN MARTIN
King of the Road

Michael Freedland

ROBSON

First published in Great Britain in 2004 by
Robson Books
151 Freston Road
London
W10 6TH

An imprint of Anova Books Company Ltd

ISBN 1 86105 882 9

10 9 8 7 6 5 4 3 2

Printed and bound by Creative Print and Design (Ebbw Vale), Wales

This book can be ordered direct from the publisher
Contact the marketing department, but try your bookshop first

www.anovabooks.com

For Fiona and Robin, Dani and Dave, Jonathan and Sarah – who have grown up so brilliantly in the years since I first started dedicating books to them.

Contents

Acknowledgements

Dean Martin was quite an entertainer – and quite a surprising one. I met him a number of times. I saw him at work in Las Vegas and in London and, more significantly, I saw the way he had with people – and how people reacted to him. All that came out in the number of people interviewed for this book and for the BBC Radio Two series that preceded it.

I first wrote a biography of Dean Martin twenty years ago, a time when, for legal reasons, there was much that could not be written about him, particularly about his relationships with Frank Sinatra and the Mob. These restrictions ceased to apply after his death. Also, his life changed radically in his last years. For these reasons, I thought it sensible for this new approach to the story of the man known to his friends – and his public – as Dino. And there is also another reason. As I have explained in this book, amazingly, his fame and his popularity remain as strong as ever, a fact to rock the rock generation and those that have followed them.

I am extraordinarily grateful to Hollywood-based British journalist Barbra Paskin for interviews – originally conducted for the radio series – with Mrs Jeanne Martin, Ms Gail Martin Downey, Peter Graves, Shecky Greene, Alan Livingstone, Greg Garrison (to whom I also spoke) and, not least, with Jerry Lewis, giving his first insights into his former partner Dean Martin for many years. I spoke to Jerry, too, in London. Barbra is always such a wonderful help.

Among the other people I have cause to thank (although, alas, many are no longer with us) are: Joey Bishop, George Burns, Abby Greshler, Sammy Cahn, Dan Defore, Polly Bergen, Janet Leigh, Nina Foch, Wilfrid Hyde White, John Anderson, Elke Sommer, Tina Louise, Walter Scharf, Hal B Wallis, Billy Wilder, Albert Salmi, Sammy Davis Jnr, John Wayne (in a previous interview), Ruta Lee, George 'Bullets' Durgan, George Cukor, Cyd Charisse, Jack Rose, Melville Shavelson, Hal Kanter and Arthur Marx. To those people, who wished the subject of this book only well, my profound thanks.

Above all, my thanks to my dearest wife, Sara, who tolerates so very much.

MICHAEL FREEDLAND
Bournemouth, 2004

Prologue

Dean Martin had a hit record called 'Memories Are Made of This'. But what was 'this'? If you could answer that question as easily as you could ask it, you would have unravelled a secret – the reason why, years after his death in the previous century, the name Dean Martin still conjures up pictures that bring smiles to the faces of people who continue to go into record stores to buy his records, why Dean Martin tunes are being downloaded from the Internet and why, all those years later, he sums up a relaxed style that today's rock singers wouldn't begin to understand.

'This' was indeed a remarkable man, but a man with a mass of contradictions. He was never happier than when at home or playing on the golf course. Yet he travelled widely, and all over the world he would always be greeted by adoring friends. *King of the Road*

He made a sensational living by talking and singing about all the drink he consumed. Yet most of the evidence seems to indicate that, until a horrendous tragedy upset his entire life, he was never even slightly intoxicated. 'Oh, I love to drink,' he would say, 'but I'm never drunk.' And he'd list the drinks he loved . . . whisky and soda, a Martini, 'anything'. To countless fans and observers, Dean was seen as the perfect representation of the philosophy 'wine, women and song'. It was how people saw Dean Martin's attitude to life. How did *he* see it? 'Women and song? I'm not so crazy about wine.

I love to sing and I love women.' You could have written that on Dean's tombstone, except that it would have been a too light-hearted attitude to his death. *Mr Booze*

'This' was a ladies' man. Nobody doubts that. It was part of his appeal. It was what made women swoon when he went on stage, why they queued to see his movies, why they sent for autographs, why they had his photograph over their beds. A ladies' man, but not a womaniser – although one man would claim to have seen letters from women who claimed to have been made pregnant by him (at least a hundred of them). A womaniser? Not according to the one woman to whom he went home every night of almost every week – the woman he married, divorced and then, after a short new marriage, went back to. They were never to remarry, but neither of them ever thought there was a need to do so. They had one marriage, signed one lot of papers, there was no need for more. Love was pretty powerful with him. *Everybody loves somebody sometime*

'This' was a city boy, born in Steubenville, a steel town in Ohio, a place with other tough city boys who thought nothing of solving their problems with fists that were frequently mangled in the steel mills. Yet he loved the West, loved riding a horse and singing Western songs like 'Houston'. He enjoyed the countryside, which could get him all philosophical. *Little green apples*

'This' was a loner whom even people who considered themselves his friends never got to know properly, who never even went into the office of his TV producer. Yet 'this' was also the man who achieved amazing success – so amazing that nobody ever imagined he could survive its ending – as the partner of a comedian whose name would for years always be linked with his. The contradictions are so strong that, to this day, there are debates as to who was responsible for their break-up. *Pardners*

'This' was the man who refused to rehearse for his TV shows – at least, in any conventional sense. Just so long as there was a golf course at hand, he had a place to sing his songs. The picture in the mind of those privileged few who knew him is of a fellow who was never happier than when lying on a couch watching TV. So was he lazy? Not according to the folks who worked with him. It was just that their own definition of perfectionism was not his. He was the most punctual man that the people at NBC knew. That was just the way he did it.

The immaculate Dino would have had little truck with today's entertainers with their long unkempt hair, jeans and sports shirts. For him, that was the outfit you wore at home, at a barbecue or visiting friends (which, of course, he rarely did). On stage, there was always a tuxedo that cost up to about $3,000 a throw (and he had a dozen of them), a superbly pressed shirt, a bowtie and a red handkerchief in his breast pocket. That was his uniform. No one else wore the red handkerchief – he regarded that as his own identification mark, rather in the way that a lead dancer would always dress slightly differently from the girls in the chorus. It was his . . . *Style*

'This' was a man who summed up an old-fashioned view of America and Americanism. He wasn't terribly political, but Ronald Reagan never had a more devoted follower (or insulter, if you took account of what happened at his famous 'roasts', in which he mercilessly ribbed willing celebrities). He wrapped himself in the Stars and Stripes. And yet, much of his heart was in Italy. If his fellow performer Tony Bennett left his heart in San Francisco, the man who was known as Dino left his in Rome. 'Point the Italian,' he'd tell people, speaking of himself like some historical character in the third person. *Arrivederci Roma*

'This' was a man who knew where it all came from, who knew the source of his first inspiration – Bing Crosby. If Dino's two thousand records (twelve of them platinum) could really be put down to that,

Crosby had a lot to plead guilty to. As Dino explained: 'I just loved to sing when I was small. I just sang. I never missed a Bing Crosby picture when I was young . . .' From there, it just escalated into a career of his own. He knew that he was in good company with that: 'As most of us did, Frank and Perry Como, they'll tell you the truth that everybody copied Bing and in time they developed their own star. But it was the man Bing who started it all. Rock is out with me. I can't stand rock but I like nice easy smooth singing.' *I wish I could sing like Bing*

'This' was a man who was known as the wittiest man in showbiz, who made his name with a routine called 'Sex and Slapstick'. But he was also a remarkably strong actor, more consistent perhaps than his fellow Rat Packer Frank Sinatra. Watching a Martin performance in movies like *The Young Lions* and *Some Came Running* could be an overwhelming experience. And it helped him create a public for his work, millions who experienced what was part of a love affair between them and him. *That's amore*

And for all those things, 'this' was a man who will not be easily forgotten. *Memories are made of this*

That's My Boy 1

They came in their millions – in ships that had already been condemned as unseaworthy, in conditions that defied most of the rules of human dignity. Mothers breastfed babies surrounded by vomiting elderly men. Young married couples made love amid dirty-faced children, picking their way through the holds, gasping for air one moment, chasing and fighting the next. Middle-aged women tried to create meals from practically nothing in conditions of indescribable filth.

The languages varied according to the port of embarkation. In one ship, the Eisenhower family spoke to their fellow passengers only in German. In others, the tongue was essentially Yiddish. A young Asa Yoelson – within a decade to become Al Jolson – and an even younger Israel Baline – he would call himself Irving Berlin – knew no other way of conversing with the others on board before their ships docked in New York.

The Kennedy family had no language problems when they arrived from Ireland, but the new world beckoned to them with as much fear as hope. From Italy, the Sinatra and Como families paced the decks in wonder, one moment consulting the priest who had come over with them, the next asking themselves if the decision they had taken had been right. On another such boat Gaetano Crocetti was planning the exciting future he was convinced was just ahead of him. He was young, barely nineteen, with the respectable trade of a barber already firmly in his grasp and he had made up his mind that he was going to be an American with an American name. Almost immediately after his arrival that day in 1913, he called himself Guy.

But there were formalities to settle first. The Statue of Liberty, with its message of welcome from Emma Lazarus to the 'huddled masses, yearning to breathe free', was more than just a monument. It was a symbol – and a warning. Horrendous stories had swept back to the ghettos and hamlets of Europe of families being sent home after going to a mysterious island that was either America – or wasn't. It was a convenient mystery to the immigration department that had set up Ellis Island as a spot on earth that was of America but not in it. If a prospective immigrant was discovered to have TB or glaucoma or an incurable skin disease, anything that would make him either a health risk to his new neighbourhood or a drain on local services, he was sent back from whence he came – as far as the men sitting behind inhibitingly high desks were concerned, they not only had never been in the United States at all, they hadn't existed.

Crocetti had no fear of that, and neither did the doctors or immigration men who examined him. His health was robust. His skill as a barber – and the Italians were regarded as the best – meant that he would work hard.

But where? New York was where everyone was going. It was the port of entry and most of the immigrants had no desire after their long journey to go much further. But there were others who had heard about spots on the map that seemed more like home.

Whether Guy Crocetti believed that Steubenville, Ohio, was just like Abruzzi, his own patch of central Italy, is a matter for conjecture. Two brothers had settled there before him, so it was obvious he would join them. The trouble was that they had been there for so long, he thought he would no longer remember what they looked like. Neither did he know their addresses. It was only moments after getting off the bus, walking through the first street in which he found himself, that he saw a face he thought he might know.

'*Eh – tu sei Guiseppe?*'

Guiseppe Crocetti it was. '*Si,*' he replied. '*Eh – tu sei Gaetano?*'

They had exchanged recognition, names – and huge bear hugs. Gaetano had come home. It was a good omen. Steubenville was one of America's steel towns, just a stone's throw – by American terms, that is, more likely a guided catapulted stone's throw – away from Pittsburgh and itself the home of the Weirton and Wheeling steel mills.

Before long, Guy found himself a job – and a girl from an Italian family. Angela Barra was studying in a convent. Within two weeks, they decided they were wildly in love and got married. Guy couldn't speak English, Angela couldn't speak Italian, but her parents had come over from the old country just before her birth and she would learn, so it became their natural language of conversation.

Guy was making thirty dollars a week when, in 1914, Angela gave birth to their first son. In keeping with the Crocettis' new spirit of being Americans – a spirit that still did not include the necessity of speaking anything but Italian – they gave him what they considered to be a typical American name, William. For ever afterwards he would be called Bill. Three years later, their second son arrived. There were fewer inhibitions now about keeping to the traditions of their origins. He was named Dino – Dino Paul.

No one would call the Crocettis rich. But in the early Twenties they did have a car of sorts, the kind where you never heard the engine because everything rattled so loudly. Dino himself had a bicycle, which had probably belonged to two or three other boys before it reached him, but was his own, nevertheless. By the time his father had become what Dino years later was to say was a 'very successful barber', they were well established in the community.

Mama Crocetti's meatballs and spaghetti were well enough known for people to try to obtain invitations to her table whenever possible. There is good reason to think that this just summed up the spirit of a town that had a reputation for being 'wide open' – with enough illegal gambling to give it the sobriquet of 'Little Chicago' (no one had yet heard of Las Vegas).

By the time he got to tenth grade at the local school, Dino decided he knew more than his teachers, and left. It was an event that, despite all the future bravado, would haunt him for years, prompting what seems a totally unnecessary inferiority complex.

It may not have been hell's kitchen, but there was no better way for a boy from an Italian family to stake his claim in Steubenville society than with his fists. Dino decided to take up boxing as a career. Because few people at the time bothered to analyse the meaning of words, there seemed nothing terribly wrong with the fourteen-year-old Dino Crocetti describing himself at the time as an 'amateur prizefighter'.

His prizes weren't that great and nor was his fighting. But it was something to do and he thought it earned him the respect of the other kids in the neighbourhood. What earned even more was his adeptness at petty theft – hubcaps from cars, ties from shops. 'There wasn't much else to do, except a little stealing,' he'd recall years later – and with no noticeable sense of shame either, as if it were very much part of the way of life for an Italian boy in Steubenville, Ohio. Which it was. The culture in his home town was centred around work at the steel mill, women who were easy lays, cheap illegal booze and fights between rival gangs. As Dean's future wife, Jeanne, would say about the Crocetti crowd in Steubenville: 'Italians from that kind of environment are not sitting around discussing Shakespeare and reading poetry.'

James Cagney once told me of a whole collection of boys with whom he played in New York who ended up in the 'hoosegow'. In Ohio, there were more than a few tongues wagging that the Crocettis' younger son was likely to have a similar fate. Or worse. As he once sang in a parody of himself: 'Back home in Steubenville, they're doubting all this I swear. They're still betting six-to-five I get the chair.'

Indeed, from the time he left school, his aunts were warning Mama Crocetti that young Dino was going to end up on Death Row. 'You're crazy,' she would reply. 'My son's gonna end up a star.' She had heard Dino sing – and thought there was something very sweet about the sounds that he made.

But for the moment, he was a boxer. Dino the welterweight gave a few older fighters time for pause. When he was a little more established, he had a name for himself: 'Kid Crochet'. Occasionally, he even came away with twenty-five dollars for a successful bout. Even so, protective Italian families rarely relish the idea of their sons getting bashed to pieces in the ring. Papa Crocetti gave Dino five dollars to enrol in the local barbers' school. Not only was he keen on his son following in his own footsteps – to any immigrant father who thinks he hasn't done at all badly for himself, the epitome of joy – but he knew it offered a sense of security. Dino thought otherwise. He had seen his father in his shop and the notion of clipping the sides of men's heads ten hours a day, six days a week was unnerving. Any mention from the local priest that this would be a nice honest way of settling down made him feel even worse. Dino had inherited his family's Catholicism. He prayed regularly to the Virgin Mary, but he was a lot more religious about making appearances at boxing matches than he was about attending Mass.

No one, however, should get the impression that young Dino was fighting and stealing simply because it was easier. He did try his hand at more honest and less dangerous forms of toil. He was a soda jerk in a local drugstore – and if he consumed as much ice cream as he dispensed, that was only for his boss to worry about. He worked in a filling station. The Steubenville people had a name for that. He was a gas jockey. Just before Franklin D Roosevelt came on the scene, Dino was doing his own little bit to maintain Steubenville's reputation as Little Chicago: he was humping bootleg booze around the town. At other times, he worked in one of the steel mills, bundling wire. He gave up when a bale of red-hot metal landed virtually on his feet. There were more comfortable ways of making a living – to say nothing of dying – even in those fringe years of the Great Depression.

But it was the fight game that seemed to offer most. If it mangled his hands to a degree that would still be evident half a century later –

his manager knew even less about binding hands under the gloves than he did, and he never forgave the man for his neglect – it was still better and more rewarding, it seemed, than other forms of work. When his nose was distinctly bent in a fight, he shrugged it off as part of growing up.

He possibly also thought it was of assistance in the necessary task of getting girls – although he really had little reason to worry. Despite the apparent extrovert nature of the fight, he was basically shy and quiet in company. But girls flocked to him like bluebottles to the barrels of beer he and the other bootleggers had delivered to the neighbourhood speakeasies. He was slim, with dark curly hair and with a large nose that, before it got bent, travelled to his forehead in a single sweep without a break at the top. Grecian, he called it, once he had learned the word. His nose and his hands weren't the only casualties of his chosen profession. Once, he broke his collar bone – not in a contest with another fighter, but with a punch ball. And any close look at his lips would reveal unusual cracks, further proof of the effects of the ring.

He worried in those days about his hands. It was the one reason he didn't jump at the chance when he was first offered a job in one of the local gambling joints. It was suggested that he might make a good croupier. When Dino found out what that meant, he held back. Show all those people his hands? The inferiority complex seemed for once to be backed by reason. It would take time before he became a lot more confident.

Dino was also worrying about another gap, as he saw it, in his personality. Not only would he have to show his hands to strangers, he would be expected to speak to strange women – and suddenly that notion held him in fear. Talking to the girls he met at the fights or the ones he had come across at the gas station was no great problem. Many of them were prostitutes in a town that was as rife with the practitioners of 'the oldest profession' as with the other elements that made Steubenville Little Chicago. But now he worried about the sheer exercise of conversation. It was all right to speak Italian at home – his parents still never spoke anything else – but the women he would meet in a gambling establishment were different. And, as he admitted years later, he couldn't be sure he was ever completing a sentence in correct English.

Eventually, he decided the time had come to make a change, and gambling seemed to offer the best opportunities. He was rarely making more than ten dollars a bout – occasionally having to be satisfied with an Ingersoll watch that he would sell for five or six dollars, and he would then have to split the proceeds with his manager, the one he resented for damaging his hands. If only for that, he was glad to get out of the business.

His father still wanted him to become a barber. But Dino was cute enough now to see the pressures of that job on his dapper, moustachioed papa, and he made up his mind not to let work be the ultimate factor in his life. With his last 'purse', Dino gave Mr Crocetti a fountain pen, and announced he was moving on.

Guy and his wife hadn't always known what their younger son was up to. They were liberal, Dino recalled years later, but not *that* liberal. He remained convinced that had they realised some of the trips he made to Canonsburg, Pennsylvania, were dedicated to carting around bootleg hooch, they would either have disowned him or collapsed in disgrace. Certainly, the priest would have been called in for advice.

It isn't certain whether, when he did reveal to them he had a job at the Rex cigar store in Steubenville, he told them the whole truth and nothing but the truth. He was offered a job at the Rex. He *did* accept a job at the Rex. But he wasn't picking Havanas out of boxes or offering shiny new briars to visiting worthies or providing scented cigarettes to the more well-to-do ladies of the area. His work was distinctly behind the counter – and behind closed doors. Just as speakeasies operated at the backs of establishments as varied as undertakers' parlours and coffee houses, so gambling was conducted as serious business behind other concerns. It was almost traditional that a tobacco store would have its gambling concession – perhaps because the smoky atmosphere fitted in perfectly with the merchandise out front; perfectly enough, certainly, for the local police to feel entirely justified in accepting 'protection' money that guaranteed there would be no unfortunate interruptions to the job in hand. Besides, it was a way of life in Steubenville. There was one gambling joint or another on practically every street corner.

Later, when Mrs Crocetti did hear about her son's activities, she was appalled. Gambling! It was sin incarnate. 'No, Mom,' he told her. 'I'm not gambling. The people who come into the store, they're the gamblers. I just move the stick around.'

He became 'stick man' and 'apron man' at the roulette tables. He was croupier on the blackjack tables. And he was good at it – no one appeared to notice that those mangled hands of his were also fairly slick at moving dollar bills up his own sleeves.

Dino was so proficient that word got around. He moved from cigar stores to local casinos like the High Hat Club and the Plantation. Word was that he was a young man to watch on the gambling circuit. So worth watching that it was to be hoped he would expand beyond the boundaries of Steubenville. The young wizard of the tables would say eventually that he was taken on as a croupier 'in self defence'. He had got to know so much about the way the games were operated, how the wheels spun, and cards were dealt and so on, that he had been 'beating the house at its own game'. So it was safer to have him join the operation than try to beat them.

He was 'loaned' out, much as Hollywood was loaning out contract players from one studio to the next. The money was earned by the employee, but it went to the original employer, who paid the usual salary. Dino wasn't sorry to do it. It was good experience. He was seeing more of the country than any Crocetti had previously imagined possible and he was building up his confidence – with girls in particular. He was also earning incredible money. Once in Florida – and he was still only nineteen – he clocked up $125 in a week, a veritable fortune in 1936; certainly as much as his father had ever earned in a month.

Grateful winning punters were adding to his total with three- or four-dollar tips every time their numbers came up. And so were the silver dollars he picked up without anyone knowing very much about it. He and a friend had a racket worked out. They would stand next to each other while dealing – and hand a few bills or coins to the partner in the process. Croupiers are supposed to clap their hands at the end of a dealing session – to prove they haven't any money in their palms. Dino became so proficient at this that he could have two silver dollars adhering to his hands and still clap them.

The picture remained much the same for the next five years. His motto might well have been 'Have Tuxedo Will Travel'. He went where the money was. Florida, West Virginia, Washington, DC. And people got to know him. They liked his casual approach to a very serious game – which they knew was deceptive – without always understanding his motives. They enjoyed his personality.

They also discovered he had something more to offer than most of the other croupiers or the men with the big sticks. While dealing the blackjack cards, the handsome dark-haired Dino could be heard humming. After a short time, he found the courage to turn the hum into words. He would sing softly to himself. Before long, wives and girlfriends were persuading punters to play on Crocetti's table. They said they thought that the songs would bring them luck. More truthfully, they thought his voice sounded sexy.

A gambling establishment is a highly organised small community, where everyone knows precisely what is going on. They have to. In a business where it is practically unheard of for the operators to go bust for the benefit of their clientele, every movement is recorded in the back office. The message had struck his employers – and the people who frequented their places of business. It was a fact particularly noted by Ernie McKay, the leader of the band at Walkers Café, where Dino and a group of his fellow croupiers would sometimes go at the end of their shift. They would have a few drinks, fool around with the waitresses and then when he felt sufficiently relaxed, Dino would go on to the bandstand and act as the semi-resident vocalist. Everything he sang sounded like an imitation of Bing Crosby, then merely on the verge of a sensational career in which for two or three generations he would be top of everyone's pops in America.

Dino denied then that he was deliberately trying to sound like Bing. But as he said years later: 'I copied Bing Crosby one hundred per cent. I wasn't alone. Frank Sinatra and Perry Como did, too. They'll tell you they did if you ask them. I bought all Bing's records.'

McKay liked what he heard and finally offered Dino a job. Fifty dollars a week, he promised him. To most youngsters in America at the time, it would have sounded like a gift from heaven. But, as he recalled many years later, Dino was not impressed. 'Hell,' he said with a degree of innocence that would before long endear him to audiences thousands of miles from Steubenville, 'I steal more than that every week.'

But the temptation of a different life doing something he enjoyed as much as singing was strong. He accepted, and the career of Dino Crocetti was on its way. Or rather, as it turned out, the career of Dino Martini – cousin of the star of the Metropolitan Opera, Nino Martini. Dino didn't know Nino, let alone was related to him, but McKay thought it was a good come-on line. Dino Martini sang with the band at Columbus, Ohio, and most of the dancers who moved to his singing seemed pleased that he did.

He stayed with McKay for about a month. But although he enjoyed the songs, he still felt uncomfortable in the company in which he moved. Whenever a girl spoke to him – and the more women he met now, the more sophisticated they appeared to be – he retreated into a self-constructed shell as though he were a snail meeting an unknown object on his trip down the garden path. He mumbled a few pleasantries when they approached him and hoped they would go away. Dino was simply frightened of what would come out of his mouth when he opened it. So he kept it closed.

He then decided he had had enough. He was going home to Steubenville. Back at the tables, he found that his former colleagues were not pleased to have him there. They had agreed among themselves that Dino's future lay as a singer, not as a croupier or even as a dealer. When he again raised the matter of money, they decided he was out of his mind – to the extent that three of them agreed to supplement his takings with contributions from their own 'palmed' profits at the casino. There was, however, a catch. They demanded a share in the profits of any future Dino Martini career.

He went back to McKay at Columbus, where he was heard by another bandsman called Sammy Watkins. Watkins was one of those men who, to use the old aviation term, flew by the seat of his pants. There was a gut instinct that told him there was more about the fellow called Martini than a pleasant appearance. At the end of the evening, when the bandsmen picked up their music, stowed away their instruments, and Dino himself was ready to leap from the platform, Watkins approached him with an offer.

The next day, Dino penned his name on a contract that he didn't bother to read – a habit from which he would suffer recurrent symptoms in the years to come. What he had signed for was a singing engagement with Watkins's band at Cleveland, the biggest city in Ohio. He had also given the man options on his work for the next ten years – which unions in other occupations would have declared tantamount to slavery. But Dino signed. He also agreed to take a new name: Dean Martin.

Bells Are Ringing 2

Dino's metamorphosis into Dean Martin wasn't painless. Watkins was a tough bandleader who demanded two pounds of flesh for every one that other orchestras expected. Dean not only had to sound like Bing Crosby, he had to *be* Crosby and if occasionally the still immature Martin sounds didn't measure up, he was told so. He was on his feet all the time there were dancers on the floor and it was not as though he were really prospering.

The money was terrible. Fifty dollars a week – even with the occasional supplements from the boys in Steubenville, which were now drying up – sounded like big money to men on the breadline, but Dean was already used to what he thought was the high life. If his salary wasn't going far when he first arrived in Cleveland, before long it was going nowhere at all. Suddenly, Dean was not finding it as difficult to have attractive girls swarming around him as he had always imagined he would. He was dating regularly – with practically anyone he wanted lining up for his attentions. One of the girls was Elizabeth McDonald, daughter of a liquor manufacturer, a brunette with the kind of breasts and hips that made the Martin brain forget most of its doubts.

Her background was very different from his. Betty – as she inevitably was called – was Irish, he Italian; she had had a college education, he considered himself practically illiterate; her family was wealthy, the Crocettis were just about getting along, although they still considered themselves comfortable. But she thought he was marvellous, good-looking, funny, intensely masculine. Since he was equally enamoured of her, the decision to take Betty on a journey to Steubenville was only to be expected.

She may have anticipated walking through the door of the Crocetti home before they did anything else, but Dean had other ideas. He was shy. He needed moral support – and found it at the Rex cigar store where the gang who had staked his beginnings in show business were on hand to provide the necessary wolf whistles that Dean accepted as general approval. From the store, they moved on to the Crocettis. Guy kissed Betty warmly, Angela smiled and offered to make some spaghetti.

On 2 October 1940, 23-year-old Dino Paul Crocetti married Elizabeth McDonald at the Catholic Church of St Ann's in Cleveland – with a special dispensation to marry within twenty-four hours granted by the local bishop. Mrs Crocetti, senior, made her daughter-in-law's wedding dress. The band – who were at the ceremony in force – were due to move out of town and Dean wanted to be sure that the marriage ceremony could be held before they left.

Betty became a band wife and went where they went – not an easy thing to do when the band husband seems to regard his relationship with his spouse as less important than that with his buddies. But they had an obvious sexual compatability. And then, twenty-two months after their marriage, Betty gave birth to their first child, a son they named Craig.

They weren't easy days for the young couple. Betty wasn't cut out for show business. She would have preferred having her husband to herself and her child in the evening. But he was working every night. If she accepted that with equanimity, what he did after the dancing had finished was another matter. He stayed behind in his dressing-room, playing cards.

Sometimes the band went on tour, giving dancers in other parts of the States, and occasionally the border cities of Canada, an opportunity to hear what Cleveland took for granted. They weren't always noticeably delighted. But once in a while, there were people who saw him and thought he had something that the trade would have called 'superior'. If he hadn't enjoyed being so languid, he might have decided that for himself, but Dean didn't want pressures. There was no need to trouble himself about getting to work on time or bettering himself. It would just be too much like hard work at a period when he was basically quite happy – even if Betty wasn't.

But among the people who thought he *could* do better for himself were the ubiquitous agents who hung around dance halls and similar establishments, not seeking a good time themselves but with miserable expressions on their faces trying to work out what made other people happy. The band's own agent Merle Jacobs was aware of this and suggested that Dean might like to consider going his own way. Whether Dean had a good hand at that moment, or had a few more drinks inside him than usual, or even perhaps because Betty was finally getting through to him that she was unhappy with things as they then were, we shall probably never know. But Dean accepted the suggestion.

At first, it seemed a good idea. From place to place he went and he began making an impression. In Philadelphia, in 1942, a young soldier home on his first leave – Dean had not yet been called up himself – was persuaded by his wife to see a man she had found exciting. 'I went,' Joey Bishop told me, 'and I didn't know what to expect. But I ended up falling off my chair.' What so enchanted this future member of the same 'Clan' of which Dean would become second-in-command was the song that the young Martin sang. The spotlight was on a commanding figure in a tuxedo, and the band struck up a bolero rhythm. It was a very well-known sound. The music was 'Temptation' – and Dean started to sing:

> Yous came, I was alone
> I should have known
> That yous was temptation.

'I had never seen anything like it,' said Bishop. 'I thought anyone who could be so funny with a song like "Temptation" and have the audacity to say "yous" was fantastic. He was more than just a singer.'

Nevertheless, it was as a Bing Crosby sound-alike that Dean Martin's appeal was at its most potent. And as an Italian. Crosby's principal rival in 1943 was an Italian former barber called Perry Como. At the same time, a younger man from a similar background was dragging the customers into the Riobamba night spot in New York. He, too, had Crosby as his idol, although he didn't sound all that much like him. However, he had something that made young girls swoon, girls who waylaid him in alleyways near the club and asked him to sign his name on the most intimate parts of their anatomies. But Frank Sinatra was so popular that he was moving on – and the Riobamba wanted someone else. Dino Crocetti's background seemed to allow him to fall into the Sinatra niche very comfortably indeed. And, if anyone had known it, very much into his temperament, too – despite his easygoing manner. They met, shook hands and parted. Neither had any idea of the extent to which their paths would later cross.

It was at this time, when Dean was giving his perfect demonstration of what today would be called 'laying back', that someone referred unpleasantly to him as a 'greaseball'. Without bothering to finish his song – it was, naturally, a marvellous follow-up to 'Temptation' – Dean jumped on the table and punched the man in a spot that guaranteed he would never want to be quite so rude again. (As Dean said years later: 'The only one who can call me "Dago" or anything is Frank. I call him "Dago", too. With anybody else, there's a fight, 'cause I never call anybody Chinaman or Jew, so why should they call that to me?') As we shall see, that would not prove entirely true.

Merle Jacobs offered his client's services, and the Riobamba accepted them. Dean Martin may have had a great voice, but in 1943 he was no Sinatra. He took off at the Riobamba something like a lead balloon. That certainly was the opinion of the *Variety* correspondent who noted that in the eight minutes in which Dean appeared at the Riobamba, he cut no ice at all: 'Cleveland's entry in the swoonstakes is Dean Martin, a thin-visaged dark-haired baritone who's making his New York debut with this date. The New York competition is apt to be a little too tough.'

What really worried the writer was Dean's dependence on electronic aids at a time when the top names in entertainment thought that the truest test of success was the ability to get through to audiences purely on lung power. 'Martin, seemingly, would be lost without that mike. He's lacking in personality, looks ill-fitting in that dinner jacket and, at best, has just a fair voice that suggests it would have little resonance without the P.A. system.'

On the whole, the Riobamba clientele agreed with *Variety*. He didn't last long at the establishment and moved on to less salubrious surroundings. He was in Montreal when Betty was in Pennsylvania with her parents – and giving birth to her second child, in March 1944. The baby was named Claudia.

There was not much excitement about the career of Dean Martin. His income dropped with the quality of the bookings he received. One man who did have faith in him was another agent called Lou Perry who thought that he needed above all an opportunity to shine. But he didn't think Dean could do it the way he looked. The build wasn't bad. The weight was about right – certainly more potential there than the skinny Mr Sinatra. And the face . . . the face? On Perry's advice, he wanted a new image for himself. But how? The answer was staring him in the face every time he looked in the mirror. As plain as his nose. In fact, it *was* his nose.

Perry consulted a plastic surgeon who said that for a consideration – amounting to about $500 – he could do something with the Martin nose. Dean took the plunge – and according to some accounts more loans of $500 to do the job than Zero Mostel had backers in his film *The Producers*. The money would be honoured in time, but the operation provided an opportunity not only to improve his appearance, but also to help his even more crippled bank balance.

The operation was an amazing success. The result was surprisingly good. Suddenly, the young dark Italian had become an Adonis. The fellow with the strange bent nose now looked positively handsome, although not for the moment handsome enough to get a great deal of work. He shared a double room with Perry in a low-grade New York hotel. On some occasions, Betty moved in, too, although she was spending most of her time with her ever more disapproving parents.

She hated the life even more than she had that of a bandsman's wife. Dean himself was to decide that New York was his least favourite place on earth – and remained so for the rest of his life. He was out of work more often than he was in, and when he had an opportunity to drive a yellow taxi, he grabbed it with as little ceremony but as much gratitude as he had previously taken hold of a plate of his mother's meatballs and spaghetti.

'I starved in New York,' he said years afterwards. 'And I was humiliated, and I hated every moment of it.' That is why he subconsciously vowed never to go back there if things ever got better.

Dean didn't escape the draft. But he didn't stay long working for Uncle Sam's World War Two effort. He was called up and stationed at Akron, Ohio. He stayed there and in the Army for fourteen months. Then he was invalided out without leaving the base. Doctors found he had developed a hernia. He wasn't sorry to discover that physical disability. Nor was Betty, who was pleased to have him home again – or rather once more on the road.

Things did start to get better. If he never tried to work at obtaining better jobs while still employed as a band singer, he now had all the get-up-and-go of first-generation immigrants like his father. Previously, there had been no real need to rise – he wasn't a brilliant success, but he was richer than anyone he had ever known. Now, he was poor and there was an intense need to get out of the mire. He borrowed more cash as 'milk money' to provide for his children – from others working in the same shows. He also had other mouths to feed – even if Betty's parents' neighbours were already tut-tutting about the ne'er do well that the McDonald girl had got tied down to.

The fact that she was expecting another baby soon after Claudia's birth didn't exactly help the Dean Martin public relations campaign. 'Hell,' he said in 1945, 'all I have to do is send Betty a telegram and she gets pregnant.'

In April of that year, Gail was born – this time in the Crocetti home in Steubenville.

He certainly benefited from not being away in the Army. There was a distinct shortage of readily available talent and a number of nightclubs on the Eastern Seaboard of the United States were now agreeing that Dean Martin was precisely that. He had his first record contract – recording discs at $150 a session. In the late Forties, the Woolworths buyers were putting down a few cents in the American stores or a couple of shillings in England to hear him sing numbers like 'Far Away Places (With Strange Sounding Names)', 'I've Got the Sun in the Morning' and, surprisingly this, a collection of songs made famous by Al Jolson, like 'Toot Tootsie Goo'Bye', 'About A Quarter To Nine' and 'I'm Sittin' on Top of the World' – which indeed before long he would be.

Even if he wasn't in uniform for long himself, Dean joined the parade. Those Woolworths buyers put songs on their turntables like 'There'll Be a Hot Time in the Town of Berlin', which contained momentous lines like, 'We'll take a hike through Hitler's Reich'.

Jobs came, and with them all the money he could earn. As has already been established, one of both the nice and unfortunate things about being in Dean Martin's kind of show business was that people talked about the folks practising the art. Now the word was that this man with the brand-new nose had a certain amount of sex appeal. It reached the New York offices of the major film studios. Both Harry Cohn of Columbia Pictures – who after the Rita Hayworth films and in the midst of his biggest gamble to date, *The Jolson Story*, had decided that the future of the cinema lay in the musical – and Joe Schenck of MGM expressed interest in the singer whose Italian antecedents would have looked very good in a press release. But for various reasons, both rejected him.

Cohn called for a screentest – but discovered that the fellow whom he heard had done so well after the floor show at La Martinique nightclub didn't know how to open his mouth when fed the dialogue of a film script. Schenck didn't even get as far as a test. He thought there were too many singers on the studio's books anyway and let the idea drop. Which was how Dean got himself a spot on the bill of the Glass Hat in Manhattan.

The Glass Hat was situated in the Belmont Plaza Hotel on New York's Lexington Avenue. It was in its last years of being a middling type of nightery. The days when it was regarded as swank and fashionable had gone, but the hotel had not yet entered the somewhat seedy phase of a lot of New York places which resemble *grande dames* all dressed up with nowhere to go.

Also on the bill at the Glass Hat was a young manic-looking performer called Jerry Lewis.

Pardners 3

Jerry Lewis would probably say he had show business in his blood, although his grandfather would have preferred him to be a rabbi. Nevertheless, what Jerry was doing at the Glass Hat was fairly closely related to what his father was doing in the Catskill Mountains.

Danny Lewis was a performer in waiting. Waiting, that is, for the big break that would do for him what the Borscht Belt had done for a score of entertainers from Danny Kaye to Mel Brooks. It never came, although he had regular bookings from hotels which expected him to tell jokes that were as Jewish as the gefilte fish served as an hors d'oeuvre at every meal, and to fill their recreation hours with impersonations of the men whom they regarded as their patron saints – Jewish-American success stories like Al Jolson and Eddie Cantor.

Danny Lewis, né Daniel Levitch, did it well enough, aided by his wife, Rea, who was also in the act and helped him with his musical numbers. By the time he was at an age legally to stop going to school, their son Joseph had decided he wanted to get into the business, too. He liked his father's show-business name, so called himself Lewis, as well. As for Jerry, it just sounded 'more American' than Joseph – or even Joey, his parents' pet name for him.

He hadn't had an easy life. Danny and Rea were usually working 'on the road' and he had been brought up by Rea's mother, Sarah. When 'Boobah' Sarah died, Joey was left very much to his own devices – which led him to finding his own spot in the world of entertainment.

He made a name for himself quicker than did his father – although that name wasn't always very good. He was a crazy performer who did little more than mime to gramophone records – frequently the same Jolson records that his father regarded as virtually holy writ. Only, he made faces when he mimed and the audience reacted by appearing to be in a state of oncoming epilepsy. When he did speak, it was with a voice that sounded like that of a child who had just taken the wrong end of a red-hot poker.

At twenty, he was nine years younger than Dean. He looked younger than that. 'I'd have said he was about twelve,' Martin joked a little while after they met on a street corner. Jerry remembered: 'We shook hands and I said, "My God, he's an Adonis." I fell in love with him immediately. He made the welcome in his handshake. He knew I was a kid and I looked at him as superior material when he was no bigger than I was, but he saw something in my "hello", and I saw something in his "hello" which touched my heart and I found a hero.'

Although Jerry and Dean were on the same bill, it was some weeks before they met. Various people take credit for what happened when they did – the doorman at the Belmont Plaza for introducing them, Lou Perry for bumping into them in the street at about the same time and Abby Greshler who was Jerry's agent. Greshler had been that ever since he first discovered that Jerry could do funny things with a gramophone record. Lewis was fifteen at the time.

As Jerry tells it, it was he who heard Dean was looking for work and had the idea while at the 500 Club in Atlantic City that he might do him a favour. Lewis and Martin had done nothing more concrete together in show-business terms than spend an evening reminiscing about the past and playing their favourite Billie Holiday and Louis Armstrong records.

It was a new life for both of them. And not just for them. Quite fortuitously, the local chapter of the Mafia had found new family friends.

The relationship with the Mob was cemented (like a cement over-coat) at precisely the same time as that between Martin and Lewis – and at the start they were always billed as 'Dean Martin and Jerry Lewis'. 'Martin and Lewis' – like 'Laurel and Hardy' and 'Abbott and Costello' before them – took time to register with the public.

The 500 Club was owned by Skinny D'Amato who, in addition to being a legendary figure in second-draw nightclub circles, was a prominent member of the twisted nose and long overcoat fraternity.

Jerry had barely got started with his act when the singer due to perform there became ill and the boss asked Jerry if he had any ideas. There was one stipulation: he needed another performer, but he didn't want another singer. Jerry told him about his pal Dean. He sings, Jerry told him, and, before the gangster could protest, he added that they did a great comedy act together. Jerry recalled: 'I do my act and leave, and the gangster says, "We have to have a talk." Dean doesn't know anything about it. He overhears the gangster say, "If he doesn't do what you said he does, he'll be wearing cement boots."'

Abby Greshler remembered the story slightly differently. 'Jerry had been working with a girl in his act and things weren't going too well with them. He was quite desperate and asked me, "Can't we get Dean?"

'I put the idea to D'Amato who was a great friend of Frank Sinatra and was the man who at that time, in 1948, said that gambling would come to Atlantic City. By the time it did come, he wasn't running the 500 any more.'

According to his own book, *Jerry Lewis In Person*, Jerry suggested to D'Amato: 'Why don't you book my friend, Dean Martin? He's not working.'

'Tell me just for my edification,' Lewis recalled D'Amato saying, 'What's a Dean Martin?'

'He's a terrific singer,' Lewis said he replied. 'He's played some good places.'

But by all the accounts, D'Amato took the gamble on Dean and Jerry. Nor is it in doubt that their first performance together was fairly terrible, not to say disastrous. D'Amato actually told them, Lewis remembered: 'If you're not using any new material by the next show, you're both out on your asses.'

They walked out of the club and in the alleyway came to a decision. Dean would sing and Jerry would put on his old junior waiter's 'busboy' jacket. And that's what they did. Dean sang – and acted the fool. Jerry acted the fool – and tried to sound as if he were singing. They did frightening things with plates (both empty and filled with food) and juggled and horsed around with them till the people watching felt that they couldn't eat another thing and laugh at the same time. They chose laughter in preference to food and Mr D'Amato was over a nightclub-shaped moon, as the experience was repeated show after show, four shows a night.

Their own perception of their success matched that of their audiences. Both decided they ought to look important, too.

They went to the smartest tailor in Philadelphia. There they were, two somewhat callow-looking men, both younger in appearance than their years, ordering two new tuxedos of the best material ever to be touched by needle and thread.

'You don't understand, they are $200 a piece,' said the tailor, whom Dean had previously understood to mean he charged $200 for the pair, which he thought was still a hell of a lot of money. 'With or without the hangers?' asked Dean. Jerry ordered four – two each.

It was formula that counted – at least as much as material. Dean wanted to go on stage wearing a nice grey suit with a striped tie. Jerry – who, according to legend, has gained the reputation of wearing some of his suits only once for fear of putting on clothes that might be creased – insisted on each of them paying indecent sums for tuxedos which they would then ruin by falling on the floor. That gave the pair a comical edge – if an expensive one. But it worked. Says Jerry: 'I knew we had lightning in the bottle.'

As Abby Greshler related the story, the Martin-Lewis double act was totally his own inspiration. And since Abner L. Greshler was an important figure in the American agenting business, where a handshake is as good as a contract – some would say almost as authoritative as the kind The Godfather specialised in – there could be reason to accept his story. It was certainly in his character to negotiate a deal that other people may not have thought feasible.

Whatever the cause, the result that time in July 1946 was mayhem – the kind that has bank managers lining up to offer to finance the very next episode of organised anarchy. Not since Olsen and Johnson had had audiences running around like headless chickens after seeing their *Hellzapoppin* had there been anything like them. There was Dean trying to sing a song, while Jerry was playing a 'busboy', dropping plates as Dean dropped the notes. Jerry conducted the orchestra with his shoes and Dean managed to wisecrack his way through their performance from eight o'clock in the evening until four o'clock the following morning.

When Jerry threatened to take over the whole show himself, leaving Dean with nothing to do, his partner found himself a suitcase and walked through the centre of a rapidly collapsing house. It was as though they had been playing the parts together for years, not simply putting them into an act for the first time.

It was like that for six weeks. As Dean was many years later to tell the *Saturday Evening Post*: 'It was wonderful . . . doing all the funny things I had always wanted to do. I love to hear laughter, but I couldn't get laughter just singing. Hearing a whole audience laugh is like getting drunk.'

But drunk they were – Dean only partly aided by alcohol, Jerry strictly with the magnetic pull of an audience. And the magnetism spread with the word of their success. They were flooded with offers of more work.

Meanwhile, Jerry wrote them a routine which, he was to say in his autobiography, was the first double act that was not based on two milkmen, two electricians or two plumbers. 'For the first time, here we have a handsome man and a monkey.' No one should get the impression, however, that Jerry saw himself only as a monkey. That was far from the case. From the first word typed on the first sheet of paper he took out of the brown-paper packet, he was making it clear he regarded himself as the brains of the outfit – a fact that would lead to much of the tension that was to develop between them. What is also sure is that they needed each other.

Dean was never the stooge, the role that history has accorded him. Double acts have to be just that – double, with each of the partners having a vital role to perform. Dean Martin and Jerry Lewis depended on each other from the moment they nervously went on that first night at the 500. (Dean was to joke in later years that he changed his own name because it didn't sound too good having a show-business partnership called Crocetti and Levitch). The great achievement was not so much the effect they had on audiences, but the fact that they were, within days, receiving the supreme accolade – the admiration of other entertainers, particularly those who were giants before either Martin or Lewis was born.

In a New York theatre treasure trove of an archive is a letter from Sophie Tucker – the Last of the Red Hot Mammas of show-business royalty – which states in terms leaving no room for doubt that she considers the new pair the greatest find in modern entertainment. Later she told newsmen: 'These two crazy kids are a combination of the Keystone Kops, the Marx Brothers and Abbott and Costello.' As they say in the theatre, she spoke a book. And she spoke it loud and clear to Abby Greshler who was back home in New York. 'Soph' got on the line to the agent and thundered an ultimatum louder than any of the instructions she was accustomed to delivering on stage to somewhat ageing matrons.

'Abby, do you know what you've got here? You'd better get down to Atlantic City and find out.'

What he found out, Greshler recalled, was a line of people winding twice round the block.

Instantly, a pattern emerged – not so much of the way they worked, but the way they lived. Jerry was the frenetic one, unable to sit still for more than a couple of minutes, devising routines for the act. Dean, on the other hand, was, to use the modern phraseology, 'laid back', wanting to enjoy the financial benefits of his newly found fame playing golf – and enjoying the adoration of the women who surrounded him. When he got home to Betty and the kids, it was a bonus. The family would have preferred it if he had done just that more often.

The act moved on to Florida – and more of the same kind of success. They were already regarded as, at least, the number-two nightclub act in the States.

Jerry's idea for their act went beyond the horrendously expensive tuxedos. His idea of 'lightning in the bottle' was to run an act that he called 'Sex and Slapstick' – a title later adopted by *Life* magazine to describe their routines. Plainly, Jerry was the man with the slapstick indicator in his brain cells. He was also the first to realise how different was his partner – the man with the sex appeal in every pore.

The impression given by their act was that Dean was the sophisticated one, while Jerry was the unworldly kid. In at least one way, they could not have been more different. If Jerry was the man with the ideas, he was also the one who bought the comic books when they came on sale – for Dean, who went through them just as legend would later have it that he went through whisky bottles. Jerry agreed that it would be easier for him to pay the ten cents over the counter than for his partner to do it himself. As he told Barbra Paskin: 'It was all right for me to go and buy them, but for this handsome hunk to buy them?'

In Chicago, Greshler booked them into the city's top club, the Chez Paree – but as the supporting act to the dancing star Paul Draper. 'I insisted that they take "extra-added-attraction" billing,' Greshler recalled. 'It helped them to mature their act, to continue to be the "surprise" which, if it works, overshadows everything else.' It was a sound philosophy. Draper's act ran for three weeks. Dean and Jerry stayed for thirteen. 'And there were street lines again,' Greshler recalled.

They appeared at the Havana Madrid nightclub, and shared the huge sum of $1,500 a week. They were at the Capitol on Broadway.

It meant that wherever they went – in New York or outside – they could command star money. At the Latin Casino in Philadelphia, they earned $3,000 a week. The bookings kept coming and the money kept rising. All to the intense satisfaction of Abby Greshler who had by now bought Dean's contract and was running the team as agent, manager and wet nurse.

He was also furthering the single career of Dean Martin. They were in Philadelphia in October 1946. It was the month of the Jewish High Holidays of New Year and the Day of Atonement, Yom Kippur. The Levitches had never been used to working on these holy days themselves and didn't want Jerry to work on them either. He agreed that on the eve of Yom Kippur, the sacred night of Kol Nidre, he would take the time off. 'I felt that the management couldn't say no to that,' Abby Greshler told me.

What he did not know until afterwards was that Jerry didn't spend the evening at a synagogue service. 'He was entertaining in the window of Lindys,' Greshler recalled. The famous Broadway delicatessen-restaurant, renowned for the best cheesecake on that side of the Atlantic, rocked to Jerry Lewis's calculated madness on an evening when the theatres across the street can't even give tickets away. 'Meanwhile, Dean was having a marvellous time on his own, ad-libbing beautifully and singing the way he liked to sing.'

He also knew how well he was doing. At the end of the one-man show, he turned to Greshler and whispered in an aside: 'Do we really need Jerry?' The agent assured him that he did, but the thought was already a haunting one.

A considerable amount of animosity later existed between both Martin and Lewis and Greshler. He always took credit for crafting their careers. Both Martin and Lewis said he was the lucky one – to have worked for them.

In January 1947, he had booked them into one of New York's most prestigious movie theatres, Loew's State. *Variety*, which had been so scathing of Dean Martin's single performance, liked immensely the way he performed with his new partner: 'This new act, composed of Dean Martin who at one time began making an impression on the crooner parade, and Jerry Lewis, a young comic, has a good future. Deriving maximum benefit from the fresh, clean, youthful appearance of the pair, the turn does a smart job of tickling customers' funny bones at the State, which is playing to capacity houses with *The Jolson Story*.

'Though there's a pattern to the act, based on Martin's neat vocaling and Lewis's complete lack of inhibition, it seems to the customers to be almost completely ad-lib. The two combine to work over "That Old Gang of Mine", Martin foiling for Lewis, decked out as a moronic bartender, do vocal take-offs of various top stars etc. All they do cannot be detailed, but virtually every bit of it is good for solid laughs. All in all, these two kids have themselves a fine act. There are rough edges, but they'll wear away and what's underneath will wear a good deal longer.'

That was what Abby Greshler had been thinking for some time. He thought there was one place where they deserved to have the pleasure of rolling customers in the aisles – with or without Jerry's now favourite prop of a soda syphon: The Copacabana – the smartest nightclub of them all. Greshler was convinced that not only were the pair he was already calling Martin and Lewis ready for the Copacabana, but the Copacabana was ready for them. So they took it on, and won hands, feet and head down.

It was a strange situation for two brash newcomers to what has sometimes been called the toughest brand of show business – the kind that has audiences ready to eat entertainers they don't like. The fact that they sit at tables, instead of simply in bolted seats, that they have in front of them stainless steel knives and forks, seems to give them a licence to compete with the people in the spotlight. If they don't actually bang their cutlery, they chat to each other wildly. Only a riveting performance out front can be sure of guaranteeing the kind of attention players like to consider their right.

Dean and Jerry didn't give anyone else a chance at the Copa (as everyone knew it). They dominated the place, even though they were only third on the bill – which, considering how enthusiastically they were being spoken about in the trade now, gives some idea of how important the club was.

The real star of the show was Vivian Blaine – who before long would earn a lasting reputation as Ever-Loving Adelaide in the first production and the movie of *Guys and Dolls*. But by the time she was introduced by the club's MC, the audience was still applauding Dean and Jerry.

It put the club's management in a predicament. Without either tact or heart, they came to a conclusion which left the star with no alternative. It was suggested that Miss Blaine might like to change places with Messrs Martin and Lewis. The poor girl had her fur coat and her make-up kit out of the star dressing-room before Dean could clear his throat.

The new stars had their fee increased to $5,000 a week – and were given a six-week contract, a very long time indeed for an establishment that likes to think of its customers repeating their visits. And that is precisely what they did. Regulars who normally wanted a change of entertainment came once and booked again – because the Martin and Lewis show was never the same at two performances, let alone on two evenings. Even more important, these regulars persuaded other people who had never been to the club before to come, too. Dean sang 'Won't Be Satisfied', while Jerry borrowed another page from his father's talent book and sang Jolson's 'Rockabye Your Baby With A Dixie Melody' – and demolished another pile of plates. Nothing succeeds like success and Dean Martin and Jerry Lewis were succeeding.

The New York press had a good deal to do with all that. And, strangely for a comedy pair, it was the comparative straight man, the singer Dean Martin, who came out well in the *New York Times* review – or so it at first seemed. 'Dean Martin,' the piece began, 'is a personable baritone of Latin caste' – the paper felt it needed the intellectual approach – 'who sometimes manages to get off a completely romantic song in a husky, casual style often likened to

Bing Crosby.' And then came the rub as far as Dean was concerned: 'Equally often, however, he is verbally or acoustically shanghaied into serving as a hapless foil for the strident and nonsensical but compelling antics of Lewis, who makes his actual age of twenty seem alternately much too young and much too old for his nonstop defiance of realities.'

Variety was continuing its new love affair with the couple. 'Dean Martin and Jerry Lewis really hit the big-time at their opening last Thursday at the Copa. Both have been around singly and jointly, recently at the Capitol on Broadway, but not until their Copa bow did they truly arrive as potential comedy stars. Here's a case of two being better than one; usually it's after a team splits up that one or another component steps out into real stardom . . . The audience has given both a neutral one hundred per cent for individual talent; Lewis for his comedy and Martin for his vocalisations. Both are versatile in each other's specialities plus everything else from legmania to knockabout acro-antics and the blend goes together like Park and Tilford.'

They were heady times. (Jerry would later recall being struck most of all by Dean's wardrobe. No concerns now about whether he could buy two dinner jackets for the price of one, with the hanger thrown in. His cupboards were filled with handmade suits of the very best quality.) As the tables at the Copa filled, so did the offers from other establishments, too. Abby Greshler, never one to turn down the best ten per cents available, studied them all with the contempt of one who knows he is on the right side of a sellers' market.

But if Dean and Jerry were to maintain their position, they would have to get what today would be called the media behind them. They made their TV debut in 1948 on the number one edition of Ed Sullivan's *Toast of the Town* show – the very first appearance by the man who became America's first television superstar, introducing the most talked-about acts in show business.

It was a frightening experience for the pair – if only because the lights in use in those early days were so hot that they melted their make-up and sent the remains streaming down into their collars and on to those $200 tuxedo lapels.

They were, as Abby Greshler would have predicted, made – and in demand on other TV shows, too. Later that year, they were working with Milton Berle, the other leading TV performer of his day, in *Texaco Star Theatre*. They had to promise not to ad-lib and stick to an act – the show was live in those black-and-white days – that would last no more than eight minutes. Neither of those conditions was met – in fact, Jerry pushed his face in front of the camera at one stage and mocked: 'Milton Berle! Big Deal!' Since that was precisely what Milton Berle thought he *was*, that was dangerous talk. But the public liked them and demanded more of the same.

They also had their own radio show, sponsored by Chesterfield. But their zany humour was strictly visual. After ten miserable, abysmally rated weeks, the cigarette firm cancelled their contract. It was their first joint failure, although it mattered only as far as pride was concerned.

Mr Greshler used to worry people who met him for the first time. He didn't look as though he was in the best of health, but by all accounts he'd always looked that way, and he died at an advanced age. What is more, his 'track record' had always shown him to be a man of great business strength. He was a businessman who could just as easily have sold either dresses or grand pianos. He chose to sell entertainers – from the time he organised sales conferences with the kind of razzamatazz previously reserved for circus parades.

There was, however, one parade that was more than just enjoyable for his client Dean Martin. He and Jerry were playing at an hotel at Miami Beach at the time that the 1948 Orange Bowl Queen was being chaired through the city. It was Christmas and Dean was loaded down with gift-wrapped presents as he watched the float pass by. When he saw the queen herself, the guy who always had an eye for a pretty face was captivated. The queen was Jeanne Beigger – Jeannie to her friends.

She was nineteen years old, studying at Miami University – and Dean fell headfirst in love with her, although he tried to keep the matter quiet.

Greshler himself had no desire to break up an apparently happy marriage. It was good for business for there to be amity all round and not only were Dean and Betty apparently over their previous difficulties, but Betty and Jerry's wife Patti were good friends, too. The Martins now had a home near New York's fashionable Riverside Drive – although he still said he hated the city and had developed a virtually unmanageable disability: he was frightened of travelling in elevators. Every time the door of one closed, he was gripped by a claustrophobia that sent him into a cold sweat. It wasn't known to people who saw him perform, but it was a problem that could quite easily have destroyed him, had not Betty been around to calm him and offer stability.

Above all, Greshler wanted Dean to concentrate on his money-spinning work. It was not a time for complications. His clients were now the hottest property he had, and he treated them with the dexterity of a chef masterminding a soufflé at 212 degrees Fahrenheit. What he engineered for Dean and Jerry – convincing them, with total justice, that he knew best at all times – was a trip to the West Coast. It would be the start of a new life, the place where all three central figures in this drama would make their homes.

Hollywood or Bust 4

Slapsie Maxie Rosenbloom was the big-time operator in the Californian nightclub business. His club was not just Hollywood's answer to the Copacabana – even if the former prizefighter no longer controlled the place entirely himself, he was seen as the nightclub equivalent of Sid Grauman who owned the famous Chinese Theatre, or Mike Romanoff who ran the restaurants frequented by the stars.

Hollywood has always been a strange place in that regard. The top figures in local society are in the film business. They are either the stars or the men behind the stars, the studio bosses, the top producers and directors . . . and the agents. But whereas their opposite numbers in New York and other big cities of America want to be entertained in nightclubs, the Hollywood élite go out in the evening either to see movies at star-studded premieres or to visit each other's homes for the plushest parties ever devised by mankind.

When they went to Slapsie Maxie's, it was more often than not a strictly business occasion. Abby Greshler, who had done his home-work like a bespectacled student approaching a degree course in applied mathematics, knew that well enough. He wasn't merely looking for the $10,000 a week he was sure Martin and Lewis could command from the club, he was excitedly anticipating the reaction of the audience. He knew it would be loaded with people who had read their copies of the 'trades' – *Daily Variety* and the *Hollywood*

Reporter, which had both been publishing details of the lightning career of the pair who were already, it was said, going to knock Abbott and Costello off their pedestals.

Knowing the studio men would be in the audience was one thing. Being sure of what to do about that fact was something else entirely. Like all good agents, Greshler's mind spun with the speed of an electronic calculator at a time when other people still depended on abacus frames and their own fingers. He thought there was a good chance of cleaning up with a nice big movie contract before the evening was over. But what sort of contract? Dean and Jerry were getting excited at the mere notion of seeing a series of noughts that looked like telephone numbers on a piece of paper above their names.

Jerry was himself full of ideas. Dean was happy to let his partner figure out the details. Besides, by some mysterious coincidence, he had seen Jeanne Beigger in the first-night audience at Slapsie Maxie's. Greshler just wanted the boys to perform. The business details were his patch and no one, particularly any one of his clients, was going to be allowed to move in on it.

Louis B Mayer had been the first to make overtures for Greshler's impressive new clients. He hadn't quite forgiven Schenck for turning down the opportunity of having Dean on his books. He still thought there was a market for Italian singers – especially if they had what Mayer had already decided was Dean's sex appeal. The town was rife with the story that he had said: 'I wouldn't mind the guinea (Dean) but what do I do with the monkey (Jerry)?' He was used to making his own gods and the fact that Martin and Lewis were tops on the nightclub circuit really held little interest for him. 'I tell you what,' he said to Greshler, 'give me the singer and I'll make that skinny Jew kid a producer.'

He was offering Dean $50,000 a week. 'I said no,' Greshler later maintained. 'I didn't see any point in separating them. I knew that the studios would be more than interested,' he told me. 'But I also knew that they wanted all the rights.' What was particularly cute of Greshler was to realise that the rights that would be likely to count most would be those for TV – a burgeoning medium for which few people then had any real respect.

A few years later, George Sanders would express the views of many in the legitimate theatre when, in *All About Eve*, he answers Marilyn Monroe's question, 'Do they have auditions for television?' by saying: 'My dear, television is nothing but auditions.' The studios themselves were frightened of it – Warner Bros. wouldn't even allow a TV screen to dress a set – but none of them took it seriously. Greshler believed it could mean big money for his clients.

That night, his predictions came true – all of them. The pair had been together for a year when they appeared at Slapsie Maxie's. Dean would subsequently recall: 'In our first show, everyone was there. All the producers.'

Neither of them could believe his luck. Subtly, they expressed their insecurities in one of their best radio routines – starting out saying how great it all was, how they were destined to become radio stars as well as movie successes and famous actors with their names in lights. But then, said Jerry, it could all change. Their film career could come to an abrupt stop, they'd end up with their noses pressed to a bakery shop window. 'Dean,' said the little boy Jerry, 'I'm hungry!' It got the required number of laughs and nothing seemed less likely.

Among those present at the club were Bette Davis and Edward G. Robinson – as usual saying terrible things about Jack L Warner – James Stewart, John Garfield and Gary Cooper. Also present was a certain actor fairly low on the Hollywood totem pole but who would one day do slightly better, Ronald Reagan.

Dean sang like Bing Crosby and helped Jerry destroy the props and most of the other things surrounding them. In a few weeks, both had matured into seasoned players – each buying Cadillacs and expensive jewellery and planning the homes they were about to buy.

He and Jerry sang 'That Certain Party' and, highly appropriately, 'Pardners'. They told inane jokes like: 'Did you take a bath today?' 'Why, is there one missing?' Or there was: 'Hey, Dean. Do you remember those corny vaudeville jokes of 1924?'

'Well, certainly.'

'You know, "Can you stand on your head?"'

'No, it's too high!'

Jerry knew their value as a comedy act, although he later said: 'Do you think that . . . material was worth $230 million? Hardly.' But what was worth that money was their partnership.

Jerry was the one with the imagination to team up as a regular partnership – or 'pardnership' to adapt their song title. Today, he recalls for Barbra Paskin telling Dino: 'Do you know that 63 per cent of the US public hate to go to work and hate their jobs, and they see us getting thousands of dollars to play like kids in a sandbox?'

Abby Greshler's ears at Slapsie Maxie's were not tuned in on his clients' performance, but on how Louis B Mayer and Jack L Warner were enjoying the show. He studied the numbers of iced champagne bottles being rushed to the tables – a sure sign of how a turn is doing; a poor act isn't worth staying for, so no point in buying another bottle. He wormed his way round the tables, listening to the conversation – and the laughter.

When it was all over and the people out front were standing in applause, Greshler pushed his way through the mound of dropped napkins and discarded cutlery and had his chats, moving from table to table. There were six offers that night altogether. But he rejected them all out of hand. 'I wanted television rights,' he explained to me. 'The studios wanted to keep everything for themselves, but I knew they wanted Dean and Jerry enough to do a deal.'

Before they went back to their hotel, Greshler had an agreement with Hal Wallis, an independent producer working out of the Paramount lot. More important, and more significant, he was the man who had virtually invented the Warner Bros. gangster film and had later given that studio a mass of magic ranging from *The Story of Louis Pasteur* to *Casablanca*. He was a man who knew every sprocket of the movie business. Now he was promising to make Dean Martin and Jerry Lewis international stars in not just one picture, but a whole run of them. Abby Greshler believed him. He had also secured an agreement that he (Greshler), not Wallis, would control their TV output. It was a deal no one had achieved before in an age when the studio system still reigned supreme.

That was also the night when Greshler and Martin and Lewis decided to sell up everything they owned back East – in Dean's case not a great deal – and buy a house in Los Angeles.

Wallis didn't come to the show at Slapsie Maxie's blind. He had already seen Martin and Lewis at the Copacabana. 'They were just terrific,' he told me. 'I was interested in doing a deal then, but their manager insisted that I wait until they came out to the Coast.'

It was a recognisable ploy. Greshler knew how good they were and he was prepared to play a waiting game. Stall on a deal until they arrived in California and he reckoned he could increase the stakes. Sitting on the TV rights enabled him to do just that. As the final negotiations proceeded, the other aspects of the Dean and Jerry act were being honed to the degree of perfection they themselves knew they could attain and which Greshler insisted they did.

There were discoveries to be made. The most notable one was that this singer-comedian could be a pretty good actor – and always, when the occasion demanded, with a superb sense of comedy and timing.

And yet the guy with whom Jerry Lewis had joked about taking a daily bath – 'Oh Dean, I'm so unworthy of you!' – could also bring tears to the eyes, and not just the kind that went with holding your sides. Alongside that, however, was the pressing feeling which others in the business diagnosed as a sense of insecurity.

Even their shows at Slapsie Maxie's were not merely carbon copies of all that had gone before. They were as usual constantly inventing new material and just as constantly involving the audience in ways in which audiences hadn't previously thought they wanted to be involved. If a man laughed a great deal, Jerry thought he deserved to become part of the act – so he took out a pair of scissors and cut the man's tie in half. Dean happily joined in, singing at the same time, serenading the man's partner adoringly so that she wouldn't object. By the time the Slapsie Maxie run was over, there were men who left the club not merely without neckties, but sometimes with the shirts literally hanging off their backs – cut to shreds. The fact that the men could say afterwards that they had never enjoyed themselves more says a great deal for the way the act went over.

People saw them and heard them with equal enthusiasm. They were guests on six Bob Hope radio shows – and the audiences were more enthusiastic about Martin and Lewis than they were about Bob Hope. That hadn't happened before with any other guest artist.

The amazing thing about Dino's laid-back attitude was that he took his working process into the recording studio with the same amount of success as he would later enjoy on TV – and with the same apparent lack of effort. Alan Livingstone – then the artist and repertoire manager and later chairman of Capitol Records, the ones with the Capitol dome just above the hole – had signed both Martin and Lewis before he knew what to do with them. Dean, he knew, could record any song they put before him and before long stand a good chance of making it a hit. But Jerry? There wouldn't be a lot, although at first there were the comedy routines with both of them.

Abby Greshler would take credit for the Capitol contracts – and for the label signing Jerry at the same time: 'You had to be very careful not to upset either of them by favouring one in favour of the other. Very careful.'

When in 1948 the musicians of America went on strike, Dean flew to Mexico to record.

Before long, however, Dean was managing more conventionally, recording worthwhile but also-ran discs like 'Powder Your Face With Sunshine', 'Johnny Get Your Gun' and 'That Lucky Old Sun' in 1949. His 1950 record 'Muscat Ramble' did better.

The real announcement of their arrival in the entertainment capital of America seemed to come with an invitation to appear in a cabaret specially put on by the B'nai B'rith organisation – a Jewish brotherhood group which, nevertheless, frequently went beyond the borders of the faith to do good works and fight racial discrimination. The entertainment was held to mark B'nai B'rith's presentation of its Man of the Year Award to the head of Twentieth Century-Fox, Darryl F. Zanuck. The trouble was that, like so many other similar occasions in Hollywood, the 'bill' was oversubscribed. It was full of as many top performers as there were frames in a film's love scene. By the time the likes of Jolson, Jack Benny, George Burns and Danny Kaye had stopped singing and making their audience wipe their eyes, the organisers had decided they were ready to get on with the real business of the evening, making the presentation.

Mr Martin and Mr Lewis were informed that their performance would not be required. Now that had greater significance than might at first seem apparent. It was not just a question of their attending the function, having a slap-up free meal and then being told there was no need to sing for their supper after all – they weren't getting paid for it. Much more, they were being denied the opportunity of letting the highest-paid, most influential names in Hollywood see how good they were.

Instinctively, when the master of ceremonies announced that they would scrub the rest of the bill, Jerry put his head through the curtain and demanded to know who this Mr Zanuck was anyway. Dean made a similar query – and proceeded to mangle the pronunciation of the name in so doing. When the MC protested, Dean grabbed a soda syphon from a nearby table and squirted it down the front of the poor man's shirt.

The MC may have been soaked, but it was the audience who were saturated – by a mass of Martin and Lewis mania which had them literally rolling in their places. The next day, it was *their* performance that hit the front pages of the 'trades'.

While the big talk in Hollywood was of the success that these previously almost unheard of comics were having wherever they appeared, Betty was having to content herself with the news second-hand. While Dean was in California, Betty was at her parent's home having another baby. She phoned Dean with the news. It was in the early hours of the morning, and Jerry it was who answered the phone at their room in the Roosevelt Hotel – which in itself gives an interesting dimension to the couple's status at the time. Not only were Dean and Jerry staying at what had by then become a second-string hotel, but they were sharing the same room.

He decided that the bearer of the tidings was plainly off her head, put the phone down and went back to sleep. Later, he realised what he had done and woke Dean with the happy news that he had another daughter, who would be called Deana.

But it was the last brief interlude of happiness in the Martins' married lives, although Dean, as usual, tried to pretend that there were no real problems. He brought Betty and the children to live in a house in Holmby Hills, now best known as the residential district favoured by Barbra Streisand, Gregory Peck and Rod Stewart, but then where Fred Astaire and Bing Crosby lived. At last, Dean was close to Bing physically as well as merely resembling him in voice. It seemed like paradise – except that Betty knew Dean was still seeing the former beauty queen, Jeanne.

He was now making more money than ever before in his life. But he was spreading it around, too. While his marriage was plainly floundering, he was sending cash home to his parents, helping his mother's brother, a small-time comedian and eccentric dancer called Leonard Barr, and giving a leg up to his brother Bill. After a short time, Dean had set Bill up in a laundry business.

The money came from all the Martin and Lewis joint ventures. But the fortune was in the contract Dean and Jerry signed, at Greshler's behest, with Hal Wallis who at first began to regret having succumbed both to his own instincts and to their agent-manager's persuasion. Astonishingly, the magic this pair had weaved across the continent had appeared to dry up. As Wallis told me: 'We made a series of tests with them playing a number of roles. But they didn't come off at all well. They seemed awkward and ill at ease.' Or as Dan Defore, an actor who tested with them, put it to me: 'They were deadly unfunny at the time.'

The tests were for a film that Wallis had ready to go into production at the Paramount lot called *My Friend Irma*, about a dumb blonde and a singing soda fountain assistant. It was based on a highly successful radio series that CBS had been networking since 1944, starring Marie Wilson. Following the pattern of those days, it seemed only a matter of time before someone would give a visual dimension to the voices millions of Americans had known as well as the brand of cereal they had for breakfast. Hal Wallis decided to be the one to do it. He bought the rights and waited till he had a comedy team to do what he had in mind. Martin and Lewis, he now considered, were the pair who answered his needs.

The deal he struck, via Greshler, was for seven pictures in five years, worth $75,000 a picture to the new stars – which seemed huge money, even in the town where fortunes were made as regularly as they were lost on the tables at Monte Carlo and before long would be at Las Vegas, too. In the meantime, Dean and Jerry, on Greshler's advice – he was acting as producer as well as their agent – formed their own company, York Productions, which would make the one independent picture a year they were allowed under their contract with Wallis. *My Friend Irma* would be the film to get it all going.

Both Dean and Jerry were given parts in the picture to run through for the test cameras. Wallis was convinced they would be just right. By the time he had seen two lots of tests, he was coming swiftly to the conclusion that they would be well advised to stay in the nightclub business.

It was that idea that convinced Wallis to rethink his strategy. Undoubtedly, had they not already been signed to a fat contract, he would have let things rest there and not pursued it any further. Now he had to think of something new. 'I decided to write in two completely new characters – and just let them do with them what they would have done in a nightclub.'

The action was set at an orange juice counter with Jerry squeezing the fruit on screen so menacingly it was obvious he'd be squeezing laughs out of audiences off screen. 'They were hilarious,' said Wallis.

Any casual visitor to the *My Friend Irma* set would have had the feeling that it was Jerry who was the harder worker. Dean gave the distinct impression of taking it all fairly in his stride, while Jerry worked and worried about the planning of routines like a panzer general deciding his strategy in his next tank battle with the Allies.

Dean had to do something to alleviate both the tensions and his occasional feelings of inadequacy when it was so obvious that his partner was the master of the situation in hand. Dan Defore, who played with them in the film, told me of Dean's solution to this problem. 'He climbed into the flies while Jerry was working below – and threw water bags down on top of him.' Such are the frustrations of performers not allowed to mature. Frustrations that were then only in the embryo stage but were about to grow like a virus in a laboratory.

From that point on, Wallis initiated a formula that hardly changed for the next fourteen films they did together.

Wallis insisted that he had no idea of inventing a new Laurel and Hardy or Abbott and Costello. 'They were plainly very different and Dean was much more romantic than any member of any other comedy team had ever been before.' Dean was also happier at this time allowing his partner to do the unpleasant work of talking deals – although in truth it was Greshler who was doing most of that – and of getting all the laughs. Dean sang and people all over the world were startled at just how much like Crosby he was. Jerry got the laughs. Inside, Dean was beginning to feel uncomfortable – but he didn't let it get him down in public.

At home with Betty, however, the tensions were showing. Not only was he quite clearly in love with the Orange Bowl Queen, but he was finding Betty's company less stimulating. All the things that were so easy to bottle up on the studio floor found their outlets in his explosions at home. But you wouldn't have known of any of these tensions if you were a member of the now burgeoning Dean Martin and Jerry Lewis fan club or of any cinema audience from Hollywood to Hong Kong.

The *New York Times* critic Bosley Crowther liked Jerry more than he liked the movie, and didn't have a great deal to say about Dean.

Of Jerry he wrote: 'This freakishly built and acting young man, who has been seen in nightclubs hereabouts with a collar-ad partner Dean Martin has a genuine comic quality. The swift eccentricity of his movements, the harrowing features of his face and the squeak of his vocal protestations' were all well worth noting. 'Indeed, he's the only thing in it that we can expressly propose for seeing the picture.'

Other critics expressed much the same sort of sentiment, but it didn't affect the box office. The word of mouth that Martin and Lewis had something to offer had gone way past the nightclub set. The film took every penny at the movie theatres that Hal Wallis could have hoped for. *My Friend Irma* was such a hit that plans were drawn up for a sequel. The usual idea in those days was to find a title that recalled the previous film. *Irma* had been young and pretty, so they couldn't risk any opprobrium generated by the country's moral groups by adopting the most conventional titling of all and calling the film *Son of Irma*. Instead, the new movie was called *My Friend Irma Goes West*. The film amounted to precisely nothing in cinema history, but Martin and Lewis were better than before and Hal Wallis's contract was worth at least double the price he had paid for it.

The hostesses of Hollywood knew that, too. Dean tried to get out of parties. He always said he found them boring. Betty wasn't a party person either. Sometimes he went alone – usually when there was a way of making sure that Jeanne was there, too. But it was at these parties that Dean's insecurity surfaced yet again. Fellow guests would talk to him and get, instead of scintillating conversation, grunts or a view of a hastily rearranged back of his head. Years later he admitted: 'I'd sit in a corner not saying a word. [People] thought I must be conceited or drunk or something. It was just that I was afraid to open my mouth because I knew I wasn't speaking correctly.' What words he *was* saying, he was slurring. It was already an attractive, idiosyncratic style, but he didn't yet know it. What he did know was that the day at the studio began soon after six in the morning, and he liked getting to bed early.

What Betty had by now come to terms with was that what he liked most was getting into that bed with Jeanne – who would say about his relationship with Betty: 'He was a sad case. He was unhappy and couldn't talk about it. He specially couldn't talk to me. He didn't want me to know that he wasn't all right. He had no friends. He wasn't close to anybody.'

There was a lot of opposition to the relationship – none more than from Jeanne's family. 'He was the kind your mother tells you to stay away from,' Jeanne was to recall.

But Betty refused to contemplate a divorce – until, that is, she was faced with a situation that even in the crazy matrimonial world of Hollywood was probably unique. Friends started phoning her saying they had received invitations to Dean's wedding to Jeanne. Why had she so hushed up her divorce? It was the last straw. She saw her lawyer, agreed on a settlement that would give her a vested interest in the continuing success of Dean's career and filed for her marriage to be ended. Part of the agreement was that in addition to $1,000 a month alimony, she would get another $1,000 towards the upkeep of her children, and an extra $1,000 which was, by various legal quirks, not to be taxable. Dean certainly seemed content enough with the settlement. He never worried about mere money. That was something that was usually taken care of by Abby Greshler and his other advisers.

When Betty baulked at the idea of having a Nevada divorce in Las Vegas instead of a California settlement which would take a year to finalise, she was persuaded to accept a further $100 a week for life. It was a settlement that had tongues wagging even in Hollywood, a town where divorce talk was common currency.

In September 1949, Dean and Jeanne were married, with Abby Greshler as a witness and Jerry as best man. Patti, Jerry's wife, didn't approve of the match at all. She and Jeanne would never become friends and for years there was talk of a definite feud between them. But with two performers like Dean and Jerry finding a reaction from audiences that was little short of adulation, it didn't matter all that much.

Dean and Jerry had now signed up for their own TV show, the *Colgate Comedy Hour*, in which they headed a bill of several acts. It was worth $100,000 to them for their first show and $150,000 for those that followed. In his book, Jerry said that for them every day was the Fourth of July for them. To Dean it was more like Good Friday.

Jerry was a lot kinder in later years about the man who was his partner in those days than Dean remembered. He said that his role was like that of a high trapeze artist, while Dean's was the catcher below. Dean was not just a catcher, 'but the greatest straight man in the history of show business'.

What is undoubtedly true is that each knew he complemented the other and admired his partner's talents.

1951 was the year that Martin and Lewis topped the million-dollar mark for the first time, clocking up close to 60,000 miles in so doing when they weren't working in the studio. By the end of 1951, both Dean and Jerry had gone through their customary routine in four films, most recently in *At War With the Army*, in which they played a couple of rookies. It was the first made for York Productions. Dean was the good-looking, intelligent one who got the girl. That had been tried before, and *That's My Boy*, which was a college story about a hypochondriac, was virtually the same recipe. Jerry might have proved to be the poor victim of his personality on screen. On the set, he was the master – while Dean, to all intents and purposes, seemed quite content to let him remain in that role, despite the consequences for everyone else.

Polly Bergen, the beautiful actress who a generation later would surface as the naval wife and grandmother in *The Winds of War* saga, remembers the experience of being a co-ed in the film. 'Dean was one of the nicest people I have ever worked with,' she said, although she didn't enjoy working with Jerry quite as much. 'Dean never gave himself the credit for being quite as funny as Jerry, and would put on the best face imaginable. I don't think he was ever conscious of the power he then had as a really top box-office star.

There are some comics who are effective only when they are working against someone. Jerry's humour depended on having this laid-back guy on whom he could unload all his frenzy.'

As far as Polly Bergen was concerned, Dean found his happiness not in booze, not in womanising, but in country music – which was her passion, too. 'I was brought up on that music and when Dean heard that, we became very good friends. He found it very difficult to learn new songs. It was so much easier not to have to learn them. But, nevertheless, he worked himself to death on them.'

Anyone sitting in an audience, watching Dean Martin and Jerry Lewis in person, might have had a similar feeling about the way they both performed. Dean may have been the 'laid-back' singer, but on a massive stage in front of a vast audience, he had to work to keep the act going. It was a fact that became a phenomenon, and was noted by practically every critic who took the trouble to see their act.

They were probably at their best on television – which once again was proving Abby Greshler's idea so right. The shows seemed to work brilliantly – much better than had their radio series a year before. Somehow the tiny screens of the day seemed to have been tailor-made for the kind of work they did.

The *Colgate* shows, transmitted from New York, succeeded in spite of themselves. One of the writers objected to Dean taking a holiday before the show was aired for the first time. He said he had to get to know his subject closely. 'No one gets to know me closely,' said Dean, 'not even my wife.' Now it was Jeanne who would have said 'hear-hear' to that.

'Dean Martin and Jerry Lewis took up a regular television assignment last night,' wrote Jack Gould in the *New York Times*, 'and it may be a long time before the National Broadcasting Corporation is quite the same again.'

They were also still hotly in demand on the nightclub circuit, and their films were still burning to be made. In addition, Dean was cutting records – most of which were featuring numbers he had sung in his pictures. The discs made profits of sorts and every teenager who saw a Martin and Lewis picture was a potential record buyer. On the other hand, Paramount was delighted, too. Every time someone, somewhere, spinned a Dean Martin 78, it was an advertisement for the latest movie. The films took enough at the box office, although not enough to get into Martin and Lewis's pockets. It seemed that the profits made were all gross and not net – which meant that the two stars didn't get the percentage of the take they thought they should. Salaries, publicity and a host of assorted sundries accounted for the difference specified in the contracts' small type. But the cinema still offered the greatest room for them to show their real potential.

Everything seemed just as good in their private lives. Within a year of Dean's marriage to Jeanne, the first baby, Dean Paul – sometimes called Dino Jnr – was born. Then came Ricci. Dean seemed to have the same effect on Jeanne's reproductive system as he had had on Betty's – although now he wasn't joking about sending any telegrams.

Jeanne was the practical one. Dean was the doting father. You could see that by watching the way he sat on the floor with the kids and flooded them with presents. The problem, as Jeanne was to say time after time, was that he didn't take on the role often enough. When he was away, he left her to look after the children – and, she complained, he didn't think enough about them when they weren't actually together. He would respond by saying he was working very hard – for the family's benefit.

When *That's My Boy* was released in 1951, a *Life* article became a cover story, a paean to the men who were now the most successful performers in American show business. Inside, the magazine showed not just queues of people waiting to get into the Paramount Theatre in New York – where Dean and Jerry had a guarantee of $50,000 a week, plus half the theatre's profit over $100,000; Abby Greshler had earned his ten per cent, all right – but youngsters thronging the fire escapes to catch a glimpse of their idols. 'The strange street scene above,' said *Life*, 'marked the climax of one of the maddest marathons ever seen in show business. During a personal tour of their newest movie, *That's My Boy*, the young comedy team of Martin and Lewis made history inside and outside theatres in New York, Detroit and Chicago.' The real success of the show was that they were governed by the times of the movies – the more showings the managements could arrange, the more brief appearances the pair made on stage, the higher the take for all concerned.

To Jerry, in particular, seeing all those people was like a whole basin of milk placed before a greedy cat. Jerry wanted the people out of the theatres so that he could get a new crowd in to buy more tickets, but he also couldn't resist the opportunity to clown some more for those who had already proved so appreciative. He settled on a ploy worthy of his and his father's joint god, Al Jolson. The man who had died less than a year before would stop complete strangers on the street and say, 'My name's Jolson and I sing – do you want to hear me?' They always did want to hear and Jolson always did want to sing. Sometimes he would ask an entire audience to follow him into the café next door – after he had sat in the box office himself and gauged the potential size of his crowd.

Jerry did something very similar. He promised all those who left the theatre a continuation of the show – on those fire escapes outside the Paramount. He was true to his word and both he and Dean clowned to their hearts' content – to the sheer amazement and despair of the police who had to halt the traffic. It was indeed a scene that even Broadway had rarely witnessed before. When it so clearly emptied one house of the theatre and filled the next, it was an experiment that was repeated again and again. It was an event worthy not just of Jolson, but of Frank Sinatra, too – who ten years earlier had seen girls swooning and wetting their pants rather than leave those same theatre seats.

Four weeks after the tour began, Dean and Jerry had netted for themselves something like $260,000. And in 1951 at that. By then, the two were so exhausted that they called off the final week of their tour. By the end of 1951, they had, between them, earned $1.5

million. (Needless to say, most of that money went in tax.) 'They wreaked more havoc than a typhoon,' noted *Life*.

'We laugh at each other, so we don't care if the audience laughs,' Dean said charitably. '*We* think we're funny.' Jerry did, certainly. Dean did what he could to keep up with his partner – and sometimes surprised himself with just how successful he was. He may not have had much of an education, but he did have an ability to say witty things on stage, even if he still hesitated to say them in more intimate surroundings. It was a strange paradox, but true. To him, being on stage was a kind of disguise, as if, like an ostrich, *he* knew he was hiding but thought no one else did.

But neither did he think it important that when their act opened up for business at each performance, it was Dean, not Jerry who had the girls out front screaming. They were *his* songs they heard before Jerry came out and started treating the whole performance like the storming of the Bastille.

In show-business terms, Martin and Lewis were themselves revolutionary. A whole series of legal battles involving the right to represent them was in train. One of them in 1951 involved Screen Associates, with which Abby Greshler was connected. The company and Greshler wanted a million dollars from MCA (America's biggest talent agency), Paramount, Hal Wallis, Martin and Lewis because he charged they were due to make more films with him. The matter was finally settled without a judge's decision being necessary – and Greshler officially ceased to be the agent of the team he had brought together. MCA took over where he had been before.

It was such a familiar story that legend had it that when Dean was asked at their wedding ceremony whether he would marry Jeanne, he quipped: 'Can't we settle this out of court, Judge?'

His humour didn't, however, stop a brand-new Cadillac being unceremoniously driven away from Dean and Jeanne's new home – the method adopted by one creditor to get what he claimed were his just desserts.

It was beginning to look very much like that at home, too. After a couple of years, it seemed as though Jeanne and Dean were reaching breaking point. It didn't do much to help Dean's idea of security. He took offence at a great deal. When he heard people making fun of Italians, he came out and told them what he thought. When one of these men was more specific, he took more direct action. Like the time he heard a couple being rude about his father, a man who still hadn't learned to speak English terribly successfully.

'I picked 'em right up off the floor,' he said years later, 'and said, "You aren't gonna say somethn' about a guy who can't talk English well, 'cause he has been a barber all his life on thirty dollars a week."' The men agreed that such ideas were furthest from their thoughts. Meanwhile, Dean was having a few new thoughts of his own.

The Stooge 5

You didn't have to be a terribly close observer with an acute sense of perception to realise that all was not well between Dean and Jerry. There was an inherent bitterness that manifested itself on their TV show.

Jerry decided it would be a good idea to allow his father to appear on the show, doing the same kind of Jolson interpretations he had been performing on the Borscht Belt. Of course, he wouldn't have had an opportunity to do it on, any other programme. Dean saw it as unnecessary nepotism. 'I think I'll put my mother on the show,' he said. 'She can sew.'

Dean and Jerry were short of ideas for playing practical jokes on each other. Jerry got so angry about Dean's arriving late for a stage performance that he thought he would cash in on the Martin habit of stepping straight into his dancing shoes and going immediately on to the stage for their tap routine. Dean put his foot inside his pumps – and had no choice but to go on, swimming, it seemed, in a sea of raw eggs. Jerry couldn't control his mirth.

The times they were in agreement with each other in spirit as well as merely in person was in their rows with agents and then with writers. It was well known that Jerry would decide which material went into the *Colgate* show – despite the fact that there were fully competent producers and directors on the payroll and ready to do the job – while Dean took the easy way out and went home to bed rather than risk a confrontation. Norman Lear and Ed Simmons had been paid $10,400 a script for the show by the pair – only to have the words they wrote thrown into the wastepaper basket by Jerry – another expensive practical joke on his part, and one that hurt.

He behaved in much the same way on the film studio floor, doing his best to let people, off screen as well as on, see that he was the boss. When there were press conferences to give – and there frequently were – it was Jerry who spoke to the reporters. It was Jerry who pushed himself forward. It's also true that Dean allowed himself – sometimes wanted himself – to be thrust into the background. Again, the reason was probably his insecurity. 'The reporters,' he said afterwards, 'couldn't understand why I let Jerry do the talking. Well, I didn't know what to say or how to say it. I was using "deses" and "doses" and "aints".' But he *was* getting worried about it – and so was Jeanne who still wasn't exactly bosom buddies with Patti Lewis.

'It's always Jerry, Jerry, Jerry,' she told him, and it seemed only to add a little more salt to an already festering wound. Quite quickly they were creating a new image for themselves. In *My Friend Irma*, Dean was a definite personality in his own right. Now, the picture of him painted by those press conferences was being transferred to the movies they made. Dean was quite clearly the more handsome of the two and – to quote any number of young, impressionable and sexy bobby-soxed, pony-tailed leading ladies – he sang divinely. Hal Wallis, as he told me himself, knew the Martin value. He understood what his rapidly growing audience wanted – to swoon at Dean and to laugh at Jerry. Because they were laughing at Jerry, he had the best lines. Sometimes it seemed he had the *only* lines. As Dean was to say years later, 'I hated those terrible films. They were great for the audiences. But they were terrible for me because I had nothing to do. Jerry would say, "I'm goin' down to the drugstore" and I'd say, "Oh, you're goin' down to the drugstore?"'

Jerry had few singing pretensions at the time, so he didn't mind Dean having the songs or the girls. His role – while ensuring that audiences paid to see their act – was to look stupid, croak in a childlike voice and make it seem that his top lip had vanished in a jaw like a pelican's. All that was more than OK with Jerry. But Dean regarded his own lack of good lines to be a reflection on his lack of education. It was confirmation, as he saw it, that he was practically illiterate. Nobody else saw things that way, but the fact that *he* did was enough to unnerve him.

The titles – and the tensions – mounted up. *Sailor Beware*, *Jumping Jacks*, *The Stooge*, *Scared Stiff*, *Money From Home* all made big money and all followed the same formula. But Dean still said very little to Jerry about his feelings, although they were becoming more obvious.

He left voicing his complaints for when he got home and, just like Betty before her, Jeanne had come to expect his outbursts. Although he did not realise it, she was good for Dean. It all seemed very nice at first, if not to say idyllic, with Jeanne being both the perfect sexual object and a marvellous mother figure for the children. Few people had any idea there was trouble brewing between them; fewer than those who knew there were problems with his other 'marriage' to Jerry. The pair were earning between them in the region of a million dollars a year, but as their bank balances increased, so did the jealousies they experienced.

Dan Defore, a supporting actor much seen in indifferent comedies of the Fifties, watched it coming on the set of *Jumping Jacks*, in which they appeared in 1952, playing fledgling paratroopers. 'I could detect an increasingly bad atmosphere between them,' he told me. 'By the time they made *Jumping Jacks*, it was much more pronounced. I had thought right from the beginning that Dean was the one with the greater talent and that the stone was simply not polished.'

One of the toughest criticisms of Martin and Lewis (at a time when people were not doing much in the way of criticising the top comedy team in America) was that they seemed to ignore the people to whom they had to be most grateful of all. Dean had an answer to that. 'The appeal,' he said, 'was not that we didn't care about the audience. But we never looked at the audience. We would work like I am talking to you now, we would work to each other. We were very different, did different little situations . . . a dance or two.'

Dean had other talents which manifested themselves at about this time. 'This is when he began to show for the first time that he was an exceptionally fine golfer,' Dan Defore remembered for me. 'While working on the film, he'd pick up a number six iron and start practising. In those days, he not only hit the ball, he chomped a lot of weeds, too. He became a damn fine golfer. It seemed to be a great diversion for him.'

Jeanne would have charged that he principally needed diversions from her. They were of completely different temperaments. There were stories going the rounds of Dean getting his sexual fulfilment elsewhere. Jeanne, who had enough confidence in her own allure not to worry about that, didn't make the suggestion. What she was angry about was the fact that Dean liked going to bed early – and if necessary alone. She said she was young and wanted more out of life. He said that he was either too tired or wanted to study his next day's shooting script, no matter how inadequate he thought it might be.

'Dean is engrossed in his work,' she said at the time. 'So engrossed that I'm taking a less and less important place in his life.' When a wife admits such a thing in public, red warning lights are flashing. 'I feel he does not need me. I seem to be just a figurehead around our home. Someone looking as pretty as I can, but not a real partner who's sharing his problems.'

Eventually, in 1953, they split up. 'He can't communicate with me,' she explained. 'He never talked to me or to anyone else.' In a more telling moment, she said: 'He was a bum. He was a golf bum. We never went to a party and never had people in for dinner. He would leave the house at seven a.m. and not be heard from again until seven at night and then he'd spend the evenings practising putting on the living-room rug. We had no social life and practically no home life. When he wasn't putting, we sat watching TV like a couple of aged people.'

They were apart for three days – Dean was the one to walk out. Then they had a meeting at the family's new home in Palm Springs. This time, according to Jeanne, it was Dean begging to be allowed back to the marital state. 'He talked,' she said. 'He, like, never stopped. But I was firm. I said, "No sir. No spending the night. Not until we get a basis of agreement."'

She didn't want to end their marriage any more than he did. But first she demanded that the two of them begin living like married people, staying together frequently and then talking to each other with more interest and enthusiasm. Once having settled that, she was adamant that he had to start thinking seriously about the way he spent his money. She had heard more than enough stories of the millions he was earning – while threats multiplied of having property reclaimed if bills were not paid.

At that stage, there didn't seem any grounds at all for believing they could reach an amicable agreement. The lawyers were called in. She probably told them what she would tell strangers years afterwards: 'I couldn't tell you why he married me. I suppose it was because of my blue-eyed college girl look. I was the symbol of something he thought he couldn't get. All I can tell you is that he took me home and he put me in a shell without realising that I was proud to be Mrs Dean Martin, but I wasn't about to give up being Jeanne Martin.'

She also complained that Dean was 'bossy', making life even more tough. But it was obvious that when it came to the crunch, the old cliché about animal magnetism applied to them more than to most people. Finally, they decided they couldn't live without each other and ended up in a clinch in the lawyers' offices that said they wanted to call the whole divorce thing off. It would be a recurring situation, but for the moment bliss reigned at the various Martin households.

When the breach was sealed, Jeanne told Louella Parsons – who loved every sniff and snuffle she would claim her interviews with the stars brought on – that she had never been more happy. She had been shocked by the break-up and had no doubt at the time that it was for real. Dean, meanwhile, was saying absolutely nothing and was reacting to the apparent passing crisis in his life with the same kind of stoicism he hoped he was showing after his numerous tiffs with Jerry – which were now a great deal more outspoken than they had been before.

What had brought Dean back was the fact that he discovered that Jeanne was once more pregnant. Now that was established, both decided they had no alternative but to make a go of things. Breaking up had been 'a terrible experience for both us', said Jeanne, cuddling her newly returned spouse. 'I think our marriage is going to be better than ever. We'll be much more careful [not to hurt] each other. The important thing is for Dean to get everything settled in his own mind and I'm sure he has now. We've both had a lesson, but we love each other and that's the important thing.'

Later that year, their third child together – and Dean's seventh – was born. They called her Gina.

The break-up had been well reported by the world's press – in practically every country that had ever seen a Martin and Lewis film. They were both strong personalities and both needed to vent their spleen at each other. Dean because of his relationship with Jerry. Jeanne because, for all her protestations about being a simple college girl, she had relished all the attention she had received as a beauty queen and now resented being just the other half of a big star. Since Dean's idea of socialising was cuddling a glass of Scotch and soda (or beer, or brandy, or a margarita or a Martini), she didn't even have the consolation of mixing frequently with the colourful, beautiful people of Hollywood.

She was even more annoyed when she discovered that far from being so upset – as he claimed to be – about the apparent end of their marriage, he was having a very good time indeed on the set of *The Caddy* in 1953. As far as any casual visitor to the set could tell, Dean and Jerry were as much a double act off camera as on.

Very, very occasionally, there was real adverse criticism of their act in the press. As far back as 1949, *Variety* had commented about the return visit they made to Manhattan's Copacabana: 'Maybe their best friends won't tell them, or their management seems unable to see it or control it, but the fact is that people are beginning to talk about Dean Martin's and Jerry Lewis's dialectics. The ever-growing accent on Martin's Italian extraction and Lewis's Yiddishisms are annoying and unshowmanly. The personable singer, furthermore, is evincing his dialectic predilections by throwing in some other Bronx patois and all this tends to make for a needless hurdle for two of the freshest, upcoming comedians extant . . .'

These comments were altogether a lot kinder than those which followed their 1953 opening at the London Palladium, known throughout the entertainment world as the temple of variety. The British audiences had been spoilt by a whole succession of top American artists who had not merely had audiences cheering excitedly at their performances, but saw them lining up as an act of worship. Danny Kaye had been the biggest sensation of all. The Royal Family had cheered loudest and longest. He was followed by names like Bob Hope, Judy Garland and Betty Hutton who each drew rave notices. When Martin and Lewis opened there, they might have expected – in fact, they knew for sure – that they would be received equally warmly. But it didn't happen like that. They were slaughtered by the British press. One paper described Jerry as a 'gargoyle'. Another said that Dean was left on stage with nothing to do.

The only critic who thought well of them was the London *News Chronicle*'s Richard Winnington who said: 'The gangling, jibbering, grimacing Lewis and the smiling, crooning Martin were finally identified as two well-dressed, courteous, subdued young Americans on their first visit to London. They had deliberately waited to come to London until a week after the Coronation of Elizabeth II. "For us to have been there would be like wearing sneakers with a dress suit."'

Martin was described as a 'thirty-six-year-old Texan [who] supplies logic and the relaxed attitude' – which just goes to show you shouldn't have believed everything you read in your papers in 1953.

Both Dean and Jerry knew what was going to happen after their first night. An audience that had seemed to be so responsive early on had stayed till the end – to boo. For the first time since their joint careers had rocketed at Slapsie Maxie's, they had experienced something that seemed like a professional nightmare. The people out front at the Palladium had anticipated what the critics would say – and for the rest of the week, it was the same. Or rather it was worse, because from the second night on, there were empty seats in the house. That was also something neither of them had experienced before, at a time when the taste of the response at the Paramount Theatre was still on their lips – to say nothing of the lovely warm glow that was experienced every time MCA sent them a summary of their earnings.

It was a case of extreme disbelief. They couldn't understand it. From then on, Dean sat himself in his dressing-room and didn't want to see anyone – just like in the days when he was with the Watkins band. Only this time, he wasn't enjoying the cards – or the girls – quite as much. For his part, Jerry responded to callers with what might be considered his now customary aggression. He answered knocks on his dressing-room door with a bitter look on his face. One journalist told me that Jerry came out of the room wearing nothing more than a pair of underpants and a belligerent expression. In a more reasoned mood, Jerry said he thought it had been due to the fact that the previous day, President Eisenhower had ordered the execution of the Rosenbergs, the American alleged atom spies who had gone to the electric chair just hours before the first Martin and Lewis performance. (Metaphorically speaking, Dean and Jerry thought they were being executed, too.)

A more likely explanation had been the curtain speech in which Jerry bent over backwards, sideways and forwards to say what a wonderful audience they had had – when it was obvious that no one appeared to like them that much.

When they returned home, they let out their anger in no uncertain terms. 'British critics stink,' said Dean, taking over the job of spokesman for the first time on record. 'And put that in capital letters.'

It was indeed a strange time in Anglo-American relations and certain sections of the United States press, led by the Hearst giant, took the whole episode as being symptomatic of the way things stood between the transatlantic partners who appeared to be having the same sort of trouble as Martin and Lewis. It was just about the most stupid assumption to which a responsible journalist could jump. No one had mentioned the adoration of Danny Kaye being responsible for perpetuating the British-American Entente Cordiale – even when George VI had gone to the Palladium following his daughter, Princess Margaret, who had continued to rave after her practically nightly visits to the theatre.

But a new Queen was on the throne. People were calling for a start to a new Elizabethan era and there were grumbles in America that the country which had been helped back on to its feet by Marshall Aid was being a little too cocky for its own good and was not showing nearly enough gratitude. All patent nonsense. But not nearly as nonsensical as Hearst's display of his own anti-British prejudices in the form of allegations that the British were being anti-American – and by implication ungrateful.

His New York *Daily Mirror* said it was all a symptom of a masked campaign of anti-Americanism in the British press. 'Most of the British press is whipping their anti-Americanism. Part of that press is Socialist . . . the Labour Party were constantly complaining that all too small a part of it was, but that wouldn't have concerned Mr Hearst] and takes its line from Aneurin Bevan, a noted hater of America.'

Dean and Jerry had had their enemies before. But nothing previously had ever made them a part of an international incident with political implications. As Paul Holt wrote in the (Labour) *Daily Herald*: 'It was the clowns themselves, not the critics or the audience, who were aware of an anti-American sentiment.' At the time, Dean stuck by the 'critics stink' line. 'The critics drank our booze and wrote that we were earning $7,000 but didn't mention our show,' he said. To which Mr Holt responded: 'I think Martin and Lewis are big boys now; too old to cry. What does matter is what a critic is there for. A critic, Mr Martin, is a checker of quality. He goes to the theatre to report for his readers what a show is all about. Whether it lives up to its predictions.'

Dean replied: 'The British press didn't like us before we got there. I don't know why but they reviewed our nationalities, Jerry being Jewish, and me Italian. But they didn't review our show . . . If they continue to review and treat American acts the way they did, there soon won't be anyone going over there, and that's a shame.'

The Communist *Daily Worker* retorted that Martin and Lewis 'can't take it'.

But the British press were not the only people who were angry about Dean's comments. Hal Wallis, always the epitome of Hollywood respectability, was afraid that the pair had gone much too far. 'I'm extremely annoyed,' he said at the time, concerned, as much as anything, at the effect their behaviour might have on the sale of Martin and Lewis pictures in Britain.

Dean wasn't perturbed by his boss's comments. 'Wallis would like to put us into the way Abbott and Costello make pictures,' he said. That in itself was reasonably true. Abbott and Costello, now at the end of their careers, had had a successful formula and most people *did* see Martin and Lewis as their natural heirs. But the Abbott and Costello films were poor and never stood the test of time. Even when they were still making their own last movies, the first pictures they had filmed at the start of their professional lives no longer bore a second viewing.

At times like this, it was encouraging to know that there could be defenders of the Dean and Jerry stand. One, quite surprisingly, turned out to be America's idea of the perfect English gentleman, David Niven. 'You can say the most horrifying things about British critics and probably be right,' he said.

There were those who thought Dean and Jerry were not right often enough. Particularly to each other. The truth was that while they were putting on a united front for the world's press, privately they were squabbling bitterly. They had made *Money From Home* in 1953 and *Living It Up* in 1954 to the now totally expected and accepted Dean and Jerry pattern.

Living It Up was their first film for which Walter Scharf, an outstanding cinema musician, wrote the score. It was a remake of the 1937 Fredric March-Carole Lombard movie *Nothing Sacred* (Jerry played the Lombard role) about a girl (in this case boy) whom the press turn into a celebrity when it is discovered she (he) is suffering from a rare disease – only to find out that the diagnosis was incorrect.

Scharf told me that he was impressed with the way Jerry handled the business arrangements. The film was made for the pair's company York Productions – 'and it was obvious that Jerry was in charge of that sort of thing. Dean was much more self-effacing. When we recorded, he always seemed reticent.' In fact, says Scharf, Hal Wallis wondered if there was any need to have him there at all. 'Who's going to sit around and wait for the romantic song from a second banana?' Scharf says that Wallis asked him. Scharf said he replied that the picture needed the 'balance'.

Janet Leigh, who co-starred in the movie, said she found Dean very easy to work with and very cooperative with everything he was asked to do.

'That's the thing about Dean,' said Walter Scharf. 'He would do whatever you wanted him to. When he was by himself, he was marvellous and knew just what he wanted to do. But when he was with Jerry, he seemed to retreat into the background. He backed off . . .'

When he heard that Bing Crosby was in the Paramount studio at the same time, Dean went into a shell. After all those years of being compared with Bing, he felt very uncomfortable knowing that he was there, says Scharf.

If you want to know anything about old Hollywood, you could do worse than go to Melville Shavelson. Mel, as his friends all know him, has worked with them all. Over the years, I have met and talked with Mel from early afternoon until the early hours of the morning. He and his writing partner, Jack Rose, wrote the script for *Living It Up*. His favourite Dean and Jerry story? 'It's the one I tell you all the time because it's the one that most clearly illustrates the difference between the two: Dean was easy to deal with as far as work was concerned. He just got on with it. Jerry, on the other hand, drove everybody mad.' Mel remembered visiting the Paramount lot when Lewis was directing a movie. Like many an artist, he could be intensely superstitious. On this occasion, he insisted on having a basketball basket outside his dressing-room. 'He wouldn't go on the set until he had thrown a basket – and, because he was the director, consequently nothing could happen on set until he had done it. He got to be pretty good at basketball.'

Dean, whom Mel Shavelson always said represented nothing but a good influence on Jerry, got his partner out of trouble on more than one occasion – like the time Lewis was meant to introduce a radio broadcast of the Academy Awards ceremony. Lewis refused to work with a script – with the result that, twenty minutes before the scheduled end of the show, he dried up. Fortunately for him – and for the radio network and for the audience – he spied Dino in the audience, invited him up and got him to sing, and they spent the rest of the broadcast time 'schmoozing' with each other.

What the writers did was try to incorporate the ad-lib feeling that Martin and Lewis always had in their nightclub act (when they discarded any semblance of a script) into a movie.

Mel Shavelson remembered the Martin and Lewis nightclub act for me. It was a very simple formula: first on stage was Dean, singing a nice relaxing number like 'A Slow Boat to China', then Jerry would enter the fray, spoiling everything with a gag or a line of dialogue, of which Dino might or might not have had prior warning. That was all right. Their whole act was each trying to put the other off his stride.

Shavelson says they always seemed to have a strange relationship, 'as though Dean was Jerry's father'.

In *Three Ring Circus*, made in 1954, two former servicemen decide to join a circus – it is not difficult to guess who they were. The principal trouble was that both men hated the script even more than they hated each other. Said Dean, working over his post mortem, years later: 'There was no sense of me being in that picture at all. The picture was on thirty-five minutes before I sang one song. Then it was an old one, "It's A Big Wide, Wonderful World", and I sang it to animals.' When Dean looked at the script again after the first day's shooting, he tapped the director Joseph Peveny on the shoulder and said: 'Don't forget I'm in this picture, too.'

But Hal Wallis had other problems. 'Jerry was always clowning around,' he later recalled. 'Dean was always easy-going. I never had any trouble from him. There were no drink problems. No problems at all – until he finally got wise with what was happening to him.' And that was the tell-all line. What Hal Wallis discovered was the beginning of the end, even though it took time for those words to appear on the screen.

Everything was difficult, not least the familiar difficulty of integrating music with humour. 'That was always a huge hurdle to jump,' Wallis said. But this time, getting a song to fit into the middle of a comedy routine was nothing. They were wasting time and a great deal of money – caused not by the clowning around, but by their rows, which got more and more intense.

He shuddered as he remembered the horrendous time the whole outfit was having at Phoenix, Arizona. 'When they started filming, they weren't speaking. There was no humour with what they did. When the director would say "cut", they'd just walk away. I saw the first two or three days' work on location there, called them in and said they were not only ruining the picture but spoiling themselves.' Had not so much been hanging on this, Wallis might have washed his hands of the pair and called in the insurance assessors.

Despite all the casualness ascribed to him, Dean was always fairly disciplined about his film work. He knew his lines. He did his best to learn the words of the songs – even the ones he sang to the caged animals – and he had the 'business' off pat. One day, during the filming of *Three Ring Circus*, however, he arrived late – and was duly chastised by Pevney. 'Why the hell should I show up on time?' Dean thundered in a real display of emotion. 'There's not a damned thing for me to do.'

Hal Wallis told me he saw it coming all along. He recalled shortly before his death: 'At the end of the scene, they would cut and walk in opposite directions. That went on for three or four days. I then had the film sent up to me and I could see it was pretty bad. I called the two and told them to come and see it as well. When they came, I said: "You two are the ones who are going to suffer if you carry on like this. Now, if you'll forget your personal differences while you are making this film, I'll reshoot all we did in the first three days because it isn't any good." I reshot it and they finished the picture.'

Complaints about the picture should come from both Dean and Jerry very early on, with Jerry apparently leading the fight on Dean's behalf – which doesn't fit into the stories about the Lewis selfishness at all.

According to Wallis, it was Jerry who complained that Dean didn't appear before the script was already into its eleventh page. They had a meeting with the producer, with their lawyers present.

'Dean is a very well-liked person. I never had any trouble with him on his own,' Wallis told me. The trouble, he said, was when they got together. The meeting was called because Jerry said that neither of them was going to report to the location centre at Phoenix, Arizona.

'What Jerry was complaining about was the late introduction of Dean into the story, which occupies the first ten pages of the script. I said, "Is that it?" and he said, "Yes". I had a script on the table in front of me and I tore out the first ten pages and threw them in the wastepaper basket. I said, "Does that answer your question?" He said, "Yes".'

Wallis then turned to Martin. 'Does that suit you, Dean?' he asked. Dean, he said, replied, 'Anything my buddy wants . . .'

'Right,' I said, 'we start the picture on schedule.'

But that wasn't the end of the matter. The company arrived at Phoenix – all, that is, except Dean and Jerry. Everything else was laid on – including the Clyde Beatty Circus which had been hired for something like $40,000 a week, and had set up its tents in readiness for the start of shooting.

'I had to call our attorneys in Los Angeles, who sent a telegram back saying that Dean and Jerry would be responsible for all the expenses involved.'

The pair came on the next plane. It didn't bode well for a successful movie.

In his book, Jerry blames the row over *Three Ring Circus* on the writer Don McGuire. Yes, he agrees, Dean was relegated to a secondary role, and he confirms that he insisted on a change of script – which, he says, came back without it being very different.

Jerry says that Dean 'kept blowing his top at me' and that he, himself, got 'pretty hairy'. Dean came to him and exploded: 'Any time you want to call it quits, just let me know.' As Jerry put it himself, from then on they were in the midst of a display of psychological warfare.

Once, at a Hollywood party, they actually traded blows – after Jerry alleged that his partner had said some very unpleasant things about Patti.

All this became part of the local gossip, although it was escaping the notice of the press. *Time* magazine, however, revealed that all was not well. Dean, who had previously believed it politic to smile when he was out with Jerry and pump his spindly back whenever there was a cameraman present, was talking about it only between the magazine's lines. His denials were themselves adequate confirmation. 'What's the difference if we don't fool around?' the magazine quoted him saying. 'To me, this isn't a love affair. This is big business.'

It certainly was – even if the $75,000 they earned between them was not big money by today's standards, when a superstar can write his own seven-figure cheque for as many minutes on the screen. But in the early Fifties it was a very respectable amount indeed.

What Dean also said at the time was that he was fed up to his back teeth with being nothing more than a stooge. But there *were* times when the two did say nice things about each other. When Jerry was taken ill with a sudden fever – the diagnosis was overwork – Dean accepted the booking the pair had for a show at the famed Ciro's night spot. He did so well that Jerry later sent him a telegram. It said: 'DO YOU KNOW HOW GREAT WE WERE LAST NIGHT WE WERE WONDERFUL THANK YOU YOUR LOVING PARTNER JERRY.'

What Jerry didn't understand at the time was that it was an extraordinarily good practice session for any future solo career that Dean planned. Something he was thinking about a lot. And it was inevitable that it wouldn't be long delayed. Not only did Dean object to Jerry being the principal partner, he also didn't think he should take all the credit for helping victims of muscular dystrophy – which in years to come would be the cause for which Lewis invented the 'telethon' TV fundraiser. He said it wasn't true that Jerry had done all that work for the cause on his own. He himself had helped the campaign from the start. Dean said he would rather earn $100 a time in a nightclub than continue to play second fiddle to Jerry. Even so, Jerry had had a profound influence on what Dean did.

When his younger partner decided on a practical joke in which a third party was the fall guy, Dean fell in with the plan enthusiastically. Sometimes their behaviour was much more cruel than funny. That, certainly, was the observation of actress Nina Foch, who later became a more important name in American theatre and cinema than some of her early roles, including one in *You're Never Too Young* in 1955, which had followed *Three Ring Circus*, would indicate. *You're Never Too Young* is about a young barber (Jerry) who dresses up as a child to escape a threatened murder. It was another typical film that Americans – and dozens of other nationalities – still thought it worth while queueing for in 1955. Off screen, they behaved exactly as they had done at Slapsie Maxie's – cutting up the ties of men who happened to be on the set, and in one instance – as Miss Foch recalled – actually cutting a shirt (which they later replaced) from an executive's back.

Nina Foch suggested to Jerry at the time that he star in *The Importance of Being Earnest*, but he said it didn't interest him. Nevertheless, Dean was to say that one of Jerry's cultural aspirations was a reason for their gradual mutual dislike. 'He read a book about Chaplin. At some point, he said to himself, "I'm exactly like Chaplin," and from then on no one could tell him anything. He knew it all. Before that, if we made up a sketch or a joke, he asked me if I thought it was funny because he knew I wouldn't con him. I had never broken up deliberately – you know, pretending to an audience that I thought he was funny when he wasn't. When he didn't get the kind of laughs from me that a second Chaplin should have had, he began to try his stuff out on six guys we had around us as court followers. You might call them professional idiots. I could say, "My father's got pneumonia" and they'd guffaw. So Jerry didn't come to me any more for my opinion. He tried out his stuff on our idiot claque.'

Jerry might not have thought so, but to people like Nina Foch, Dean had a special ingredient that allowed him to overcome these problems. 'He had tremendous charm,' she told me. He was going to need it.

Wrecking Crew 6

There were all sorts of reasons why Martin and Lewis were no longer getting on. One was that Dean alleged that Jerry had fallen in love with his own definition of great art. 'He took a picture with a Brownie camera – I think it was a picture of a lamp – and it turned out very well. I could see him saying to himself: "Hey! I'm a great cameraman!"'

It was very much an oversimplification, but it gives an idea of the bitterness that was developing at the time – even though it wasn't always apparent to everyone else because Dean continued to give the impression that life was one big ball and he wasn't going to spoil it by getting angry on the set.

After *You're Never Too Young*, Jerry was to say that Dean – whom he had previously regarded as a brother – was now a stranger. If Jerry wanted to make changes in the script, he would have to give Dean the impression that he himself had thought of the idea first.

Another row developed when they decided to hold the premiere of the film – with all expenses paid – at the hotel in the Catskill Mountains where Jerry had begun his Borscht Belt career in show business. Dean had approved the idea – and then not turned up for the celebrations. Instead, he took Jeanne off for a holiday in Hawaii. An explanation could have been that Dean himself had never worked in the predominantly Jewish area and would have felt out of things.

The matter ended up at the offices of MCA where, like an East-West summit meeting, the partners agreed to be *Pardners*, the title of their next picture which was based on the 1936 Bing Crosby film *Rhythm on the Range*.

They each had a different attitude to the job at hand. Jerry would stay behind at the end of each day's shooting, studying how they came out on film, but not merely viewing the rushes. He wanted to study the cameras, the lighting, the techniques used by all the people on the set. All that Dean wanted to do was to go home or to the golf course. As Sidney Sheldon, who wrote *Pardners*, put it: 'Asked if he had any questions, Dean said, "No, I have a golf date." Jerry said, "I have a few questions," and we were there for two hours.'

They came to Atlantic City at the time the governors of the United States were gathering in conference. They were photographed with the politicians underneath theatre marquees advertising *Pardners*.

People complained frequently about the governors. Only occasionally about the Pardners. Once, someone said that they seemed to ignore the audience completely when they played 'live'. Dean was to explain once more that they made people laugh by playing to each other.

There were compensations for the complaints. Dean had the comfort of his records. Between 1948 and 1953 he was extremely busy in the Capitol studios, an ever growing public appreciating yet another Italian singer in the Perry Como-Vic Damone tradition (to say nothing of Sinatra) who sounded a lot like Bing Crosby even if he hadn't yet found himself a 'Pennies From Heaven' or a 'Blues In The Night' and certainly nothing like 'White Christmas'.

Then, in 1953, he recorded the theme song from *The Caddy* – 'That's Amore', which finally separated the man Martin from the other boys. 'That's Amore' was written for him by Harry Warren, as big a hit as any from the composer of '42nd Street', 'Lullaby of Broadway' and 'I Only Have Eyes For You' and as different from any of them as a plate of spaghetti from a New York steak. Dean didn't think much of it when it was first offered to him by the Capitol executives. But then he had little input on what he recorded. 'We just gave him a song to sing, he'd look it over and start to sing,' one Capitol executive remembered for me. Even so, he had to be persuaded to add 'That's Amore' to his repertoire. Before long, however, it would be associated with him – and would be so for ever after. Whenever there was a TV scene or a movie clip featuring a love affair between two Italians, it was 'That's Amore' we heard in the background – and usually with Dean singing it.

At last, he didn't sound like Crosby. At last, he went back to what really sounded like his Italian roots. The song certainly was as Neopolitan as a plate of spaghetti – although when Martin and Lewis went on their TV show in the midst of the number's first bloom of popularity, Jerry substituted 'gefilte fish' for pizza in the line, 'When love hits your eye like a big pizza pie'.

But it was Dean who collected a gold disc for his trouble. Nobody could ever specifically identify the secret of a success like Dino's in the recording studio. Often it was a matter of luck – like the luck of Capitol recording a song by a calypso group called 'Memories Are Made of This'. Someone suggested that Dean sing it instead. There couldn't have been a cleverer move. 'Memories Are Made of This' could easily have been called 'Success Is Made of This'. The song spoke of 'the kisses you gave me'. Jeanne had every reason to give Dean plenty of kisses for the wealth that tune bestowed on the Martin family.

All this confirmed Dean's position in the American millionaire stakes. And it did other things, as well, which affected his relationship with Jerry. The records were made as Dean Martin, single. Not as part of the Martin and Lewis partnership. They made him realise that he didn't have to be in the Lewis shadow any more.

There were other ways, however, in which they needed each other. Both of them required the act as their staple income on which all else was built.

Jerry took it all, however, as a spur to assert his position as the senior partner. Again, rather than have rows, Dean concentrated on his golf – or on learning new songs, which he still found difficult. And together they went on to Las Vegas, where, in those early days of the gambling city's role as a top entertainers' Mecca, they were putting away $25,000 a week. Sometimes it was $10,000 *a night* in theatres and hotels.

Their films continued in the old pattern. *You're Never Too Young* was followed by *Artists and Models*, which had nothing to do with the famous Broadway revues. And then there was *Hollywood or Bust*, which seemed like a rhetorical question – and a well-deserved one. It was a terrible picture about two men who win a car and decide to drive across America in it. If there was a warning in that film, it was that people didn't seem too willing even to drive across the street to see a Martin and Lewis film. But it was a situation that would before long resolve itself.

They were fighting quite openly now. 'And,' recalled Walter Scharf, who again did the music on the film, 'it was like husband and wife arguing. I always thought truly that they idolised each other personally but the arguing did get a bit heavy.'

Scharf was only one of a number of people around who said: 'Oh, cut it out, fellows. Let's get on with it.' Jerry didn't deliberately try to suppress Dean, he thought. 'It was just the character he was made to play, the way it was written.' On the other hand, the situation in Dean's home seemed to be resolving itself in a different way. In 1956, he once more found it a lot easier to take things out on the beautiful Jeanne than on Jerry. This time, it was Jeanne who decided to walk out.

Once again, Dean himself appeared as concerned as his wife – or that, at least, is what Louella Parsons wrote. Ms Parsons – who seemed to be permanently perched underneath the pillows of the Martin marriage bed – said that the break 'came as a great disappointment to friends of both Dean and Jeanne'.

There was a long session between the two in which both husband and wife tried to sort out their problems. Dean promised not to go straight to bed when he came home at night – *when* he came home –

and Jeanne endeavoured to find a way of settling for a quiet life. But it didn't work. 'We tried hard to work out our difficulties,' said Jeanne, 'but there doesn't seem to be any solution.' Once again, there were discussions with the lawyers, which didn't bode well for Dean's financial state. Paying alimony to Jeanne would not mean he no longer had to pay it to Betty. Jeanne, for her part, told her attorney that like many another showbiz wife, the 'other woman' was her husband's audience.

Yet, as before, it wasn't long before the lawyers were told that they wouldn't be needed. Dean and Jeanne had made it up – Jeanne possibly thinking that she was better off financially, as well as psychologically, sharing her life with him and Dean deciding that the various pleasures with which Jeanne provided him were not easy to do without.

Things in Dean's other 'marriage' with Jerry were not so easily settled. It was now fairly obvious that he had had enough of playing the dumb, bland singer in films for which audiences paid good money to see Jerry making a fool of himself. Dean was also worried about his much younger partner not merely taking all the glory for himself, but deserving to do so.

From Dean's point of view, the problem seemed to be that Jerry had grandiose plans for 'art' films in which Dean quite clearly had no place whatsoever. Jerry wanted to make a film of the Damon and Pythias story, which he was going to direct but which Dean said would be too clever by half. Jeanne and Patti Lewis were not getting on well either, which didn't help.

Hal Wallis thought that the solution to all the problems would be to let them work separately in one picture each, but that wasn't enough either. Then, Jerry came up with an idea for another script, called *The Delicate Delinquent*. Jerry had written the piece himself – and provided Dean with the part of a policeman.

'You mean I'm going to play a cop in uniform?' Dean asked.

'That's it,' said Jerry, 'a cop.'

'I won't,' said Dean.

'Well,' replied Jerry, 'then we'll have to get someone else.'

Years later, Dean recalled that his response to all that was to say: 'Start looking, boy,' and then walk out. As he said on another occasion: 'I resented being a stooge. It was getting to me, and I was learning more about myself.'

He vowed it was the end. Jeanne said 'wow!' and then gave him what he described as 'the biggest kiss I ever had'.

The Martin and Lewis partnership had lasted ten years. There were sixteen movies between 1948 and 1956.

'How can you give up thirty million dollars?' Dean was asked. 'Just watch,' he answered. 'It's over. It's through. Get it?' Jerry, Wallis and Jeanne and the lawyers all got it. The Martin and Lewis partnership was over and nothing was going to save it.

Scared Stiff 7

Dean could be kind and funny. Sometimes he could be funny while trying to be kind – and giving a somewhat different impression. As he told me: 'The two greatest things that happened to me were meeting Jerry, and then . . . leaving Jerry.' Like most pat sayings, that was only part of the truth. Neither of them really knew, when the tempers had cooled and the ink was dry on the documents that severed the union for good, how they were going to manage. Pride dictated to them both that they would be better off as independents. They were big enough names for it to work – in theory at least. Indeed, if Dean would succeed at all, the business thought, it would be with his records. His was an easy name to have on the books – easy for Capitol, that is. The label chose his songs, organised the arrangements and didn't bother to consult him – simply because he did not want to be consulted. He didn't need to be involved. He heard a tune, read the lyrics and sang it. With the Martin nice-'n'-easy style, that's all you needed.

Just about the only problem was actually getting Dean into the studio. Now, that wasn't because anyone thought he would be difficult, simply that he suffered from claustrophobia and every time he went into an elevator to the studio he still felt sick.

Since Jerry's zany comedy *had* been the thing that people paid money to see at the box office, it was reasonable to expect that they would continue to do so in films in which Jerry Lewis starred alone. The fact that he had always been billed as Jerry Lewis and not part of a surnames-only team had to help.

Similarly, Dean's record sales would be sufficiently remunerative to pay his alimony bills and for most of the other trappings of a life to which he had grown accustomed. They would only get better. At times, he did still sound like Bing Crosby, although there were those who knew them both who would say that the old 'Groaner' had the edge. Dino would probably have agreed. In one of the Martin and Lewis films, Dean sat in a corner smoking a pipe and played the Bing caricature for all that he thought his audiences considered it worth. He even recorded a number entitled: 'If I Could Sing Like Bing' which went: 'If I could sing like Bing, how happy I would be . . . ba . . . boo . . . ba . . . boo.' But would he ever be as big a hit – in movies as well as on disc – as his idol?

Jerry himself had just scored a significant breakthrough in the record field.

Most people believed that Dean broke up the team. But that's where the stories get confused – rather like a Martin and Lewis movie. What was so remarkable about the break-up was the fact that the pair were doing so well. 'We had made millions and there were still more millions to be made,' was how Jerry put it to me when we met. But success wasn't enough.

True, the rows with Jerry were the talk of the trade, even though it was clear that Lewis held his partner in considerable awe; yet, when the break-up happened, there were stunned faces all round, not least at Paramount Studios.

Was this just a failed marriage? I met Jerry in the late 1990s when he opened at the Adelphi Theatre in London, in the British production of the revival of *Damn Yankees*. We talked about the show, about his own beginnings in the Catskill Mountains resorts that forever gloried in the name the Borscht Belt. We talked about his Jewish background and our mutual love of Al Jolson, his father's idol. We inevitably talked about Dean Martin. At the time, the story was still that they had had an acrimonious break-up. 'Oh no,' he insisted. 'I loved Dean. He was wonderful. You have no idea how much I missed him when we broke up.'

So who was actually responsible? For years, there has been as much speculation about that as there once was about their iconic status. Hollywood lore had it that it had to be Dean himself. Plainly, he had regarded it as a long time coming. This was a man who was fed up being the stooge, and not being seen as a vital member of a partnership.

'It took about four years,' Dean said, 'and then it started getting to me because I was learning more about myself, how to become a better actor in those terrible pictures.' Ideally, he would have had a possible solution in mind. 'I would sneak off to some drama school and work harder.'

It might have been easier for him if audiences had known that here was a genuine wit and no mean actor if given the chance – not one who would easily step into the kind of slapstick humour that was Jerry's trait. Indeed, Dean was so witty that the best lines would come to him as he stood before the cameras on a movie or TV set or in front of a mike on the stage. In fact, it was all so natural that you could never be sure whether he was deliberately trying to be funny or not. But because he was so funny and witty, said the gossips, he couldn't handle the feelings of jealousy that this brought out in his partner.

Jerry will deny to his dying day that there was any jealousy between them. He always liked to say that Dean was his big brother, yet it was this very family relationship that made the break-up all the more bitter, even though Jerry now says it was totally necessary.

The funny men had come to the conclusion that they had to be serious. Whenever he could, Dean would emphasise just how dreadful were the films that he and Jerry were making: 'I had nothing to do but learn some songs, repeat what he said or slap him in the face.'

Hal Kanter, who wrote their film *Money From Home*, accepts that Dino was capable of doing more than he was ever asked to do in those days, but he didn't suspect he was unhappy with what he was doing. As Kanter told me: 'He was a very nice man. I liked him an awful lot. I enjoyed being with him. At the end of a day's shooting, he would go off to play golf. Jerry, on the other hand, wanted to stay behind and learn how to be a film maker – which, of course, he would be. He became a god in France and a somewhat lesser person in this country. He was very ambitious at that time. He was also very, very kind. The son of my cousin was in hospital in Atlanta, Georgia, and I asked Jerry to phone him – which he did. The boy was thrilled. What Jerry did was one of the greatest *mitzvahs* [Yiddish for 'good deeds'] that anyone could do.'

As far as Jerry himself was concerned, Kanter now thinks, one of the greatest *mitzvahs* would be to get out of the partnership. That was his secret. But it didn't remain one for long. As Dean said: 'Everyone on the Paramount lot knew it. I had to get away. I wasn't going to spend my life doing pictures like that, so I just quit. There was a big meeting at Paramount. They said you can't walk out. I said, "Just watch me."'

But according to Jerry, it was he who pulled the plug – and it was all for Dean's sake. As he told Barbra Paskin: 'I saw him take years of that crap. I finally said, "This cannot go on," because we were both unhappy.'

And for years, he maintains, he had wanted to do something about it. There had been a hugely successful show in San Francisco back in 1950 which, Jerry maintains, was the biggest thing the city ever saw until the arrival of the Beatles (presumably excluding that little show in 1906 called the earthquake). Jerry says he was angry that the *San Francisco Chronicle*'s review didn't even mention the Martin name. Today, Jerry remembers the man who called him 'little brother' saying he could tolerate the close to one million dollars he earned while being ignored.

But after nine years, Jerry says, Dean decided he himself could stand it no longer. 'He said, "I want my own moment." I said, "You have to have that, Dean," so I broke it up.'

Observers at the time couldn't understand it. Dean was the one they thought could not do without his partner. Jerry says he knew otherwise. If that were so, it was a gesture of extraordinary generosity on Lewis's part. He knew that Dean as a professional performer was dying under his make-up. The saddest thing, he says now, 'was that it was necessary. We had contracts totalling $235 million. It didn't mean anything to either of us.'

Jerry says that he knows he hurt his 'pardner' as much as he was hurt himself. It might have been easier had they been 'knocked through the ropes', but, as it is, they went out on top, a fact to which the writers of 300,000 letters testified. The correspondents couldn't understand how such a decision could be reached without consulting them – the audiences.

The gossip around town was that Dean Martin had allowed his ego to get the better of him. He probably had enough money to live comfortably for the rest of his life, but everybody also thought they knew that Jerry would be the big star, the one talented enough to go it alone. But Dean? He was just a sidekick, wasn't he? He didn't have an act. He didn't have a personality. As for Jerry, he was brilliant, with an unusual style. He couldn't go wrong. Jerry went it alone, made a whole shoal of movies, became a cult, particularly in France. And Dino, the sidekick, became a superstar.

Maybe they both gained from the break-up. As Jerry said: 'Before him, I was adequate. But with him, I was a giant.'

Just after the break-up was announced, Jerry earned his father's everlasting appreciation by recording the Al Jolson standard, 'Rockabye Your Baby With A Dixie Melody' in a not-unlike Jolson interpretation and taking it to the top of what was then still called the hit parade. There were other similar titles in the waxing and it seemed as though everything was going to come up rose-coloured in the immediate future. Indeed, most people were putting their money on Jerry winning the partnership break-up battle. He was doing very nicely indeed.

It was Dean everyone felt sorry for. 'That was the consensus,' Dean said in a *Saturday Evening Post* article. 'The idea was that I'd be left stranded by the wayside. People said, "Poor Dino. Seven kids to support. Tough." You know something? I believed it myself.'

Before long, the whole of Hollywood was taking bets on how the break-up would affect the boys' individual careers. Most of the money was on Jerry. An exception was the American TV personality Jackie Gleason. 'Wait and see,' he said as soon as the news filtered through to the cocktail and dinner-party circuit. 'Wait and see. In a couple of years, Dean'll be bigger than Jerry.' It was to take a little longer than that. Just a little longer. But it was a bet based on a study of form. 'Dean's got a great sense of timing,' Gleason explained to writer Richard Gehman. 'He never presses. He gives the impression that he's a nice guy, which audiences love. He's coordinated like an athlete, which means he can dance when he sets his mind to it. And I knew that once he had a couple of hits under his belt, he would develop the confidence he didn't have when he was with Lewis.'

What Gleason didn't mention was Dean's act, which was now being honed very finely and boded very well indeed for any future as a stand-up comedian. 'I got seven children,' he said on one occasion. 'One of each.'

People felt sorry for them both, couldn't really understand how such a tried and successful arrangement could be abandoned in the face of . . . what?

Lou Costello for one was unable to comprehend why they broke up. He said it was his duty to get Martin and Lewis together again. After all, it was very good publicity for his own team – and he took advertisements in the Hollywood 'trades', the *Hollywood Reporter* and *Daily Variety*, to that effect. By the time the ads appeared, Abbott and Costello had themselves broken up, never to make a movie again.

Martin and Lewis did, however, make a brief comeback together at the Copacabana, which had seen some of the greatest moments of their partnership. The season had been booked before the split and there was no way they could get out of their obligation. So when they clowned around at the nightclub, it was nothing more than a swansong – and a brilliantly executed one at that. They sang 'Pardners' from their film and then shut the door on ever being that again. The Copacabana was unquestionably the swankiest cabaret venue in the country. It was there that Frank Sinatra had some of his most memorable evenings, not least the night that he lost his voice soon after the split with Ava Gardner. Dean and Jerry could barely talk either – to each other. They had separate dressing-rooms, giving their relationship the look of the odd couple of George Burns and Walter Matthau in the movie *The Sunshine Boys*. Plainly, there was little sunshine in either of their lives. When Dean announced that he was packing it all in, Jerry burst into tears.

As Jerry later told *Look* magazine: 'I was numb with fright and shaking all over. My clothes were drenched with perspiration. I thought it would be impossible for me to work with Dean . . . Then Dean came in and we both cried. We shook hands and wished each other luck.'

The gestures were fairly empty. Neither of them wished the other anything of the kind. In fact, they were very soon revealing their true feelings. Dean accused Jerry of giving a series of magazine and newspaper interviews in which he said less than kind things about his former partner.

It was in one of these, in *Look*, that Jerry claimed the break-up was really caused by Jeanne's interference. Jeanne bravely said that she wasn't put out by that. 'Jerry's been on an "I hate Jeanne" kick for eight years,' she told Dave Kaufman in *Daily Variety*. 'I can fight a woman being jealous, but I can't fight the jealousy of a man. Jerry's resentment would have been directed against anyone taking Dean's affection. It's not me – it's any third party. After eight years of the Martin and Lewis bit, I got so used to it I'm immune to anything Jerry says. Dean knew how he felt, but whatever Dean thought of Patti . . . never got out of our front door.' (If ever there had been writing to read between the lines, this was it.) And she added: 'I think it's a shame there is such bitterness and so many things said about their association.' Even so, she maintained that she wasn't happy about the end of the partnership. (That was not what Dean was to say.) 'I thought it was a crime,' she said. 'They were just like magic together, especially in nightclubs. It was awe-inspiring and just seemed it was meant to be.'

Nevertheless, Jeanne knew that she could be seen in a bad light in all this. As she told Kaufman: 'I'm not rooting for Jerry's failure – I'm rooting for Dean's success. We've put far too much emphasis on Jerry. Dean is not malicious, not a gossip, he's just a nice guy who leaves everybody alone – and in this town that's an exception. Dean used to run away from the problems he had with Jerry, but today these problems don't exist. He's happier as a result of what happened, and consequently I am, too. Jerry played no part in our happiness, good or bad, except indirectly. Dean had the courage to face his problem with Jerry and resolve it, and as a result has confidence and is a better man for it.'

She was aware of the financial problems this could all mean. She knew of the money that was riding with Jerry and how little of it was on her husband. She knew better than most that Dean was a lot less sure of himself than she was saying. Yet she was protesting that they were better off now even if he *was* earning half as much as before.

'We wonder at Jerry's concern about all this. He's always talking about Dean, but Dean is so absorbed in his home and family he has no time for that. Name-calling is kind of silly.' However, Dean thereafter felt he was fully licensed to say whatever he wanted about Jerry. Nevertheless, as far as Dean was concerned, none of the stakes he had played for at Steubenville was as high as those he had placed on his career now. It had been Jerry not Dean who had wanted to stick it out. Once the deed was done, the Lewis cards were the ones that seemed all aces.

The Delicate Delinquent without Dean was a huge success, netting something like $7.5 million. At the same time as Jerry's 'Rockabye

Your Baby With A Dixie Melody' disc got to the top of the charts, he opened at America's top vaudeville theatre, the Palace, on Broadway, and was a sensation.

Dean, on the other hand, seemed to be plain bored. He increased his golf playing – and the money for which he usually played. It was once suggested that he lost $40,000 in one game, to which he replied: 'It's so damn ridiculous. It makes me sick. To lose that, I'd have to have $280,000 with tax. I don't have that sort of dough.'

For a time, Dean tried not to talk about Jerry. When he did, it was disparagingly. He called him 'that shmuck', which at least was an improvement on what he'd called him during a telephone conversation overheard by almost everybody walking past his Paramount dressing-room. 'You Jew!' he'd shouted. That surprised most people. It was probably mostly frustration, as Dino was never known as an anti-Semite. In later years, he got on well with other Jews in his business and he wouldn't have stayed so long with Lewis if there was any real racism in him. He and Joey Bishop were good friends in the Rat Pack days – Bishop was the one whom Sinatra called 'The Jew'. And it was Dino who would defend that Jewish one-eyed black star, Sammy Davis Jnr, when – as often happened – Sinatra complained about him.

As far as work was concerned, Dean entered the fray of an inde-pendent show-business existence with all the enthusiasm he showed whenever he was invited to a Hollywood party. Nevertheless, both he and Jerry in their own ways *were* trying to prove the same thing – that they could succeed by themselves. In a way, they were like twins newly expelled from the womb. Jerry, the smaller, runt-like brother, surprised everyone by thriving. Dean, the stronger-looking one of the twins, seemed to need the benefit of an incubator. Instead, he was given a bedroom – or rather *Ten Thousand Bedrooms*. He would have been better off sleeping in a park.

If he ever doubted the wisdom of what he claimed was his decision to break up the team, it was during that first movie that he made on his own. *Ten Thousand Bedrooms* was made in

London and he wished he could climb into any one of them and never be seen again.

MGM thought that the lone Martin would be good box office. It was, after all, the studio whose initials could conceivably have stood for Makers of Great Musicals, and Dean Martin seemed ready for a career as the musical screen idol of the second half of the Fifties. It had a story duly prepared for him – about a millionaire getting involved with a succession of pretty women in a Rome hotel. It was filmed in the Italian capital as well as in London with a co-star called Anna Maria Alberghetti, whose name sounded like the pasta Mama Crocetti still liked to make. These were the ingredients. Put together, they congealed into an unpleasant mess that no one was able to stir together properly.

The talk was still of Dean missing Jerry and Dean was reported to be terribly upset about some of the things said.

Paul Henreid was in the film. 'What a terrible picture that was,' he recalled for me. 'Just terrible. The only tolerable part about it was the fact that Dean was in it. What a very nice, easy-going man to work with! Never gave anyone the slightest bit of trouble.' That was not the impression the *New York Times* had. Its critic Bosley Crowther thought it was a great deal of trouble just having to see the film.

'More than a couple of vacancies have appeared in the musical film, *Ten Thousand Bedrooms*,' he said. 'One is the emptiness alongside Dean Martin who here plays the lead without his old partner Jerry Lewis. And that's an emptiness indeed. Mr Martin is a personable actor with a nice enough singing style, but he's just a nice looking crooner without his comical pal. Together, the two made a mutually complementary team. Apart, Mr Martin is a fellow with little humour and a modicum of charm.' Neither of those things was true. But how did someone like Dean prove it?

Louella Parsons reported in May 1957: 'He's happy that *Ten Thousand Bedrooms* gave him a chance he never had when he was half the comedy team and that is to know he can always be an attractive, popular leading man with a pleasant singing voice.' And it did also mean that he was being noted on his own and for his own efforts – sometimes nicely. When, late in 1957, Sid Grauman invited him to place his foot in a stretch of newly laid cement outside Grauman's Chinese Theatre, there was no suggestion that he had to have Jerry's toes backing up the rear – or, worse, leading from the front. Dean's feet were all his own now.

If Jeanne continued to complain – and she did – that Dean's frustrations were let out in the living-room, it was also true that, working, Dean was the epitome of easy-going charm. It was noticed, as several people working with him at the time subsequently told me, that he was beginning to drink rather too much and that he was greatly improving his golf swing. But nobody saw any example of so much as a slight lowering of his temper threshold away from home. As before, one of the reasons was undoubtedly what another international entertainer had said about himself – his 'complex of inferiority' as Maurice Chevalier described it. And for precisely the same reason – lack of education.

Sammy Cahn, the showman-songwriter who had already written a number of times for Dean, and produced the lyrics for the songs in *Ten Thousand Bedrooms*, told me: 'You didn't go out to dinner with Dean or eat with him at his home. And the reason, I think, was simply that he may not have known which knife and fork to use or was embarrassed about the napkins. Or at least, he thought he didn't, and that worried him a great deal more than it worried anyone else. Drinking therefore became a crutch.'

Sammy was probably right. A youth who is afraid of talking to girls because he may use too many 'dese' and 'dose' and then says the same thing twenty years later takes a very long time to gain a sense of security. And after his starring years with Jerry, failing alone – while his partner succeeded so brilliantly – would have much the same effect as pulling out the lowest can from a pyramid of baked beans in a supermarket.

Cahn was conscious of the professional gaps in Dean's make-up as well as his personal psyche. When Dean's agents had booked a season for him at the Sands Hotel in Las Vegas, he decided that he ought to have something more to do than sing a few songs and hope that the ad-libs would come at the right time – the time, that is, when the customers would be willing to put down their knives and forks and listen. As earlier in his career, an audience could still be tougher than that in a Lower East Side burlesque house. They may not actually throw things, but if they don't like an act, they say so by shuffling their cutlery, by clinking bottles – and by a hubbub of conversation.

Sammy was asked to try to organise a routine for Dean. He thought he knew his student – and all the antecedents of his present situation. He was not unique in still thinking of Dean only in terms of being the quieter half of Martin and Lewis. 'It was one of the great errors of the Great Casting Director in the Sky,' he said in terms of the typical Cahn oversell, and there was a lot of truth in it.

'Whatever one is, the other isn't.' On another occasion, Cahn said: 'Dean's a kind of leprechaun who makes a party go.' He meant that he had more natural humour than he was usually allowed a chance to display. 'He'll sneeze in a sitting position and throw himself round the room. He does the same for his seven kids as he does for an auditorium full of people.'

(All that, of course, presumed that he was ever so sociable. By this time, he had developed a perfect way of avoiding people he didn't like at functions he had had no real intention of attending – had not a little pressure been applied by either Jeanne or the studio. He would give a bleary smile that those who knew him instantly recognised, but which was a Martin unique. Neither was he frightened of breathing seemingly noxious fumes over people he regarded as too-friendly bores.)

Cahn and Martin worked together for weeks – but came up with nothing that Dean could satisfactorily use. Eventually, Dean teamed up with Ed Simmons who – conscious of the greatly depleted Martin bank balance – is reputed to have agreed to the writing assignment for nothing more than a new necktie. It said a lot for Simmons's instinct for a stage personality who had a watery look in his eyes and a reputation for something rather stronger in his throat.

He devised a string of one-liners for Dean that at once made him feel more at ease and established a trademark that would be his for the next twenty-five years. What made Dino special was his ability to fool – and never more spectacularly so than in what became the core of his act.

People at any one of the Dean Martin shows were treated to the experience of seeing the best drunk performance since W C Fields or, at least, Joe E Lewis (the top American nightclub performer of his day, whom Frank Sinatra played in the movie *The Joker's Wild*; no relation to Jerry). I saw it in Las Vegas myself and was so taken in, it was almost embarrassing. I knew I was supposed to laugh when the announcer proclaimed, 'Ladies and gentlemen, straight from the bar, Dean Martin!' but it was so convincing that for a time there was a feeling of intruding on some private misfortune. You saw him take a drink from a trolley, look at the audience, move from side to side, burp a little and for perhaps forty seconds – maybe even a minute, the performance was so excruciatingly mesmerising that no one was counting or looking at their watches – actually say nothing. Finally, like a drunk at a bar confiding facts to you that you didn't want to hear, he announced: 'You know, I don't drink any more.' It was as though he were saying that the one snifter they had just witnessed would be his last. 'No, I don't drink any more. I don't drink any less either.' But it was as though he thought he needed to offer further explanation. Between burps and hiccups, he told them: 'I only drink moderately. In fact, I have a case of Moderately in the dressing-room.'

George Burns nudged his wife Gracie Allen and said it was the funniest thing he had heard in years. Such a comment from one of the world's greatest comedians – who recognised the art of being able to recite other people's lines when he heard them – was the true stamp of success. Everyone else in the audience that night came to a similar conclusion. The building seemed to dissolve and a new Dean Martin career was born.

Sammy Cahn for one was amazed at what he saw out front that first night at the Sands. And a little disturbed. Martin was supposed to sing Cahn's lyric beginning, 'My darling, if I hurt you, forgive me . . .' But Dean was developing a new style. He sang: 'My darling, if I marry you forgive me . . .' (Both Jeanne and her predecessor Betty might have understood that better than the audience, who just thought it was very, very funny.)

Cahn couldn't believe what he had heard. 'I was so *angry*,' he told me. 'Dean was singing a song that had become a hit record. Yet he had to make fun of it. I told him that the audience needed a change from all that laughing. They wanted to hear his hit tune. But he wouldn't listen to me.'

'Did you hear that laugh?' Dean asked him afterwards. You couldn't mistake that laugh. It was more music to the Martin ears than anything coming from the orchestra.

Those laughing the loudest were the very ones Dean most wanted to enjoy the show – his fellow entertainers.

'I thought that was a great performance,' George Burns told me. 'Big talent.' Praise really doesn't come any higher.

Variety was excited beyond measure. Said its critic: 'For the first time since the Las Vegas casinos began importing big-name shows, a production got on and off in sixty minutes, which surprised the croupiers to such an extent they were caught with their sticks down. The credit, and it's only one of many, goes to Dean Martin, who kept his entire turn, including a beg-off speech and the introduction of a number of celebrities in the audience, to thirty-eight minutes.' *Variety* had a reputation for doing things by stopwatch. 'This is in sharp contrast to the average Vegas headliner who appears to make a contest of who can outwait the other. Besides that, Martin is a big click, delivering expertly as a nitely performer with a winning personality.'

The writer Joe Schonenfeld was not beyond comparing the Martin style favourably with that of Dean's idol Bing Crosby (there was always that similarity in styles between Dean and Crosby: 'Bing lost his tonsils and I found them,' Dean said once). And he added: 'Martin's style is surefire. Like Joe E Lewis, he obviously has the knack to sell his type of comedy for big laughs. If audience reaction is any criterion, Martin will be around long and strong as a single entertainer and headliner.'

They seemed prophetic words. So prophetic that few outside of that Sands audience really believed them. People knew Dean was a nice guy, the superb 'catcher' that Jerry would later recall he always recognised. But an individual talent? The word would spread before long. Especially when he said: 'You know where I got these muscles? It was carrying Jerry Lewis all these years!'

There was bitterness indeed for his former partner – and the gall was being mutually administered. But the *Variety* critic noted: 'Opening night, he could have heeded the customer's demands and remained much longer. He wisely quit way ahead.'

That wisdom was part of the talent. In fact, it was just as important as the rest of the act. Timing can be everything. A brilliant show running more than two hours can easily take a nosedive. Broadway is littered with the festering corpses of shows that would have been box-office sensations had someone only listened to the ticking warning of the theatre clock.

Yet the ease with which Dean Martin achieved all his goals at the Sands was deceptive. 'He was riddled with fear,' Sammy Cahn told me. 'I can never understand why people go into a business of which they are so afraid.'

Sammy saw Dean's 'drunk' act and *was* amazed. As he said: 'When the audience sees that, they are in awe. Wow!' But Dean didn't usually manage to finish it. 'You know why?' said Cahn. 'Because he couldn't take his eyes off the audience. He was so full of insecurity and fear. He was absolutely terrified.' But it didn't matter.

Dean was popular, it seemed, with everyone when he was working at the Sands – and not just the paying customers or the management who had found such a crowd-gathering attraction. The croupiers, too, liked him. It wasn't often they had a star who had his sort of gambling experience; a soul brother for the men working at the wheels and cards. Every night after his show, Dean joined them at the blackjack tables. They had never been more popular. After Dean's stint at the hotel, the full-time croupiers got together and bought him a pair of cufflinks as a gesture of their gratitude.

After the Sands triumph – for that indeed was what it was – he was in more and more demand in what *Variety* persisted in calling the 'niteries'. And with the same idea. A song or two and always, but always, the jokes about liquor and the sipping of sufficient doses of amber fluid to keep the image strong.

He took increasingly longer sips of the stuff as the evening wore on and his gait seemed to react as anyone would have expected it to. His eyes rolled, just as the audience liked them to. His syrupy style was, in truth, a lot less like Crosby's now and the effect of the booze gave it a quality that was uniquely his. Or did it?

'I took a sip of the stuff after one show,' Sammy Cahn told me. 'You know what it was? Apple juice! In all the years I've known Dean, he's never taken anything stronger on stage.'

But he *was* looking for something stronger in his career. As he said just before the break-up with Jerry: 'Any Martin and Lewis picture is sixty-five per cent Jerry and thirty-five per cent me. That's the only way it can be. But I'm at the point where I want to change. I've put up with this arrangement all these years because I liked the money better than the prestige.'

That was not the way he wanted to do things now. Jeanne could see the change in her husband and she liked it. There were signs that he was getting down to work a lot more seriously, as though realising that he couldn't put the responsibility – as well as the blame – on Jerry to see that everything happened in a proper businesslike way.

Dean gave every impression of being totally secure. But he wasn't really. He watched for news about Jerry like a hawk in search of a prey that, unknown to itself, is about to break its neck. At the same time, he looked for reasons for reassurance. Not only was he busy at Las Vegas and in the Hollywood studios, but he was very much at the top of the pops as far as the teenage music fans were concerned, a generation which by the end of the Fifties might have been thought to have idols closer to their own age. But any look around record stores in the United States would show that it was the face of Dean Martin that was beaming from glossy sleeves in the racks everywhere. 'That's Amore' had notched up three million copies. 'Volare' sold 750,000 in August 1958. That sort of success meant he was considered a solid citizen of Los Angeles – with a very successful marriage. Which was what prompted him to take his first wife Betty to court.

He said she had neglected the four Martin children and, despite the financial provisions of the settlement, had not spent enough money on them – nor had any plans to do so in future. The court looked at the case and then came to a decision believed at the time to have been unique in Californian legal history. It withdrew the previous arrangement and awarded a father the custody of his children, contrary to their mother's appeal. It meant that Jeanne was thereafter to be mother to *all* her husband's children. Someone worked out that they had a $500-a-week milk bill thereafter.

It couldn't have been easy for Jeanne. She said she didn't even know about Dean's children when they first met, but now she had adopted all four of Betty's brood and was looking after them as well and as lovingly as her own. (Betty's problems coping with the children, and constant suggestions that she was drinking too much, led to a court granting Dean custody.) The house at Melton Drive, Beverly Hills, was a virtual nursery, with the parents seemingly on the sidelines. The choice to take on the complete family was hers alone because, she said, she didn't want the children to go to a boarding school. As she said: 'When I was twenty-nine, I had all seven children.'

But it was Jerry people still wanted to talk about. It was a long time before newspapermen stopped asking Dean about the break-up or – even worse – throwing figures in his face about the great Lewis successes. Inevitably, Dean was forced to come back with statistics of his own. 'I'm doing four times better financially than when I was with Jerry,' he told Dave Kaufman of *Daily Variety*. But he was not being ungenerous about it all. 'And Jerry is, too, I suppose, which is better for the government – and I love this government.'

It was one of the first declarations that Dean had made about politics and just about the first indication he had ever given that he was, despite his immigrant origins, deep down a highly committed Republican dedicated to that other enthusiastic golfer, Dwight D Eisenhower.

There were telling reasons for his apparent keenness for the independent life. 'I am a much happier man since the break. I can do what I want. I have more time with my family. I love working for myself. If something goes over, I know it's me. If something is bad, I don't have to wonder who's at fault.'

But Jerry . . . The questions never stopped. Kaufman had the courage to ask if he would consider guesting on the Jerry Lewis TV show. Dean smiled at that. Of course he would appear on the show – 'when he has his first show on the moon'. That was bitterness real and undiluted.

What Dean really wanted was an opportunity to show Jerry – and all the people who still doubted him – that he wasn't merely doing all right on his own, he was scoring higher than his old partner ever could. Finally, something happened which made it seem that that dream would soon become a reality.

The Young Lions 8

The old relationship with the Mob comes up again just as the Martin and Lewis partnership becomes history. The story in 1952 is that Frank Sinatra, down on his uppers, needs the role of Magio in *From Here To Eternity* and brings the Mafia into play to get him the job. The legend is reinforced by the movie *The Godfather*, in which an Italian-American singer gets a big opportunity after a movie producer finds a horse's head keeping him company in bed one night.

It never happened – the horse's head, that is. But the Mob did play a part in attempting to get an Italian-American singer a serious role in films. Dick Quine, then an eminent producer-director at Columbia Pictures – the studio that made *The Godfather* – told me: 'The Mafia came to Harry Cohn [the iron boss of Columbia] and told him to give a job to this Italian-American singer who was down on his luck. But it wasn't Sinatra. It was Dean Martin they had in mind.' Harry said no.

The reason that Harry said no was that he had his own gentlemen with twisted noses wearing long overcoats, and he was threatening a turf war between the Californian families. Dean had to wait five years before he got the chance to play a soldier, in *The Young Lions*. He needed that role, and it came when he craved it most.

Dean was lying in bed when the phone rang. MCA was on the line with a question. 'Would you mind making a movie with Marlon Brando and Montgomery Clift?'

He didn't take long to answer. 'Are you drunk?' he shouted down the phone. 'Would I mind? I'd love it.'

His manager said he would have to take a cut in both pay and status. In *Ten Thousand Bedrooms* he had been the star and had made $250,000. Now he was being offered a mere subsidiary role in the film of Irwin Shaw's best-selling novel *The Young Lions*. And he would get only $20,000 for it. Dean replied that he would be happy to do it for nothing.

Brando played a Nazi in the film, Clift a Jewish soldier with psychological problems. Dean would play a draft dodger.

If Frank Sinatra hadn't taken much the same sort of deal with *From Here To Eternity* and as a result made a new life for himself as the biggest megastar of them all, it would have seemed a strange set-up. It did appear an extraordinary choice. Here was the former Martin and Lewis straight man, a crooner who had – to use the Broadway terminology – 'bombed' in his last movie, being offered a dramatic role without a song or a gag in sight or hearing distance. It seemed that the notion would be laughed out of the Beverly Hills bars and delicatessens.

The deal was all signed up by Herman Citron of MCA. Dean heard it had been finalised when he was working in cabaret in Pittsburgh. The result of that phone call was a moment of pure emotion that only someone suddenly presented with a gift from heaven could properly appreciate. When he heard that the part was his, he and Jeanne sat down on their hotel bed and cried.

Dean had always said that Hal Wallis had seen him as a Cary Grant type (a statement that had about it a certain degree of self-flattery) who also sang. *The Young Lions* would be the opportunity he craved to prove he was also something more. Not that he accepted the offer without some degree of trepidation. As he said at the time: 'Man, I'm scared. But don't get the idea I'm doing *Hamlet*. [He would repeat the allusion time after time.] I'm playing a guy a lot like me.'

Dean had rarely been happier than he was when making the picture. The result was a smash critically and at the box office.

While the film was in production, he became very friendly with – and protective towards – Montgomery Clift. Nobody seemed to want Clift around. 'Nobody would eat with him,' Dean remembered. So he made sure that he himself did just that. Sometimes Dean put him to bed at night – when the pills 'Monty' was taking took their toll. 'He was such a sad, sad man,' Dean recalled. 'And he was like a boy, so unhappy and rejected. So I said, "Come on – let's go." And I'd bring him everywhere and I'd say, "If you don't want him, you don't want me." And we'd leave the party. But first I'd spit in their faces for him.'

No one was spitting in Dean's face for *The Young Lions*. 'Dean Martin,' said the Los Angeles *Examiner*, 'contributes through his mature and beautifully shaded performance.' Other critics said much the same thing. In fact, the only person who reacted in the least negatively to the performance was the story's creator, Irwin Shaw. Looking back to that time, he told me: 'I didn't like the idea of a crooner like Dean Martin playing the part in the first place and I thought my feelings were borne out. I thought it could have been done better. But things were out of my hands by then.' What is true is that Dean had escaped his shadow. He had jumped across the threshold of a brand-new career.

There isn't much doubt that MCA was responsible for swinging the *Young Lions* deal. Just how it was done is one of those subjects open to a great deal of speculation. The story is that once the MCA people decided that Dean was right for the part, they made it clear that their other two clients, Brando and Clift, wouldn't do the film unless Dean was selected in place of the studio's original choice – Tony Randall. The agency, as one would expect of a colossus like theirs, would always deny that it resorted to anything so close to blackmail.

Dean contemplated what *The Young Lions* meant to him: 'I needed a good strong meaty part to get going.' And get him going it certainly did. It also got other people in the business going – thinking about the property they could so easily have had quite cheaply a month or two before, but who was now a highly marketable commodity. As Dean remarked to the *Saturday Evening Post*: 'The thing to remember is that when I came back to California and began that picture, people were still asking, 'What's Martin doing without Lewis?' Lewis had proved he was doing OK, too – although his initial success in *The Delicate Delinquent* was followed by films like *The Bellboy* and *Cinderfella*, made to a similar formula, which became cult movies in France but played to steadily decreasing audiences at home. Dean, meanwhile, was showing he could do just as well and, as Jackie Gleason had forecast, would soon do better.

That, of course, was just the trouble with a partnership like theirs. No matter how successful either of them would be, each would always be looking over his shoulder comparing his success with that of the other. In the *Saturday Evening Post* piece, Dean made a typically biting comment: 'Don't get me wrong. Jerry has a lot of talent. Only he hasn't got as much as he thinks.'

As Dean said, *The Young Lions* started it going for him and thereafter, 'everything began to roll for me'. It was thanks to Hal Wallis that it subsequently rolled in a certain way – although both sides of that story come out slightly differently. Wallis told me that he believed Dean was a potential star who needed to be guided in the right direction – and, with his fostering, matured into an actor of note, who deserved all the respect he afterwards received. 'I knew,' he told me, 'how necessary it was to put him into something right.'

It would seem that Dean thought himself the victim of legalised exploitation. Wallis had had a contract with the former team of Martin and Lewis for four new films. Now that the pair had separated, he was in a position to demand four films from *each* of them. Which gave him eight new films altogether at a fee of something like $37,500, half what he would have paid for a joint Martin and Lewis production.

Herman Citron saw the other side of that coin. Under the deal, Dean made, between 1959 and 1965, three films for Wallis – *Career*, *All In a Night's Work* and *The Sons of Katie Elder*. Each time, Citron asked for a $75,000 bonus. Each time, the producer refused. He was obliged to pay Dean, as he was Jerry, $37,500 a picture. Each of them owed him four pictures. If they had still been in partnership, that would have been four films altogether. Now they were apart, it meant a total of eight pictures. That, as someone said, was show business.

When there was one more picture left in Dean's contract – Jerry had gone through the same requirement of fulfilling his agreement with Wallis – Citron demanded $475,000. It sounded rather like the National Debt. He said it was based on $250,000 for the picture, and $75,000 bonuses for the other films. Wallis was, like Queen Victoria, distinctly not amused. But in 1968, the last Wallis film – *Five Card Stud* – would be made for that sum.

That was all in the future. For the moment, the fact remained that Dean had established himself as something more than a lush who didn't like to work too hard. He had found a place as one of the lions of show business. And still a young lion at that.

Some Came Running 9

Real proof of an actor's success comes when others in his business extend hands that say: 'You're one of us.' More than anything else, it was *The Young Lions* that did that for Dean Martin. The patronage that meant most for him came from Frank Sinatra, whom he had first got to know in the Riobamba days. In 1959, Sinatra was looking for someone to play the part of a womanising drinker in the film he was about to make for Sol C Siegel, *Some Came Running*. He chose Dean. Or rather Dean chose himself.

Actually, the stories have got somewhat mangled over the years. Undoubtedly, Sinatra gave him what he considered to be his second big opportunity (after *The Young Lions*). Dean told me: 'They needed someone who was supposed to drink a lot and gamble and go with women! Frank said, "My dearest friend, Dean Martin, that was made for him." And I think that role *was* made for me. One of the best I've ever done.'

On the other hand, he told gossip columnist Hedda Hopper: 'I didn't ask him [for the part]. I told him. I said, "Frank, I hear you're looking for a guy who can play a drunk and a gambler. You're out of your mind. You're looking at him." He said, "You've got the job."'

Actually, there was a little more business than that to discuss. Like price. 'All I want,' said Dean, 'is a hundred and fifty thou.' They were talking at a party to celebrate the premiere of Frank's film *Kings Go Forth*. 'When and where do I sign?'

Sinatra told him to be in Indiana the following Monday morning. The film, it was clear to see, confirmed all that most people had said about *The Young Lions*. But in his personal life, it had a more lasting effect. It established Dean Martin as a member of what was being called alternatively The Clan or The Rat Pack.

The Rat Pack had been set up by Humphrey Bogart in the days when he was *the* contemporary cult figure, when the other top names of Hollywood would gather around his table or sit at his feet, chewing whatever fat he thought worth bringing to public attention. Not that they weren't a crowd with thoughts of their own. Hollywood's court restaurateur Mike Romanoff – known as the Prince, since he had borrowed the surname of the former Russian Imperial family – was one. The others were the more illustrious members of a Hollywood community that included Sinatra, Katharine Hepburn, Spencer Tracy (of course), John Huston and Bogart's wife, Lauren Bacall.

When Bogie died in 1957, Sinatra took over his responsibility of establishing an iconoclastic society who said just what they wanted to say when they wanted to say it – and enjoyed the experience. They were there to counter the Establishment.

That was the official reason. Or excuse. In practical terms, the Sinatra version of The Clan, as it ultimately would be known most of the time, was more a laughing, drinking group that formed itself with nothing more serious in mind than that its members would have a good time in each other's company.

Frank became known as the Chairman of the Board. Dean was his recognised deputy. Others included Sammy Davis Jnr, Joey Bishop, Peter Lawford, Sammy Cahn and their one female member, the then kooky Shirley MacLaine, who had played a prostitute – with the customary heart of gold – in *Some Came Running*.

One newspaper suggested that theirs was more a Mouse Pack than a Rat Pack, whose members tried to emulate Frank, even if they only drove Chevrolets. Plainly, the author of the piece had never visited the members' garages.

Indeed, it was for long the main status symbol of the Clan (Dean excepted; he was content with his Cadillac) that its members invested in an Italian-Detroit hybrid known as a Dual-Ghia. It was long before the term Ghia was added to Ford production models and when Sinatra bought one, Eddie Fisher and Tony Curtis – sometime Clan affiliates – decided to drive them, too.

Lauren Bacall, who had to be regarded as the High Priestess of her late husband's Rat Pack, was inclined to resent the name being taken over by Sinatra and his cronies. 'The Rat Pack,' she has said, 'really stood for something. We had officers. Bogie was Director of Public Relations and I was the Den Mother. We had principles. You *had* to stay up late and get drunk and all our members were against the PTA. We had dignity. And woe betide anyone who attacked one of our members. We got them.'

Most looks at the Sinatra clan seem to indicate a similar devotion to fraternal responsibility. They didn't call Frank the Pope for nothing. It was considered a suitable nomenclature for the man whose views on life were never less than infallible.

The Clan it was originally and for years The Clan it remained. In recent years, the Rat Pack has taken over in history as the name for the gathering of Sinatra and Pals. The fact that this was the title of Bogart's mob has been virtually lost in history. In this form, it really began when Sinatra rang Dean to say that he hated working alone: 'Come and join me at the Sands,' he said. When Dino arrived with his dinner suit and red handkerchief, Sinatra himself was more relaxed – allowing Dean to get most of the laughs. Before long, they were deciding to make a movie with the rest of the pack.

Groups like his were really part of a revered Hollywood tradition. In the old, old days of Hollywood, John Barrymore had surrounded himself with hard-drinking cronies like the one-eyed director Raoul Walsh. When Barrymore died, Errol Flynn took over his set. You saw them in a score of Flynn films, those permanently inebriated pals of his like Alan Hale, Bruce Cabot and Guinn 'Big Boy' Williams. And if they weren't laughing, drinking and womanising with him, lesser members of the set were employed by Flynn cleaning out his tennis courts. James Cagney had Pat O'Brien, Frank McHugh and Allen Jenkins.

What was special about Bogart's Rat Pack and Sinatra's Clan was that these were performers, after the chiefs themselves, of largely equal status who would never be sent to clean up anyone's tennis courts, not even their own.

News of The Clan's existence started creeping into American prints in the late Fifties – but not too late for Shirley MacLaine to be described as 'a new actress' and for another fringe member, Pat Lawford, wife of English-born actor Peter, as 'a daughter of ex-Ambassador, Joseph P Kennedy'; her brothers weren't even mentioned.

There were others who were more on the periphery of things. Like George Burns who qualified for honorary membership simply because he was the funniest man any of them knew – and the ability to be funny was as much a requirement for association as the knowledge of golf is to joining a country club. Jimmy van Heusen was given special status as the song-writing partner of Sammy Cahn, and David Niven, Judy Garland and Milton Berle were awarded favoured attention.

The men in The Clan had other qualifications besides the cars they owned. Each of them had a white seersucker jacket made by Sy Devore in Hollywood for around $125 – a fortune at the time. Other groups like theirs like to think they have a group arrangement to get things wholesale. In The Clan, it was the cost of the thing that really counted. The more they spent on their clothes, the closer they were to the top of the tree.

They were all aware of the exclusivity of their existence – and the price they were expected to pay for it. As Dean said once: 'You'd be crazy to walk down Fifth Avenue without a long black overcoat and a false beard.'

It wasn't long before Dean was regarded as the number two in the ensemble. Although no one had dared describe him as the

Deputy Pope, there were alternative thoughts in mind. Sinatra was sometimes called the General. Dean was called the Admiral – possibly because he knew his way around the liquids of the world, if not the waters.

In fact, Joey Bishop would tell me that he himself was really the only non-drinker in The Clan. 'I never drank. Nor was I really very sociable in the way the others were. I was amazed that they let me be the hit I was. The reason was that I had three $300,000-a-week straight men.'

They played together at Vegas. There was always a bar on stage – mainly for Dean's benefit. On top of it was a bottle of JV whisky that looked the real thing, except that it was Dean's usual shot of apple juice. 'One night,' said Bishop, 'I took a swig from the bottle and Dean told me not to say anything. In the course of the evening, I got thirsty and drank some more. Then I heard mumbling in the audience: "Look at Joey. He can outdrink the both of them." I'd forgotten what I was doing.'

By now, Dean's drinking was the main topic of conversation about him. He was drinking more, although rarely enough to justify his reputation. In fact, Joey Bishop recalled the time someone button-holed him about Dean. 'He really drinks, doesn't he?' said the man. 'Yeh,' said Bishop. 'He really drinks – and then he's up at eight o'clock in the morning to play thirty-six holes of golf. And playing for pretty good money. So what do you mean, he's drinking?'

It was merely part of The Clan's first unwritten rule that they sterlingly defend the dignity of their fellow members. But Bishop insisted: 'I never saw Dean drunk.'

Other comedians had used drink as a prop before. Dean Martin perfected it – as much as anything as a gap filler. He knew he could refer to the bottle (if not actually drink from it) any time he forgot a line or a lyric.

He built a marvellous routine from a naturally slurring speech and a pair of eyes that would gloss over at the mere sight of a cocktail shaker. And always, from the announcer: 'Ladies and gentlemen . . .

direct from the bar . . . Dean Martin.' It was funny. It was also extremely clever.

He already had Harry Crane working for him as his principal writer, a man who thought that the best way of maintaining his relationship was not to talk about his meal ticket.

But as much as anything, Dean's gift was always to say and do the things that no writer could put into a script. That was why his friends told him not to bother about Jerry any more. But he always did. And nothing rankled with him more than that charge about not contributing to the muscular dystrophy campaign. 'Those millions Jerry raised were raised by both of us over a ten-year period, if anybody's interested. *We* did it, not he. I'm still doing it.' As he told *Variety*: 'I just don't want him taking credit for something he didn't do alone.'

Dean himself was busy with his own charities. It was more and more becoming part and parcel of show-business life that top stars worked for good causes, but Dean was undoubtedly going beyond the call of what could be considered his duty.

By October 1958, he had raised two million dollars for the City of Hope Hospital, which had opened a Dean Martin wing.

Dean and Jerry got together again, very briefly, on the Eddie Fisher TV show. It happened when Dean was in the same studio and heard that Jerry was Fisher's guest and was about to do a song on the show. Dean pushed his head through the curtain and with the camera and the microphone switched on, called over to his partner: 'Please. Just don't sing.' Jerry was thrown off his guard but did manage to stammer a 'Hey, come back', while a perplexed Eddie Fisher looked on and the producer and cameraman didn't know what had hit them. Dean didn't do any more on that show – or on any other with Jerry – for a very long time.

'If I'd stayed longer,' Dean maintained, 'they'd think we were together again.' And that for Martin would be his idea of agony, as he was never reluctant to point out.

It was to get worse. Jerry had a TV spectacular the next day. 'He has a show tomorrow? I'm leaving town tonight!' It was funny, but not since Hitler invaded Russia had two former partners had as much unfettered dislike for each other.

Once, Dean invited Jerry to his place for a drink, but neither of them enjoyed the experience and while they promised not to avoid each other in future – as Jerry had been doing whenever their paths threatened to cross – they were glad to part. As for Dean himself, he wasn't much interested in television at the time. There were too many song-and-joke men suffering from overexposure on the small screen. There were a number of suggestions that he was simply being lazy in turning down various offers of a thirteen-week season all his own. His reasons were novel and showed an inbuilt intuition that not nearly enough other entertainers had yet been clever enough to spot. The problem, as he explained to Hedda Hopper in 1959, was not so much the work he would have to do on any *Dean Martin Show*, but in honouring promises to other people. 'When I turn down an offer for thirteen shows, it doesn't mean I'm against doing that many. But when I take on thirteen, it means I'll be doing twenty-six. I'm supposed to do two shows a year, so I end up doing six. On my own show I need two guests. I had Bing Crosby and Phil Harris on the understanding I'd go on their shows. I'll have Frank Sinatra and Patti Page and I'll reciprocate with them. I've done one with Phil Harris and Alice Faye. That was a return for his appearance with me. No money exchanged. I'll have Dinah Shore for my next and I'll be doing hers. Same with Lucy and Desi [Lucille Ball and her husband Desi Arnaz].'

The business about reciprocal arrangements was to bring Dean a problem. There was a row over a deal allegedly done with Eddie Fisher to appear on his show in return for a $25,000 kitchen. It was said that he 'walked out'.

That wasn't the way Dean saw it at all. 'I told Fisher eight weeks prior to the show I wasn't going on. I said I knew what a kitchen cost and if I needed a new one, I'd buy it. I thought it would be an expensive kitchen, but it wasn't. I said I didn't want to do a show for that kind of a deal . . . Is giving eight weeks' notice walking out?'

What was galling about that set-up was that Jerry Lewis stepped into Dean's place – the way it looked, the programme was trying to rub the Martin face in the mud – and did the show for nothing, although that was probably a reciprocal deal, too.

'Many thought I was buggy two years ago when I turned down offers. Now those people are going crazy because they're on too often. You could be on every week if you allowed yourself to get too involved.'

That was why he was maintaining there was no chance of his ever agreeing to do more than two shows a year – words he would choose to swallow before very long. For the moment, however, he was saying that the only chance of that happening was 'if I am doomed in pictures'. And there was no sign of that on the horizon, either.

He was very pleased with the way that side of his career had taken off. Hedda Hopper wrote in 1959: 'Dean Martin fans who watch the easy-moving, good-natured idol singing and swapping wisecracks with the world's top talents have caught the essence of the man as he is in private life. Dean Martin the motion picture actor is another thing. In the last two years, he's surprised us with his ability to take on the colour of a character and bring impact to a dramatic situation. Since he's hot in both fields and rolls up a fortune annually with records, he's almost a photo finish with Frank Sinatra as top man in the town.'

He followed his success in *Some Came Running* with an even more impressive performance in *Rio Bravo*. It really was a brave move on his part and it came off splendidly, even though he subjected himself to playing in a Western with John Wayne. 'I'd never imagined old Dino could do it,' Wayne told me shortly before he died. But Dean was as comfortable in the picture as he was with a glass of Bourbon in his hands.

And comfortable with the company he kept. He joined a highly respected Western repertory company that included Ward Bond and Walter Brennan – and had Angie Dickinson in one of her earliest demonstrations of how sexy she could look in a cotton blouse.

Thereafter, Dean always called her Feathers – the name of the character she played in *Rio Bravo*. She would say that he always 'purred' when he spoke to her, a guy who was, she maintains, 'like whipped cream, soft and gentle'.

But it was Dean's performance in this story of a drunken sheriff and a cowboy against a band of brigands that got people talking. *Time* magazine was particularly impressed by Dean's proficiency with a gun. 'Actor Martin,' said the magazine 'makes a snap shot that snaps a horseman's reins at twenty paces.'

The film was for Warner Bros. with Howard Hawks producing and directing. Immediately afterwards, Dean honoured his commitment to Hal Wallis with *Career*, about a World War Two veteran, played by Anthony Franciosa, who makes the trek to Broadway determined to be an actor and a star. Dean played a fast-talking, small-time producer, who gives him his chance in an off-Broadway production to which no one goes.

Time was comparatively lukewarm. All it could find to say about Dean's performance was that he and Shirley MacLaine 'fairly well supported' Franciosa, but added: 'the main trouble with the picture is the perhaps inevitable one that the characters are so actorish and attitudinous that they come to seem phony and their problems unreal. They are so passionately and exclusively interested in themselves that the spectator may sensibly conclude that they do not need any interest from him.'

Tony Curtis, his then wife Janet Leigh and James Whitmore joined Dean in *Who Was That Lady?*, which might better have been called *Who's Kidding Who?* It was about a man who is seen kissing a girl and then has to convince his wife that it was all in the line of his FBI duty.

Dean was exceedingly popular on the set of that film – as he was in most productions in which he was involved. Janet Leigh told me, however: 'I felt that Dean had great depths that had not been plumbed yet. He's a naturally funny and very sweet man with tremendous potential that is still there.' People have said that he can be indifferent to things around him while working in a film. Janet said: 'I didn't find that at all. I think he's very, very nice.'

It was at a party at Dean's house that Janet met her present husband, Bob Brandt. 'When Dean and Jeanne heard that we were going to get married in Vegas, they decided to give us our wedding. Those are very nice people.'

Dean, like his mentor Frank Sinatra, was very pleased with his combined role as a serious actor and a nightclub performer. In fact, he was saying that his only regret was that he had not struck the dramatic vein a lot earlier. 'Singing is a form of acting,' he was to say a couple of years later, 'but it is not IT. Singing is a different form, a necessary training. It gives you voice. It gives you the feeling and expression, like dancing gives you a certain grace. But you've got to assemble yourself, and the only way you can do that is by acting and living and looking at yourself honestly.'

In 1960, he was not noticeably unhappy teaming up with one of the comedy geniuses of the age, Judy Holliday. The film was *Bells Are Ringing*, in which she played the girl behind the answering service switchboard, and he the man who falls in love with her voice. It wasn't a marvellous film, but it did give Dean his first shot at a musical since *Ten Thousand Bedrooms* and he was a good foil for Miss Holliday. It was also his first film since the *Bedrooms* flop in which he was indisputably the male lead.

The question arising out of *Bells Are Ringing* was whose film it was – Dean's or Judy Holliday's? The songwriter Jule Styne certainly would never have given the accolades to Dean. He hated the way he thinks Dino destroyed his big number 'Just In Time'. As far as he was concerned, it was a 'throw-away'. As he said: 'He kinda phoned it', which might be taken as meaning that Dean took the theme of the film about a telephone answering service a little too seriously. '*Bells Are Ringing* was shot very badly,' said Styne. 'It was shot very badly because if you have a comedienne like Judy, like Chaplin, you have to be in close with that camera all the way.' The songwriter was brutal in his assessment of the problem, in which Dean didn't come out at all well. 'I'd rather have had either a better actor or a better singer, one or the other, but not halfway.'

Now if that wasn't a strong enough indictment, Styne went further: 'He couldn't have cared less . . . It was a marvellous stage musical here in New York; it turned into not so good a picture.'

That was the pique of a writer speaking. On the other hand, he could have had a point. You wanted Dean to make love to the camera – to be more intense. Somehow, you did get the impression that he was taking things a little too easily.

He was to tell Don Alpert of the *Los Angeles Times*'s *Calendar* section: 'I call it a wonderful job, working in pictures. To me it's a job, a great job. And if any actor tells you it's tough, tell 'em they're full of beans. I love these comedians who give interviews saying you have to be serious to be funny! To become half a success in what you do, you have to enjoy it or else you become a griper. The good Lord gave me a talent and I'll use it until I run dry.' Which was not a word Dean Martin liked to use.

He was spending a lot of time on the nightclub circuit, although he wasn't a great believer in doing too much travelling any more. He didn't have to. When he opened at the Coconut Grove in Los Angeles, he got all the applause – and money – to which he thought he was entitled. As Kendis Rochlen noted in the Los Angeles *Mirror News*: 'Dean Martin, who says he was relaxed when Perry Como was just learning how to lather, ambles into the Coconut Grove tonight to entertain the folks nice and easy like.' As he told her: 'I'm not only more relaxed than Old Perry, I'm more Italian. At least I can sing in the language.' He was also trying to outslim him. He was able to do it, he could claim, because he had decided to go in for physical fitness.

'A while back I saw that I was getting just a trifle flabby. When my kids punched me in the stomach, I could feel it. So I've been down to my cellar every day and exercising. I've got all the equipment – medicine ball, bicycle, the whole ravioli. I'm back in shape now. Go ahead, punch me.'

At that time, the only way of punching Dean would be to say that his appeal was falling off. And that wouldn't have floored him either. He had all the evidence he needed to the contrary. He also seemed as slim as a twenty-year-old – and a lot better-looking. He was clearly a devilish performer, although not an overtly sexual one, for which Jeanne for one was grateful. His jokes were aimed at the men in the audience, not the women. There was never any question of his looking specifically at a woman in the audience, another fact which would gratify any wife.

He was also inordinately busy. There were those who could not understand how he managed to keep going. 'When do you sleep?' an inquisitive business associate asked him. 'I faint a lot,' Dean replied. That was not the sort of humour a writer could possibly have penned for him. Still, he hadn't yet got to the very summit. His money – $350,000 a film – was in 1960 only half of what Sinatra could get and he wasn't at the time considered a sufficiently hot property to justify earning a percentage of a movie's profits – which he was getting in Las Vegas. That was the town where you saw an all-singing, all-joking, all-happy Dean Martin.

'We were working once,' Joey Bishop told me, 'with Frank singing while I was tending the bar on stage. People in the audience were laughing – and I couldn't see why. Then I looked round and saw Dean behind me. He was flicking ash from his cigar on to my new jacket. I said, "What the hell are you doing?" He said, "I'm making you into a colonel." The ash was forming like a colonel's eagle. When I complained, he said, "Now I'm gonna bust you." And he blew it off.'

Dean's deputy-leadership of The Clan didn't make him any more sociable than he had been before entering it. As Joey Bishop put it: 'He was basically a loner. If you didn't see Dean for ten years, he'd say, "Hi, how are you?" – and be gone.' But, despite his own reticence, he gave some of the best parties in California at the time. 'He didn't *try* to be funny,' said Bishop. 'He and Frank and Sammy would get together and be terribly funny. Simply because Dean's a natural. There was no trying in it.'

Although sometimes his guests felt that they were being put in something of a trying situation. Every Christmas Eve, the Dean Martin parties were the ones to which people wanted invitations. It was a sign of arrival. However, the guests knew that after a couple of hours, they would be parties without a host. That was when Dean would decide he was tired and simply go to bed. The Clan laughed about it but there wasn't much else they could do.

Bishop had got into the group largely as the result of his close friendship with Dean. Martin and Lewis had followed him into the Casablanca roadside café opposite the Garden State Track in New Jersey. Dean's taste in humour appealed to Bishop, who saw every reason to join him in what he considered this monument to good fun if not taste called The Clan. 'After all, what was it?' he asked me. 'Five guys having fun.'

And fun was very much the totem pole around which they all danced. When they made each other laugh, they were paying their dues. Dean qualified highly in this respect. 'He has one of the best comedy minds in the business,' Joey Bishop told me. 'Nothing's going to throw Dean with his laconic expression. He has the best comedy delivering and timing of anybody you've ever seen. He can steal lines from men who consider themselves comedians.'

Once, when Bishop and Sammy Davis Jnr were topping each other's impressions on stage – doing between them anything from Amos 'n' Andy to Paul Muni – Dean staggered on stage looking as though he had just done a deal with the JV distillery and proceeded to demolish everyone around him with a perfect Cary Grant impersonation. When the house went wild, all he said was: 'I was doing that crap years ago,' and walked off.

What they had was a mutual respect for each other's talents. As Bishop said: 'No one tried to score off the other guy.' What they also had was a distinct ability to work with each other. Bishop had been on bills with Sinatra since 1952.

In 1960, The Clan grew up and had more fun than they had ever had before. They decided to make a movie together, called *Ocean's*

Eleven. It was arranged with a great deal of thought. This wouldn't be just a partnership of pals. It would have a distinct value that only members could fully appreciate. For these were hard-working performers in great public demand, who were not content merely to be engaged on a film. They each had their nightclub or stage interests. With this thought in mind, The Clan became essentially a top entertainers' trade union – looking after the interests of its membership, shielding each of them from the excessive demands of overwork. If the producers didn't like the arrangements they made, that would be the end of the picture. Consequently, nobody dared make the slightest protest.

Conveniently for all those concerned, *Ocean's Eleven* was set in Las Vegas – where Dean, Frank, Sammy and Joey Bishop all had shows at the time and Peter Lawford was just as diligently making his way around the casinos. They also agreed that, when necessary, they would substitute for each other on stage. It was a hotel owner's idea of paradise. And since Dean was joining Frank in control of the Sands casino, it suited them as well as anyone else.

'That was why we decided,' said Bishop, 'that the guy who had the early shots in the movie, who would have to get to the set first thing, wouldn't have to work at night. But as it developed, I had the first night myself – and found the other guys in the audience. Then, they started kidding. The next thing we knew was that they joined me up there [on the stage]. It got so we each looked forward to what would happen at the end of a show.'

The audiences weren't averse to it either. Before long, a tradition had been established. A Clan member's show was an invitation for all the others to get in on the act. It was hell let loose. No semblance of a script. No attempt at letting the public in on most of the frolics. The paying customers were invited to sit in on a private joke.

The tiny, skinny Sammy Davis Jnr was the centre of attention for having converted to Judaism. When he jumped on the stage in the midst of Dean's Vegas show, Martin picked him up and said: 'I'd like to thank B'nai B'rith for giving me this trophy.'

'I remember,' said Bishop, 'that on Sundays we never used to put on tuxedos. It was a tradition. So we decided that we'd all wear black mohair suits. Frank turned to me and said, "How do I look?" I told him, "If you're gonna look dead, you might as well *dress* dead." It was continuous banter.

'As tired as we were, working on *Ocean's Eleven*, none of us could wait until we got together in the evening. We just broke each other up. Frank would sing a few songs, I'd do a monologue. Dean would sing and joke and Sammy would do his impressions.'

By the end of the first week, all four had their names on the Sands marquee – working at the hotel two shows a night and then at 2.30 on Sunday morning doing a special performance for the other show people working on The Strip who hadn't any other opportunity to see The Clan in operation. That is an old showbiz tradition, born as much of a desire to impress one's contemporaries as to provide a public service.

Strangely, for a group so close, there is no evidence of the slightest row between any of The Clan's members. 'In fact, it worked the other way,' said Joey Bishop. 'For example, when they saw I didn't have too much to do, one of them would say, "Hey, give Joey something to say. He's standing around with nothing to do."'

As Sammy Davis Jnr said: 'When I'm with the group, I can relax. We trust each other. We admire each other's talent. People think we're troublemakers. But only two of us have escapades. Frank and I. And we have them by ourselves. There's nothing tantamount to panic when we're with the others. After all, Dean Martin has seven children. I guess we're all the sort of people who could get in a little trouble. But if one of us is in trouble, nobody in our group talks about it. When Eddie Fisher split up with Debbie Reynolds, none of us said anything to him about it.'

The film was much the same as the live performances. *Ocean's Eleven* was written as the story of a group of friends (perfectly planned casting if ever there had been any) who decide to rob the kind of casino where they all – except Lawford – now earned most of their specially baked bread and custom-produced butter. For once, the story was more important than the clowning – a fact underlined when the film was remade forty years later with George Clooney at the helm.

Joey Bishop had the toughest time. Despite their original plans, not only was he usually the first to get on stage, he was also the first to get to the studios in the morning – and, because he played an ex-boxer with a broken nose, the only one who required detailed make-up. 'It wasn't exhausting. We got exhilarated by it all, by the charisma of everyone around us. Every night, someone else showed up. Once it was Milton Berle. Then Red Skelton. George Burns. Jack Benny. They all came round, too.'

The Clan appearances were well orchestrated by the President of the Sands, Jack Entratter. It was not just standing-room only, more like perching-room. People who couldn't get tickets were haunting the aisles, the corridors, all but clinging to the rafters. It was a fire chief's nightmare.

Once, it was Dean's name heading the marquee sign. 'Dean Martin and friends'. Anybody who had ever fried alive in the Las Vegas desert sun knew what that meant. Those who managed to get tickets – and you usually had to know someone who knew someone else to obtain an entry for opening night – were not disappointed.

The tanned showgirls – each with the necessary amount of aid from Max Factor administered to parts of the body that were never allowed to be exposed in most other areas of the United States – had focused attention on the stage. The waiters had stopped pouring the wine and serving the regulation steaks. The lights had gone down for the main attraction. The customers were waiting expectantly. That was when a voice was heard over the loudspeakers. 'Hey, Frank.' It was Joey Bishop. 'I can't find Dean. Take his place until we locate him.'

The house dissolved in one solid mass of applause that sounded like one of the fruit machines upstairs delivering a jackpot. Of course, that was precisely what it was. The band was playing 'I've Got the World On a String' and the diners knew precisely that they were getting what the *Los Angeles Times* had described as 'the most expensive opening act of all time'.

Sinatra sang two or three other songs while Bishop still protested that he was being serious about not finding Dean, who had probably fallen into a vat of newly produced vodka.

Finally, Dean appeared. Almost anyone else would have seemed an anti-climax, following Sinatra in the same business. Of course, it had all been planned in advance to the last whistle and clap from an audience they knew would be eating out of their hands. But it still provided Dean with a problem: how do you prevent following Frank being anything but an anti-climax? By saying: 'I thought I didn't have to open till Wednesday' – and then being told that Wednesday it was. What Sinatra had done was to warm up that audience to the point where they would have given a standing ovation to the Salvation Army's band school.

Nobody paid Frank – or Joey. If they had, the cost in those days of the early Sixties would have gone into six figures. Today, seven – without the first of those figures necessarily being a one.

The *Los Angeles Times* critic said of Dean's performance in that show: 'Martin gives what is probably the best impression in show business of a happy drunk but don't kid yourself – this cat knows what he's doing every second on stage. He's not about to lose his image after years of building it up.'

It was the peak of The Clan's success. And it had to end. 'We kept trying to top what we had done before,' Bishop recalled for me. 'Dean and Frank were marvellous with each other. But you can't keep on like that for ever.'

The end was really signalled – as was so much in the America of the time – by the inauguration of John F Kennedy. As Bishop said: 'We'd all campaigned for him. We all went to Washington for the inaugural. What was going to follow that?' Even Dean had to agree – although he was distinctly not of their persuasion. He was so easy-going that no one expected him to argue about anything more serious than the length of a piece of spaghetti, but in politics he saw eye to eye with none of the group, not even with one-eyed Sammy. The others were Democrats, Dean was a conservative Republican. But he joined the others, officially at any rate, in lauding Kennedy on *his* opening night.

The Clan kept him busy – even if they divided up their activities. In *All In a Night's Work*, Shirley MacLaine was the only fellow Clanner, in a story about the heir to a publisher's millions. The film itself certainly didn't add to anyone's fortune.

Nor did *Ada*, Dean's second film of 1961, which was not a Clan property. His co-star was Susan Hayward who, according to another fellow actor in the film, Wilfrid Hyde White, was acting very strangely. 'We didn't know it at the time but poor Susan was already showing signs of the effects of the brain tumour which before long would kill her,' he told me. 'She was very undisciplined. Never knew her lines – and was very impolite. She never said, "Good morning". Dean, who behaved like a perfect professional on the film, would stop her and say, "Good morning" and she'd go fumbling about the script and say, "Where's that? I can't see it."'

Wilfrid, who had a reputation as the perfect elderly English gentleman, but who could be extraordinarily salty in the use of language, said he went 'blue with embarrassment' when Dean confronted her on this. He went up to Miss Hayward and said: 'You'd better say "Good morning" to Wilfrid because he thinks you're a c**t!'

Hyde White, who changed his accent to play a Southern town's mayor, added: 'She made it very boring for everyone. But Dean was kindness itself.'

But he wanted a chance to get back to The Clan. The opportunity presented itself, as usual, just when Dino needed it most. The Pack, as Dean preferred to call it, once recorded the big number from Cole Porter's *Kiss Me Kate*, beginning, 'We open in Venice'. More often, the boys opened at Vegas. They made films near by because they were bored during the day – or during the weeks when one of the gang was appearing at the Sands and the others had nothing to do.

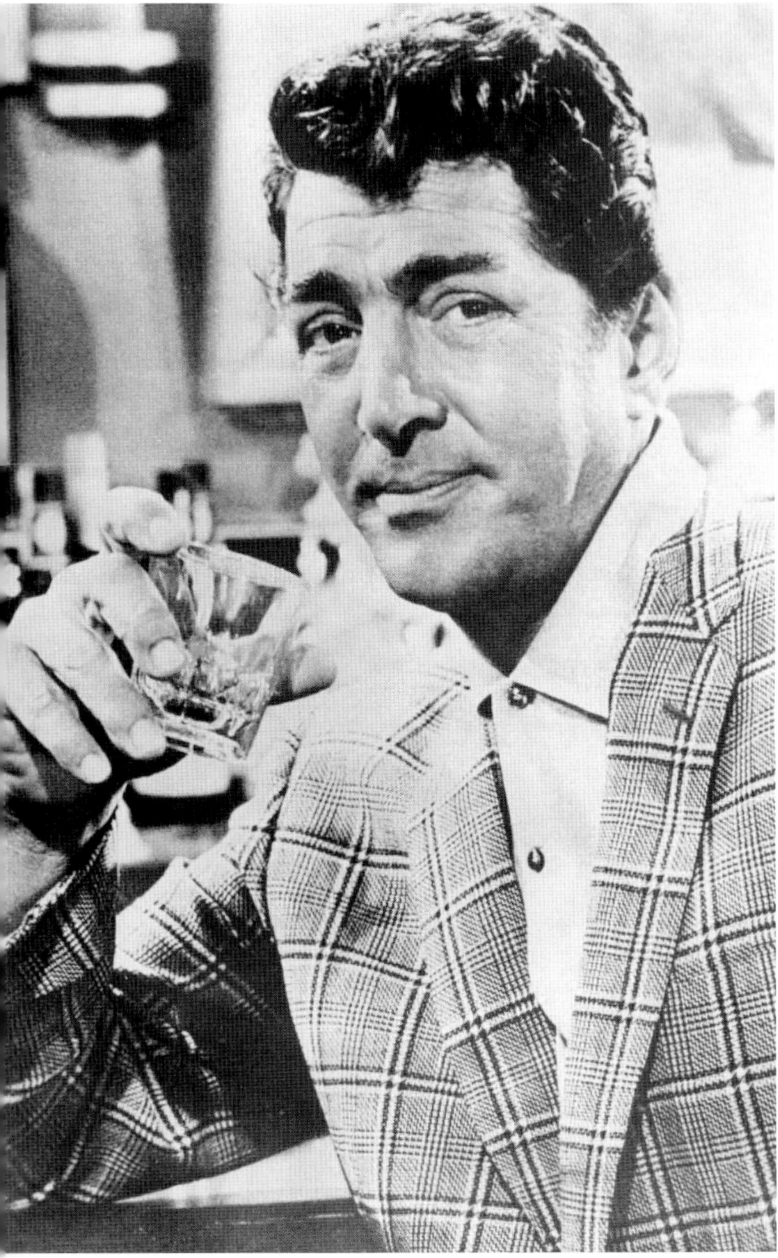

no: That's the image.

Dean, the married man.
With wife number one, Betty,
in 1948. © Bettmann/Corbis

(Right) With Jeanne, the girl
to whom he returned – and
in whose arms he died.
© Hulton-Deutsch Collection/Corbis

ways on the golf course: Dean
isn't a praying man most of the
me but with a club in his hands
d Bing Crosby, his biggest
fluence, as a partner, there had
be an exception to the rule.

ttmann/Corbis

an, the family man. In 1957
th Jeanne and baby Gail, who
uld later be the only other
artin to go into show business.

ttmann/Corbis

(Left and opposite) Martin
and Lewis – the partnersh
that couldn't last.

Posing for Little Brother: C
the set of their first movie
together, *My Friend Irma*,
1949. © Snap/Rex Features

They both had recording contracts – easy to see which one got the platinums. ©Corbis

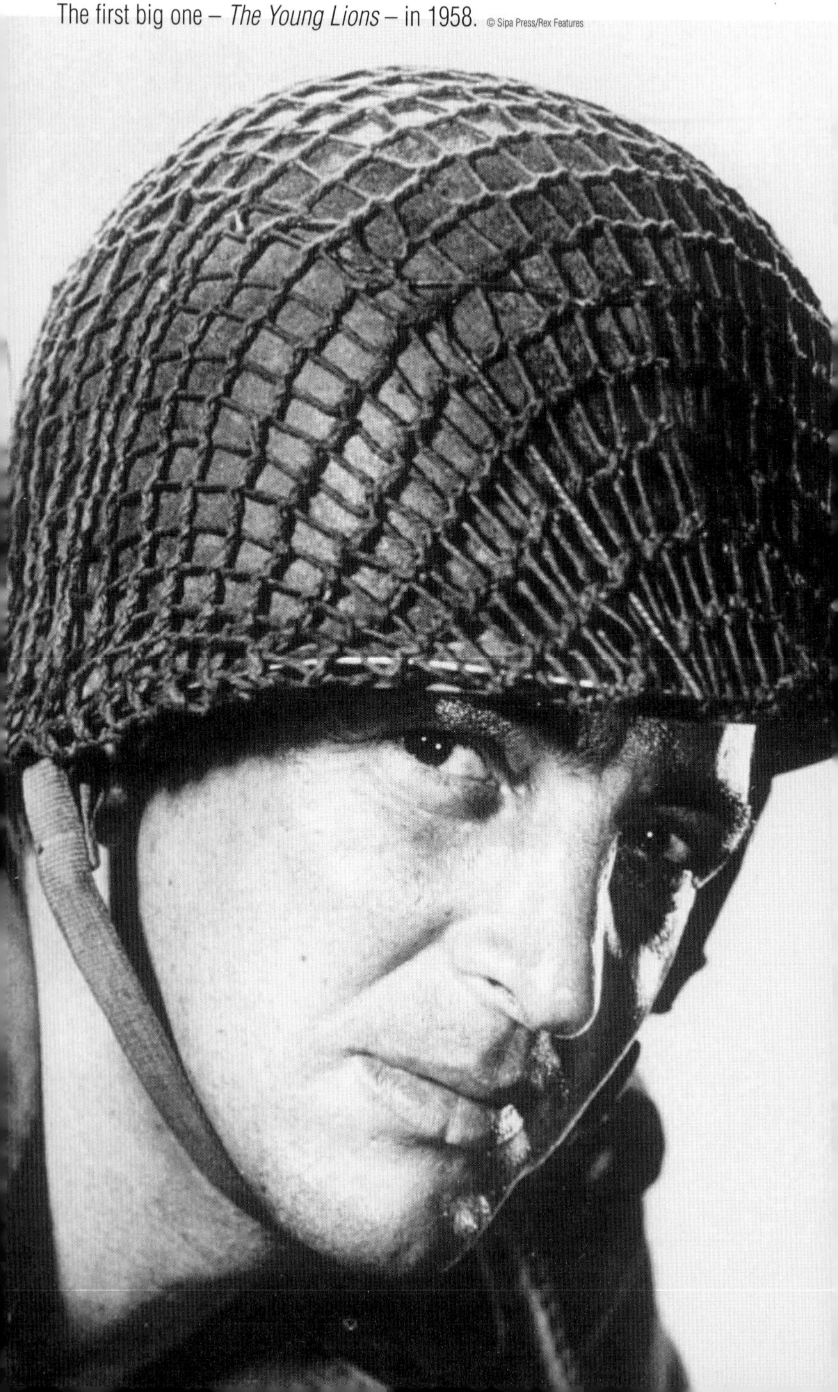

The first big one – *The Young Lions* – in 1958.

Fun time for the Pack – with Sammy and Frank.

The apple of his eye: Dean Paul – in air force uniform (opposite) and with actress Dorothy Hamill on their 1982 wedding day. The younger Dean's death was to be the great tragedy of his father's life.

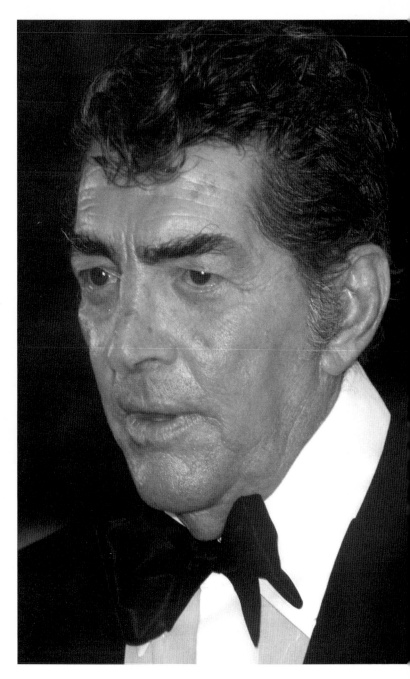

Dean in his last show – the strain shows. © Kip Rano/Rex Features

That happened when they made *Sergeants Three*, roughly based on the Rudyard Kipling *Gunga Din* stories, but set in the America of the post-Civil War era, instead of the North West Frontier Province.

Ruta Lee, then a young beauty of the kind that Sinatra loved so much, was in the cast, too. 'If Frank was down in Vegas that week, we shot around Frank,' she told me. 'If Dean was down, we'd shoot around Dean. But there were always a lot of comings and goings because we'd all go down to Vegas to see whoever was playing. There was a lot of partying going on. Frank had literally hired a fleet of planes to go back and forth.' Which was all par for Sinatra's course.

Ruta enjoyed the fun of the piece – most of which, she said, came from Dean. 'He was probably one of the most fun human beings I have ever worked with,' she told me. 'And innately the funniest man God has put on this earth. He didn't plan his jokes. He just saw through a wonderfully humorous, jaundiced eye. God, was he funny! Easy. Just as he appeared to be. Nothing rattled him. He was a laid-back man. When that expression first came out, I thought, "That was coined just for Dean Martin."

'He just automatically saw fun in everything,' Ruta said. 'Maybe I identified with it because I see great joy and humour in almost everything . . . My favourite pastime is laughing, even more than eating and counting money, so I just adored Dean Martin. When I was with that group, I was a very young girl. It was an overwhelming experience. It was not the material that was so funny, it was the time, the place, the attitude. Dean saw three garbage cans laid out in a row and made a joke about them.'

Off duty, he and Frank Sinatra maintained their friendship. Once, he and Frank had a routine that scared the life – if not the hearing – out of their victims. Dean would call a friend or business associate and then say, 'Frank wants to talk to you.' Frank would come on the line – and then take a pistol and shoot blanks into the mouthpiece, making the recipient feel as though he had had his brains shot out. The agent, George 'Bullets' Durgan, was one of the lucky ones. He had his own back. He went to the nearby hospital and had his bald head bandaged. He then called on Dean and told him he had been deafened for life by the shot.

Sergeants Three was made in Kanab, Utah, as barren a stretch of wilderness as can be seen in the West, but also one of the most beautiful, with magnificent tones of purple, of coral, of reds and rust in the rock formations. Dean would sit perched on a rock, a drink in his hand – 'I'm sure more a prop than anything else' according to Ruta Lee – and say to one of the grips: 'Listen, the great master painter in the sky screwed up. There's a stripe missing up there. We need one more stripe.

'Dean sat there, holding his inevitable drink in his hand. It had me on the sand. It was just one continuous laugh after the other. Frank Sinatra was a volatile sort of man with great highs and great lows. Dean's act, which has been refined, came out of him. That material wasn't written. You knew he had an audience rolling at this nothing stuff he did.

'He was the joke teller of them all.'

As Ruta Lee said: 'It was as much as anything the timing and the circumstance. It may lose something in translation, but when he said it, all of us were on the sand doubled up. One continuous laugh after the other. He seemed to be able to temper everyone's attitude.

'Frank was a man of great emotion, very emotional. Dean seemed to be able to calm the troubled waters.' When he wanted to, that is. Sinatra saw no reason to be calmed when it came to having the ring-a-ding time he sought. When Dean celebrated his birthday during the making of *Sergeants Three*, he flew the entire company to Las Vegas for a party. It was a suitable Sinatra occasion – with a guest list that included Elizabeth Taylor and Marilyn Monroe. It was at this party that a waiter spilled a drink over Sinatra, an event not to be regarded as a trifle. To Frank it was virtually grounds for instant execution. Dean prevented the use of the guillotine – by putting a napkin over his arm and posing as the recalcitrant waiter. 'Sammy just fell down,' Ruta recalled. 'He was always Dean's greatest audience.'

It wasn't that Dean was a great joke teller. He seemingly oozed his way into funny situations, used the right word at the right moment and found a laugh where other people wouldn't expect it.

But he had his serious moments, talking politics and revealing to some for the first time why he wasn't going quite as crazy about John F Kennedy as the rest of The Clan. If things got in the least bit heated, chances were it was a Republican–Democrat confrontation.

'He was, of that whole group, the most conservative,' Ruta told me. 'Everybody else was very liberal politically. Of the whole group, he was conservative, so far right, you meet yourself coming back the other way.

'To put it mildly,' she added, emphasising the point, 'Dean was not of the Democratic persuasion.' Frank was still very much of that 'persuasion'. 'But,' she recalled, 'nothing ever got heated because it was always too much fun.'

Dean would have fun, whatever he was doing. He was even then suffering from arthritis. 'I don't think he was comfortable, but nobody would have known it.'

They also subjected each other to practical jokes – like shoving smoke bombs under dressing-room doors. When Dean decided there was good reason to respond to one of Frank's tricks, he arranged for the Sinatra dressing-room to be smothered in balloons. 'So many,' Ruta Lee told me, 'that it was impossible to open the door. Now that was funny – until they started to pop in the midst of takes.' So the balloons had to be burst deliberately. Easier said than done. If you couldn't get into the dressing-room because the way was blocked by the balloons, how do you burst them?

Dean decided to take it easy. 'Hey, fellows,' he said. 'I'll just sit around until you get all that hot air out of there.'

If he was a man who could find humour in most things, he was also very good at covering up problems other people might consider insurmountable. Few of his fellow players on the set of *Sergeants Three* knew that he was constantly wracked with pain. He was keeping the severe discomfort – and the cause – very much to himself.

Doctors had told him that the arthritis from which he was suffering was of the spine, but he wasn't going to advertise the fact. As far as anyone else on the set was concerned, he was still the fun guy they all loved.

All of them still laughed and created mayhem around them, but the days of The Clan were plainly numbered. Joey Bishop thought the reason was television. 'TV decided it for us. We didn't ever choose a time to break up The Clan. What used to happen in the time of the nightclubs was that Frank would ring up a club and say, "I need Dean for a week, let me put someone else in for you." Well, TV was a completely new ballgame. You can't say that to a TV company. After that, we just couldn't do it.'

But for a long time, they tried. And the trade union aspect of things continued to work, to the point where it became more like a freemasonry. 'When Dean was ill one night, I was given two hours' notice to fly up to Vegas to replace him. Of course, I did it. It was for Dean after all.'

Sammy Davis Jnr hadn't seen Dean Martin for some time when I once called on him. 'If it's for Dean, I'll do anything at all,' he said. That was one part of the Clan story. The other was harder. 'We've all grown older,' said Joey Bishop. 'I don't think I could keep up with it any more.' So the Rat Pack naturally died quite a few decades before most of its members did themselves.

Living It Up 10

Even if they had grown older, and saw each other a lot less, the Clan members were still close friends, still relished the few opportunities they had to work together. Just occasionally, they could be seen stepping into Dino's Lodge – not quite the sort of edifice in which they were used to playing at Las Vegas, but a much smaller affair which in the late Fifties and early Sixties was a moneyspinner for Dean Martin. With a cartoon figure of Dean outside, this little restaurant was a top tourist attraction for the sightseers driving up and down Sunset Strip.

It was intended as a sound business venture – although Dean couldn't avoid turning it into another Clan joke. 'I figured that if Frank Sinatra could get his pizzas and pastas on the house, why shouldn't I? I always had a yen for a place where I could meet some buddies for good food and some fun and run up a tab without paying. Doesn't everybody? But my accountant straightened me out on that pretty quick.'

Dean may not always have been blessed with the kind of business brain that could be guaranteed to outsmart the agents, but he was really selling himself short there. He knew he had a potential money-spinner on his hands and it was an opportunity for him to give his brother Bill a job as manager. He had been looking for a place for some time. When he discovered that the Alpine Lodge bistro was for sale, he bought it and changed the name to Dino's Lodge. What he did not plan for was a huge potential clientele attracted to the Lodge by television. Not by Dean's own show but by a detective series.

Seventy Seven Sunset Strip was the address and *Seventy Seven Sunset Strip* was the title of a TV private eye series.

Dean liked to say, however, that the real customers came for the food. Chances are that most of them really came because there was a fair chance of bumping into Frank or Sammy or Joey there and, on a good evening, Judy Garland and even Zsa Zsa Gabor.

It was there that in December 1960, Dean threw a party. He told friends it was his twentieth wedding anniversary. It called for some speedy mental arithmetic. Had he really been married to Jeanne for all that time? 'No,' he said. 'I've been married to Jeanne for ten years, but then there was the ten years with that other broad.' It didn't sound nice, but it was funny and Jeanne was laughing with the others. What Betty said when she heard about it is not on the record.

For a time it was *the* place to go and Dean enjoyed the role of restaurateur, recommending everyone to try the Dover sole. But few fads last and Dino's Lodge would before long go the way of most of them. Dean sold the Lodge but for a number of years afterwards it continued to bear his name and to have the picture outside.

He was, in any case, spending more and more time in Las Vegas – and trying to convince people that he wasn't interested in what he had previously liked to call 'the sauce', although few believed him, and when they heard that 'Direct from the Bar' announcement, no one had a right to expect them to do so.

Now, he would stay in bed most mornings until about 11.30 when he would have breakfast. At 12.30, he was out on the golf links, limbering up. (In Los Angeles, he was a much earlier riser.) After his game, he would have a sandwich, a bottle of beer – never more, he insisted – and go into the hotel's gaming rooms, playing blackjack. There's no experience like working on a gambling table to bring out the addiction in man. Dean still had the bug as badly as when he worked the sticks at the other end of the operation back in Steubenville.

But even a man like Dean was frightened of going over the top. He made sure he was never in a losing position – by making equally sure he didn't have the money available to him. When he worked in Vegas, his salary was paid direct to his business manager – the day after his arrival in town. 'I play the tables with *their* money,' he explained. 'I deal for a while, take fifty dollars from the rack as my pay – and play with it.'

He got all the exercise he wanted on the golf course. When necessity called for more exertion, it came from walking up stairs and down again. His old New York phobia against using elevators was as strong as ever. When he stayed in a Las Vegas hotel, his rooms were always on the ground floor. He wasn't ashamed of it. Other people would admit pathological fears of flying, of dogs, of water (swimming in it, that is); Dean considered he was both old enough and big enough to admit that he was still suffering from claustrophobia and he saw no reason to hide the fact. When he had to go above the ground floor, he simply walked it – or, as was more likely, people came down to talk to him.

He usually took a shower and a two-minute ultra-violet treatment at about five o'clock in the evening, phoned Jeanne for about ten minutes (she frequently told him she wasn't any more happy being left alone in Beverly Hills while he was away in Vegas than she had ever been before) and then had a sleep.

In the course of his show, it was apple juice till the end – although more and more frequently there would be a real drink slipped in somewhere through the middle of the performance, which he would justify as being honest with his audience. When the show was over in the early hours of the morning, Dean would go off with Charley Turner, who had an interest in the Sands, for an Italian meal in one of the restaurants in the We-Never-Close town, and *say* how much he would rather be home. He told reporters that, more than anything, he valued his relationship with Jeanne and their children. 'If we have an argument,' he admitted, 'two or three hours later, one of us will say a line kidding the argument we've had. Then we're smiling again. We never go to sleep angry or without speaking to the other. We always kiss each other good night. It's terrible if you don't. I used to get angry and freeze up until she made me start talking. Once you start talking, you feel better. And before they go to school, our kids march in and kiss us. Even if we're sound asleep, they'll still kiss us good morning. Those are some of the reasons why I call it a happy house.'

That was the official Martin family line, and Jeanne herself was backing it all the way. Watching Jeanne at home and listening to her talking about her marriage was like being in the midst of a yo-yo contest. One moment, she was full of the joys of motherhood, figuratively taking Dean, his children and their children to her magnificently shaped bosom, the next she was crying 'out'. It was, quite obviously, not an easy life for her. She *was* being left alone a lot while Dean was revelling with his Clan cronies and succumbing to the hypnotic effect of his audience – if not totally to that of the booze he protested he was not imbibing. She, meanwhile, had her hands full. While still in her early thirties, she was expected to have complete responsibility for three teenagers, Craig, Claudia and Gail, as well as twelve-year-old Deana, while looking after her own children Dino, Ricci and Gina. Of course, there was plenty of help in the house, but the buck stopped at her own door.

They built an extension on to the Beverly Hills house that was really an additional home. Not only was there the expanded Martin family, but also a housekeeper, a gardener, a laundress, a nurse and a maid. 'Sometimes, I feel like a city,' joked Dean. Jeanne felt much the same.

'Seven children can be pretty noisy,' she told Louella Parsons. But although they called her Jeanne, they always introduced her politely as 'my mother', which must have pleased Betty Martin a great deal! Nevertheless, Jeanne gave every impression that she loved it all.

Until, that is, there came the periodic decision that she had had enough and announced through lawyers that she was leaving. 'I'm happy at last,' she said in 1959. 'I own myself.' The next thing anyone knew was that she was back in the house playing wife and mother. It was a constantly repeated story and one that continued to baffle both her family and the Crocettis who still adored Dean and were themselves adored in return – and kept very comfortably by their successful son, given the best of healthcare when they were sick.

But more and more, Dean's real home seemed to be Las Vegas, where the smoke-filled, low-lit gambling rooms offered a womb-like comfort to him. It was all dreadfully artificial in a land where no building has a clock for fear of bringing people back to reality. To Dean, who seemed ready to escape from the responsibilities of other mortals, it was the ideal life. He kept a suite reserved for himself at the Sands, full of pine panelling and the kind of carpet in which unsuspecting feet all too easily lose themselves.

What he always found hard was learning new material. But he did it, and only by ear. Nobody had ever convinced him that he should take music lessons, and since music brains like Irving Berlin had created vast catalogues of material without being able to read a note, there was no reason even to suggest that Dean find out the difference between a crochet and a quaver. As he once told Hedda Hopper: 'Sinatra, Perry Como and Tony Bennett are in the same boat. Dick Haymes reads music and Tony Martin does, because he once played an instrument. But Frank can conduct a band, even though he can't read. He conducted the orchestra for my new album, *Sleep Warm*, got the idea for it when we were making *Some Came Running*.' Which to him – and to most other people as well – seemed sound thinking at that.

He was king of his own little castle and now offers were being made to the throne that he knew he could never refuse.

Something's Got To Give

Dean Martin was now precisely what Jerry Lewis seemed not to be – a top box-office figure on his own account, able to sell every one of the projects in which he chose to get involved. In 1962, he accepted the film offer which his business managers were quick to warn could be more trouble than anyone imagined it would ever be worth. But to Dean it had about it practically everything he could ask of a movie. It was a fun idea, with a fairly good financial base, and most important of all, he had actually been asked by the film's star to take the principal male role. Even more significant, that star was Marilyn Monroe.

By 1962, Marilyn had become, if not a cult figure, then a household name; a part of the way of life of most people in the West. In bygone years, it had been Mae West's figure that had given a name to a new kind of lifejacket. During World War Two, Betty Grable's bottom and legs decorated the lockers of practically every self-respecting American soldier. Now, the Monroe pout, the Monroe hair and for those with either a good memory or a vivid imagination, the Monroe breasts were the sex standard of America. When Marilyn was asked if she had had anything on when she posed for that famous calendar picture, she replied: 'Of course I did. I had the radio on.' Now that required not just sex appeal, but intelligence – a combination that not only appealed to the country's number one intellectual, her last husband, playwright Arthur Miller, but had enchanted Lee Strasberg of the famous Method school, the Actors Studio, and his wife Paula.

There were, however, problems. She was now regarded as the most temperamental and undisciplined of actresses since Judy Garland – and for much the same reason. Both had mental problems based on a reliance on drugs. Both had unhappy marital relationships. Both were fighting the studios. The public knew about it, of course. Every time Marilyn arrived late at the studio or kept stars like Laurence Olivier waiting, it was headline news. No one yet had suggested that she was taking both the President of the United States and his brother the Attorney General to bed, yet there was about her a sense of public love that only the Kennedys, in their own ways, could match.

It was to this sexual sensation of the past decade that Dean Martin had been summoned and he had no intention of ignoring the command. The film was called *Something's Got To Give.* No one knew when he signed the contract that before long, *Everything* would.

The movie was to be directed by George Cukor. It was an old story resurrected, about a girl who returns, it appears, from the dead, to reclaim the husband who in all innocence had remarried.

Marilyn – an idea of her popularity and apparent power at the time is clear from the fact that no one had to use her surname – wanted Dean for that role. She thought he was extraordinarily good-looking, a man whose singing voice she adored. Dean, for his part, was singularly flattered. He considered Marilyn to be the sexiest woman in Hollywood. Her request for his services in the movie touched his ego both as a male and as an actor.

But, right from the start, it was not the movie that either Twentieth Century-Fox or George Cukor had wanted or expected. And that was mostly because Marilyn was behaving much more like a prima donna than a movie star. She was invariably not merely a couple of hours late, but she would miss an entire morning – if she turned up at all. On one occasion – it was the President's birthday and Marilyn had been deputed to sing 'Happy Birthday To You' at a vast gathering at New York's Madison Square Garden – she skipped off in the midst of a Friday and flew East for the weekend without telling the studio she was going.

When the publicity department asked her to cooperate with demands for photographs or interviews, she did it in her own way.

When she did it on *Something's Got To Give*, it was taken as cast-iron proof that she was dissatisfied with the movie and was therefore trying to wreck it. What she was, in fact, doing, was making Will Hays, the Hollywood-appointed czar of studio morals, spin in his grave. Mr Hays it was who had decreed not merely how long lovers were allowed to kiss on screen, but that they were never to share the same bed without one of the parties having at least one foot on the floor. Most vital of all, no actress would ever expose to public gaze her breasts, upper thighs or, well, worse.

Marilyn was about to shoot in a swimming pool a scene that, for 1962, was considered incomparably daring. She would appear nude. In fact, it wasn't to be nude at all. Marilyn would wear a skin-tight bathing costume, but Cukor was to shoot it so delicately that it would appear to be a shot of Miss Monroe in the buff. The studio had agreed that a few highly vetted cameramen could take stills of the scene. Marilyn poured her body into the water – and decided that the bathing costume was much too uncomfortable. So she peeled it off and then continued her dog-paddle in the altogether – raising, as she did so, not the slightest objection as the camermen leaped forward to shoot every possible glimpse of water-splashed nipple and each exposed strand of pubic hair.

The studio was not happy with the situation but made no official objections. A few days later, Dean was among the actors, grips and other people on the set who kissed Marilyn affectionately as she cut a cake specially made for her thirty-sixth birthday. That seemed like Hollywood love personified. It was. Ten days later, Marilyn was fired – and she then sent gifts and letters of apology to the extras and technicians.

Dean led a chorus of protests at her dismissal. (No one knew at the time that Marilyn was not only seriously ill, she was also pregnant.) That fact and later legal action makes it clear that Dean regarded her as badly used by the studio. Or did he?

Also working on the film was Cyd Charisse, whose legs and enviable figure had already had audiences salivating in their seats as they watched her in *Singin' In the Rain* and *Silk Stockings*. Her story is slightly different. She remembers Dean complaining about being kept waiting by Marilyn while Cukor tried valiantly to reassure him. 'We must be patient with her,' he said over and over again. 'Dean, who is a very easy-going man, was extremely anxious to get finished with the movie so that he could move over to Paramount for his next film,' she told me. The official studio line was that its star had only produced something like eight minutes of usable film after showing up for just twelve of the thirty-two days of shooting. Actually, contrary to most of the legends, Marilyn frequently did turn up on the set at six o'clock in the morning. 'We would know she was there,' Miss Charisse told me. 'We would sit and wait for her to come out before the cameras, but she never arrived. She would sit, redoing her make-up and her hair while Dean got more and more upset about the whole situation.'

That was totally at variance with Dean's own attitude – and contradicts the legends about him, too. 'He was always prepared, had every one of his lines memorised and was ready for whatever Cukor wanted him to do,' said Cyd.

'Yet we sat around for days waiting for her to show up so that we could shoot *Something's Got To Give*. He kept saying how unprofessional it all was. Finally, Marilyn started shooting and was taken off the picture. And Dean left, too.'

Dean didn't leave simply because the picture had folded. In fact, as far as Twentieth Century-Fox was concerned, they were still very much in business – and with a completely new female star, Lee Remick. Dean, for his part, said he was going to make the movie with Monroe and if not with Monroe, then with no one. There was still a great appeal in her name and her reputation – and none of the recent publicity had done any harm as far as the box office was concerned either. There was also the fact that he found her an intoxicating woman to be around.

In fact, perhaps the idea of Dean working with Marilyn was never going to work. As Jeanne said, Marilyn not only came late on to the set, but was also a 'mess' without her make-up – and that was not how he liked his women.

When the studio told him he would now be acting with Miss Remick, who was physically very attractive indeed as well as being a splendid actress, he wanted none of it, and walked out.

Fox sued Marilyn for half a million dollars. But they reserved most of their big guns for the battle with Dean. After all, Marilyn had been fired. Dean had gone without a push. To them he had simply walked out of his own volition, sabotaging everything that had been shot so far and everything that could follow.

Fox sued Dean for every cent they had spent on the movie so far – and added a further $1 million in 'exemplary damages'. In other words, not only was he going to have to make good the studio's losses, he would be punished for making them go to all that trouble, too. The bill was placed at Dean's own personal front door as well as that of his company Claude Productions Inc. Dean, said the studio, had 'arbitrarily and in bad faith refused to approve an actress designated by plaintiff as replacement for Marilyn Monroe and refused to approve any actress which plaintiff might have so designated'.

Martin was saying that, right until the last minute, he and his agents at MCA, George Chasin and Herman Citron, had been negotiating to find a way of carrying on the filming. But the studio's lawyers were insisting that 'Martin never intended to perform in said picture with any actress other than Miss Monroe, never intended to consider any replacement for Monroe and never intended to exercise good faith in the right of approval of a replacement for Monroe.'

Now that was, as they say, a challenge. Nobody expected Dean, his company, his agents or his lawyers – certainly not his lawyers – simply to apologise and write a couple of cheques, enabling everyone to shake hands and be nice, cosy friends.

They issued a counterclaim, making it all look on paper like the opening of a new series of war games, if not war itself. If Twentieth Century-Fox wanted blood, Dean demanded bones and sinew, too. He answered their demands with his own suit of $6,885,000. As much as anything it was an attempt at rubbing the studio's nose in dirt the lawyers believed they had themselves laid, a means of ridiculing the whole sordid mess. He accused the studio of 'fraud, oppression and malice'. His counterclaim took up all of sixteen pages. What was more, Dean emphasised that he agreed with Fox that he had the right to approve any substitute actress. He also acknowledged that he didn't think Lee Remick *was* suitable. However, he said that 'various other actresses would be satisfactory'.

Dean seemingly felt he was on ground that was quite as firm as the concrete surrounding the famous *Something's Got To Give* pool. In not one of his twenty-three motion pictures to date had he himself either delayed or interrupted shooting. In his view, as far as Fox was concerned, he had invited the studio to submit a list of alternative names but none was forthcoming. It was all, in short, a conspiracy in which he was to be the principal victim-cum-fallguy. Press statements about him were 'false, fraudulent and misleading', holding him up to contempt.

Certainly, there had been recriminations. Various Hollywood labour unions were alleging that he was personally responsible for their members being out of work. His own 'union', the Screen Actors Guild was calling him to account for actions that resulted in small-time fellow members suddenly finding themselves without the jobs for which they had planned and budgeted. Not only that, in addition to 11.5 per cent of the profits, he was due to receive a salary of $300,000. He received only $165,000 – which meant that Fox still owed *him* $135,000. These were not figures that could be dismissed out of hand, even if no one was taking them at anything like face value. If the suit and countersuit weren't part of a military operation, then it was a poker game or, at the very least, a high-powered Monopoly session – which required a meeting of those holding the Community Chest card before anyone was allowed to pass Go or threatened with being sent to jail.

Suddenly, the idea was to bring Marilyn back into the picture. A series of meetings was held with Fox and finally, in July 1962, it was announced that filming would recommence the following September, when Dean had finished his current nightclub commitments. Marilyn would make the movie after all.

Alas, it was not to be. A week later, Marilyn Monroe was rushed to hospital for a termination of her pregnancy – like her last, it had occurred in her Fallopian tubes – and after the operation, lapsed into fits of uncontrollable depression. In August, she was found dead by a maid. In bed. Covered only by a couple of sheets. Pills nearby. With a telephone in her hand. *Something's Got To Give* was eventually made with Doris Day and James Garner. It was called *Move Over Darling*.

Career 12

Once Marilyn had died, the vultures were ready to move in. Stories of her moral irrectitude flourished. But consciences began to prick at the same time. The lawyers involved in both sides of the *Something's Got To Give* contest were the first to meet. Almost immediately, they agreed to drop all legal action.

As for Dean, he was ready for more work in more films, while keeping nightclub audiences in fits of inebriated laughter.

Ruta Lee was by now inescapably part of the Martin-Sinatra set, as welcome at a Las Vegas shindig as ever she had been on the lot of *Sergeants Three*. As she told me: 'Not enough people know how very gracious Dean was, not just to me but to practically everyone else he knew. I don't think he singled me out to be dear or kind or sweet to. He would always acknowledge me from the stage when he knew I was at Las Vegas.'

He was the one who dubbed this somewhat booming-voiced sexy lady 'Loudy', an appellation that everyone else in what was left of The Clan adopted thereafter. He would see me and say: 'Hey Loudy, come over here, baby.' He had an almost 'Will Rogers countryish approach to things'. That was another facet of the Dean Martin philosophy that few people got to know.

Whether, however, Mr Rogers – who said he'd never met a man he didn't like – had quite the same sort of sense of humour is another matter. Certainly, Dean had never been regarded as a man strictly for the family audience. That did not prevent his associates wondering why, apart from in the odd interview, he did not talk more about his own family. 'He'd never talk about his kids,' Walter Scharf told me. 'Never. That was strange about him. He always seemed to talk like a telegram. "Fine. OK. Thanks." That sort of thing.'

Dean, however, told the world that he enjoyed a drink and friends like Ruta Lee saw another aspect they wouldn't necessarily like their children to get to know. 'We were always making up dirty lyrics to songs,' Ruta remembered. 'He did most of them but then invited me to try to top them. It was a great kick to make Dean himself laugh.' The best of the lyrics went into the Martin act – like 'You Made Me Love You – You woke me up to do it . . .'

Dean was never usually the kind to get involved in other people's arguments – a cause of some friction in years to come. When he did, it was to make a joke of it, which sometimes had the required result and sometimes did not. 'Or,' Ruta Lee remembered, 'he'd sprinkle humour over things so that it became a tease and no one would end up yelling.

'I know that everyone thinks that Joey Bishop was the comedian, but Dean was the really funny one. He laughed about Jerry a great deal, but never with any bitterness or rancour.' She plainly didn't hear everything.

He was also extraordinarily generous. Once, Ruta lost a cherished ring in the ladies' room of a Hollywood restaurant. Dean heard about it – and arranged with Frank and the rest of The Clan to make up the loss. 'A couple of days later, Dean called over to me, "Hey, Loudy." I saw he was with Frank and Joey and Sammy and it was like a firing squad.'

It was really one of the occasional reunions they allowed themselves to indulge in together – and this time with a purpose in mind. 'They then handed me a little box containing the most wonderful South Seas pearl ring, with clusters of diamonds. It came from

Rusers, which was then the number one jewellery store in town. It was much, much more valuable than the one I lost.'

That undoubtedly also went for the career that Dean Martin had made for himself now that the ashes of the one with Jerry Lewis had blown away.

The farce of *Something's Got To Give* was followed by *Who's Got The Action?* in which once more he was teamed with a sex symbol, even if the days when Lana Turner in her tight sweater had caused eyes to swivel had long passed. Now, Miss Turner, in her own autobiography *Lana*, says that she spent little time with Dean and, when one reads between the lines, cared for him even less. She says that he took two- or three-hour lunch breaks, drank a great deal more than he ate (usually heavy Italian food) and 'strolled on to the set as though he had just decided to drop in on us'.

Now, that is unquestionably Miss Turner's memory and it fits in beautifully with all the legends, but it is not what other people working with Dean at the time would have said. All the other evidence points to Dean taking things very seriously indeed on the set – even when the film project on which he was working was as stupid as this one, the story of a lawyer and his wife who can't stop winning every time they succumb to gambling fever. Said *Time* magazine: '*Action* [the magazine always did have a unique way of abbreviating awkwardly long titles] is not the merriest oatsmobile that ever came down the track, but Dean and Lana make a surprisingly smooth entry.'

The film had a somewhat dour-looking Walter Matthau in the cast – long before he had started mining the seam of comic genius that he was later to demonstrate.

As for Dean, he was enjoying himself – 'he was a very healthy male,' said writer Jack Rose. Jeanne, meanwhile, having asked her way to the divorce courts on several previous occasions, was keeping both her counsel and her marriage very much to herself. But neither of them went out of their way to show they were living in a state of connubial bliss. Neither was there always a wild welcome for visitors. Dean still liked to go to bed early, whatsoever might be happening downstairs. Once, he went to bed at midnight and then telephoned the Beverly Hills police department with a complaint: 'There's a noisy party in the Martins' house, can you get them to stop playing their music?'

He could be more sociable at other people's affairs. It was about this time that Sammy Cahn had regular parties at his Beverly Hills home at which Dean was a very welcome guest indeed. As at most Hollywood parties, the centrepoint of the evening would be the films shown. To Dean it was a great opportunity for ribald comments thrown back at the screen. He and Sammy would vie with each other for the most objectionable ripostes to the filmed dialogue.

Still, no one invited Dean to a party where he would have to use an elevator to reach the room. If travelling up several flights of stairs was inevitable, he would try to use a service lift, one of the open kinds where he could see all the cables and the rest of the works. That way he could at least tell when he was really moving. Jeanne, who was an extraordinarily caring woman, wanted him to get treatment for his condition. He always refused. He didn't want to hear what the doctors might find out.

He might also have had to reveal a compulsion that he had had since early childhood. He was a pathological shoplifter. 'When I go into a haberdashery and spend $500, I steal a necktie or a pair of gloves or a pair of socks,' he once admitted in an interview with the *Saturday Evening Post*. 'I'm sure that the owners know it, but I'm such a good customer they don't really care. Everyone has a little larceny in him, a little bit of original sin; only some of it's not too original.'

The confession brought a mass of protests flooding into the magazine's offices. 'What soft clay people are made of,' wrote a municipal judge. 'I hope no children in my court say they got the idea from the article.'

Altogether, the *Post* reported, more than two hundred people wrote in saying that it should have bluepencilled the remark. One of them wrote wondering if Dean's seven children practised the art –

and what he would think if they did. The answer is fairly predictable. About this time, the now very shapely Claudia Martin saw her father give a very healthy male reaction to a young girl coming his way wearing a see-through blouse. After smiling approvingly, he told Claudia and her sisters: 'If you kids ever wear anything like that, I'll lock you out of the house.' And Claudia added: 'He meant it.'

But psychiatrists would have told him he was simply a very successful entertainer who still had a vast number of insecurity problems. In the early Sixties, however, there was no evidence whatsoever that he had cause for concern in his work.

Who's Got The Action? was followed by a far more serious movie, *Toys In the Attic*, based on the Lillian Hellman story of two sisters, played by Geraldine Page and Wendy Hiller, who look after their brother, a ne'er-do-well.

'The play,' said *Time*, '*is* written with Hellman's customary vigour and elegance, and James Poe's script incorporates almost all of it intact. What's more, Geraldine Page slithers through her role with the sinister sweetness of a chocolate-covered cobra and Dean Martin demonstrates impressively that he can act. But something is terribly wrong with this picture. It is cold, mechanical, dead . . .'

In *Who's Been Sleeping In My Bed*, Dean played a TV sex symbol. It was the nearest he was getting to having his own show on the small screen. Was that insecurity? Probably. The Martin philosophy was always to take advantage of the things you do best, once having found them. He knew that he was good with the one-liners at Vegas and people seemed to like him in the cinema, so why should he bother with anything else? Besides, he needed as much time as possible to play golf.

In 1964, there were two new Dean Martin movies, *What A Way To Go* and *Four For Texas*, in which he joined up once more with Frank Sinatra and Ursula Andress.

What A Way To Go co-starred Shirley MacLaine, Paul Newman, Robert Mitchum, Gene Kelly, Bob Cummings and Dick Van Dyke, as impressive an assemblage of stars as most people could remember.

The story was not so impressive. It was about a girl who reveals all about her ex-husbands. Dean played a rich man whom she describes as 'overbearing, arrogant, a snake'.

The film was made by Twentieth Century-Fox, much of it on the studio's ranch at Malibu. 'I enjoy making comedies,' Dean said at the time. 'But people are slipping out of their images these days. It's because the movie industry is casting its stars out of clay. And that's good. An actor shouldn't be stuck with one characterisation. It used to be that way, but the people behind the scenes are learning to gamble.' He had plainly got to know his Hollywood quite well. 'Look around and tell me if you see any Gables, Coopers, Fairbanks Juniors, Valentinos. The industry has stopped manufacturing them. You might find one or two, but you won't find any new models.'

It was about this time that America entered its most traumatic period since World War Two. President John F Kennedy was assassinated. Dean had never been a Kennedy supporter, even if he had sung for him, but his death affected him like that of a brother. And for the lapsed Catholic that he really was, he did a strange, out-of-character thing. He ran out of the house, jumped into a car and drove to the nearest church where he lit a candle and prayed: 'Please don't let him die.'

If he made a prayer or two at this time for his career, it was obviously answered. There was a lot of work simply because he was getting so much exposure. The days were comfortably past when an actor needed an Oscar to be deluged with offers. Now, one major appearance begat another and that was the way he liked it. He wasn't saying anything bad about Hollywood either, the town that he would be the first to recognise had been good to him. 'I'd feel like the guy who's just snatched the old lady's purse,' he said.

He was, however, being fairly modest about his talent. Particularly about his singing. 'I can deliver a song with an easy style, but a lot of us crooners get by because we're fairly painless.' His record sales were proving much the same point, with a whole range of top-selling albums and reissues that took him back into the platinum disc range.

Leslie Halliwell, the ace historian of the cinema, described *Four For Texas* as a 'flabby Western comedy, tediously directed and casually performed'. The tedious direction was by Robert Aldrich who told me that it was about the funniest movie experience of his career. The main trouble though, as with the other two 'Clan' movies, was that the participants seemed to regard every step they took as an 'in' joke into which other people were not expected to be allowed to pry.

By this time, the *Los Angeles Times* was accepting that for as long as people were going to go to nightclubs – and in 1964 they still were, and not just in Las Vegas – Dean Martin was the king. Martin, said Cecil Smith in the paper, 'is the funniest human performing (even infrequently) on a nightclub floor . . . the master of the throwaway line. The small twist on a thought that makes it hilarious. He is very proud that he invents these lines himself, he has no writers.'

Dean never went anywhere, it seemed, without Mack Gray, whose duties would range from laughing when Dean told a gag, through to accompanying him on the piano, to acting as a general aide-de-camp-cum-gofer. Another of Gray's duties was to write down Dean's one-liners when he heard them. The Martin brain was very quick with inventing the brilliant ad-lib, much slower at being able to remember it afterwards.

No one would suggest that Dean saw the funny side in absolutely everything. If he thought a studio or a nightclub management were trying to put something over on him, he would make noises akin to a gorilla losing a banana – although as always he often reserved those expressions of dissatisfaction for Jeanne and home. But there was a great deal of fun to be found in anything, from the bust of a girl to that of a business venture.

In 1964, he and Sinatra had pooled a small fortune to set up a gambling establishment on the shores of Lake Tahoe, the Cal Neva. The name was taken from the first syllables of the names 'California' and 'Nevada'. Before long, it would be the centre of State Gaming Commission investigation, especially when it was discovered that

Mafia Don Sam Giancana was a silent partner. Altogether, it wasn't a good idea – 'Frank had to open his big Italian mouth,' was how Dean put it delicately. The trouble was that the California-Nevada state line ran right through the middle of the house. Gambling was then, as now, a staple industry in Nevada; illegal in California. 'Frank got the Nevada side with the gambling and the booze,' said Dean with the sort of expression on his face most people use when they hear of the death of a beloved relative. 'I got the California side . . . It's got six pay toilets and a picture of Nixon.' Whether the money he lost in the venture had anything to do with his deciding to revise his feelings on working in TV is a matter for conjecture. What is sure is that he was now embarking on what was to be probably the most successful light-entertainment televison career of all time. The really *serious* trouble was that both Frank and Dean knew of the Mob connection and were benefiting from it.

At the end of 1964, he signed to do a weekly series for NBC in which he would host a variety show. He, it was understood, would act as a kind of MC to a whole assembly of top stars. While he would have to sing a song or two and tell a couple of jokes, most of the action would go to the guest stars. As he told the *Los Angeles Times*: 'I ain't gonna work that hard. They'll do the work and I'll get the credit.' Like the drinking one, the dilatory Martin character was one that had to be fostered for the good of his bank balance. What no one knew at the time was that he was in at the beginning of a new one-man cottage industry of TV show making.

NBC believed it was on to a fairly good thing after Dean had topped the bill on a Thanksgiving Day TV special with singer Eydie Gorme and musician Al Hirt. It had a wildly enthusiastic response from the critics.

He had also taken his turn hosting *The Hollywood Palace*, another variety show which NBC ran with a series of superstar guest hosts – Bing Crosby had been among them – after, ironically enough, the network had been forced to close down Jerry Lewis's weekly shows, which they found failed to attract either audiences or advertisers. Dean said he would do the show providing he didn't have to do more than one day's rehearsing – the first shot fired in the Martin TV Revolution.

All In A Night's Work 13

Dean Martin took to television like a salmon to the Atlantic Ocean. He had overthrown the doubts of jumping upstream and was now signalling to all who wanted to take note that he was ready to become king of all he surveyed.

From his first joke – 'My doctor told me to take a little drink before I go to bed. You know, I find myself going to bed ten times a night!' – you knew this was going to be a different kind of TV show. Dean sang all his favourite songs, 'That's Amore', 'Arrivederci Roma' and 'Sway' among them, of course. There were the country songs like 'Houston' and the song that his daughter Gail says was probably his favourite, 'Where Or When'.

NBC had no doubt now that they had to trap this fish while seemingly letting him swim whichever way he wanted. Not that there weren't expressions of disbelief from the TV professionals – an ever growing band in early 1965 – at the things Dean was subjecting them to. Not only was he going to rehearse just once, if he didn't get the jokes right when the cameras were rolling, then audiences would have to get used to laughing at the way he fluffed his lines. Revolutionary? It seemed downright slap-dash, but every morning after *The Dean Martin Show* was aired – once the show's pattern was established – the ratings bounced high into the air.

What if Dean wasn't interested in joining the show's comedy writers as they formulated jokes and then digested them? When they got into the script, Dean wasn't going to bother to read them. He would wait until the idiot-board cue cards were prepared in jet-black ink. If he read them wrong, it was either the fault of the writers or the inspired good taste of the people sitting out front who found that almost contemptuous approach so appealing. Was it contempt? Certainly, it was a gesture of Dean Martin saying that he didn't take television seriously enough to work at it with as much dedication as a movie. It wasn't his idea to get into the television business and if the network wanted him so badly, it would be on his terms and no others. He was still frightened of collecting obligations to other artists, so he let his producers know that it was their affair to gather the guests. He wasn't letting himself in for free work that he had no desire to do. He told them: 'I have to be ladled out of bed and squirted on to the golf course in the morning,' and they still wanted him. He talked to them in terms of what he admitted were 'ridiculous fees' and they still said yes, come over to us.

The experts were convinced that Dean's attitude was foolhardy, but if he wanted to take that risk, it was his look-out. Few TV executives bothered to see further ahead than the end of the current season, and no one really believed that the Martin approach could be more than just a flash in the entertainment pan, which they would have to scrape clean for the following year. No one imagined that a pattern had been set which would break all records and which eighteen years later would still be the most successful in American showbiz history.

What Dean brought to the variety screen was something unique. He was the first performer to *dominate* the variety show he hosted with his own name in the title. Ed Sullivan, certainly, had had an immense success with his own variety shows in the very earliest days of American television and his programmes were legendary. But Sullivan was a newspaperman who sometimes said little more than: 'Ladies and gentlemen, the next act is . . .'

Dean turned introducing other artists into a mere device to tell the latest story he had picked up on his way from the bar. As Greg Garrison, the producer of Dean's shows for two decades, told me: 'The secret of Dean's success was very simply the man himself – truly one of the most delightful, charming, cute, adorable people in the world.' Now, it is not difficult to be sceptical about comments like that from a man talking about the provider of his food. But Garrison is convinced that Martin's genius was to portray himself on screen simply as he was. He adds that 'people were disappointed when they meet him. He was shy. He was not one of the "Hello baby, let's-sit-down-and-have-a-drink" types.' But working with Dean, he insists, was like visiting your favourite uncle. 'You loved to go and visit someone who is super nice and gives you tea.'

But Dean had never done it at the NBC studios or at Garrison's office near by. 'This was also Dean's office,' Garrison pointed out in 1983. 'He has never been here. Not once.' Which also said a great deal about the Martin approach to running a TV show.

Right from the early days of the show, any negotiations in which Dean *did* feel compelled to involve himself were conducted on the phone. 'What the hell is Greg's number?' he would ask his business manager. When he was given the number, he would dial it – and then forget it until next time. But that wasn't often. 'I've spoken to Dean on the phone about three or four times in the past nineteen years,' Garrison told me in all seriousness. 'And I can pinpoint each and every one of those occasions.'

Once, he asked Garrison for an introduction for one of his sons who wanted to get into TV production. Another time, he asked for the name of the show's designer – so that he could plan the Martin home's new dining-room. 'The third phone call was once when we did a show from my ranch where I breed horses. Dean is an animal person who loves horses and working with the wranglers. After that show, he called me and said, "I think the horses looked absolutely sensational. Fantastic . . ." Never once did he mention a song he had sung or a story he had told. He called to tell me that my horse looked sensational.'

The fourth phone call was to ask for an address of a steak house.

His relationship with Garrison and other people with whom he worked on the TV series fitted into no known pigeonhole. As he told me twenty years ago: 'I see him. I have dinner with him. Are we extremely close? Yes, we're extremely close. Are we socially very friendly? No.'

This strange, brotherly-love relationship between the two men – which is Garrison's definition of the way they existed together – began before Dean's own show started. He was a guest on a Bob Hope special which Garrison produced in 1963.

'What time are we going to start tomorrow?' Dean asked him. 'At about ten o'clock,' said Garrison.

'And what time are we going to be through?'

'About three,' the producer replied.

Dean always arrived at the studio on time – and also expected to leave at three. Actually, he had started rehearsing just like any other star. But it was Garrison who, once he came on to the operation, saw that Dean's free-and-easy style and a conventional rehearsal schedule wouldn't go well together.

'I noticed something then,' Garrison told me. 'On the first day on the set, he was absolutely wonderful. He enjoyed what he was doing. He laughed at all the jokes. He read his lines beautifully. On the second day of rehearsal, he enjoyed himself. By the time the fourth day came around, he seemed bored by it. Everything was just old hat to him. By the time we actually got round to shooting the show, he was kind of lackadaisical. He had heard the jokes so many times that they didn't interest him any more and his performance was not exactly thrilling.'

Garrison was not the first producer-director of the series. When it started, the ratings were noticeably disappointing. Dean resented being given direction. He complained about the then director during an early taping. The director told him: 'It's my job to tell you where

I think you've gone wrong. If you don't like it, you'd better tell me and I'll go.'

Dean softened at that. 'You're here because you know what you're doing. But don't mind if I tell a few jokes.'

Within weeks, however, the director had gone.

There was a lesson there to anyone who cared to stop and take note. When Dean called Garrison after that, inviting him to take over the show, the producer remembered their first experience together. They got around to talking about their rehearsal schedule. '*Must* we rehearse?' Martin asked him. Such a question had never been asked before – and to anyone else it would have seemed like an attempt at professional suicide from a performer the whole industry knew didn't give two golf balls for a career in television.

But Garrison had remembered the Bob Hope show. 'Let's just rehearse the music, walk through it a little bit and see how it works out.' It was really Dean's own idea to do it that way. 'As we got on with the show, I really took the place of his alter-ego.'

For one thing, before long it became clear that he wasn't going to rehearse in the conventional way. It would have to fit in with his golf schedule – and that's when he learned his lines and his songs.

The process was always the same: Lee Hale, the musical director on the shows, would make three cassettes. As Dean explained: 'He did my parts for me on a cassette. And I would have three cassettes. I would have one here, I'd listen to it for three or four hours. I'd take one with me on the golf course, and also in the car. I would rehearse for five hours a day. And when I went down on a Saturday they couldn't understand how I would know everything and not rehearse. They'd say, "What a brilliant guy this is." I wasn't brilliant; I was rehearsing more than they were – and most of the time, they made more mistakes than I did.'

Garrison, or Dino's friend and assistant Mack Gray, would act as his stand-ins. He would do the dance routines, tell the jokes or ask them to imagine that 'this' was the time when Dino would sing. 'I would rehearse the show with the performers,' Garrison told me.

But when he came for the taping itself, he couldn't be faulted. For one thing, Dean's punctuality was immaculate – another of those contrasts between legend and reality. As Greg Garrison put it to me, speaking from the experience of being Dean's business partner as well as his producer for all those years: 'He'd be in the building at noon. When I say noon, you could set your clock and say at five minutes to twelve, Dean would be in that door. Not twelve, not ten minutes to twelve, but five to twelve, not five after. It was his little game. Never ever late. Ever. Only once he didn't turn up at all. His brother Bill had died suddenly – and he couldn't find the phone number to tell the studio he wouldn't be coming in.'

When you deal with someone like Martin, a performer who obeyed no one's rules but his own and yet remained the favourite of both audiences and fellow performers, there had to be something very vital about him not to want to consign him to the nearest jail.

His rehearsals were not all at the golf club, although seeing Dean plan his next routine while trying to get a hole in one was something to treasure.

He could occasionally rehearse at home – although that was unusual. The best bit of home rehearsing would have been a scene in which Dino had to be lying on a couch or watching television. That he would have found tolerable. Otherwise, work was for the studio on a Saturday.

Garrison, who is a ham of the kind only a man working *behind* the scenes possibly can be, sat in for Dean at all rehearsals. Where the script called for a Martin joke, Garrison told it. When it was time for a song, Garrison would sing it – although the music was done a bit more seriously before it got to rehearsal stage. Every song that Dean was expected to sing would be recorded for him by another (lesser) artist and put on to one of the cassettes. If there were a duet to learn, there would be two singers engaged to do the song for him – in the way Dean would be expected to sing it. Usually, it would be someone from the music department who would play the Martin part. The girl in the duet would be one of the show's chorus singers. The numbers would be recorded on to two cassettes – the first with the complete duet, properly mixed; the second with one of the voices omitted, so that Dean could see precisely where he came in on the number. As Dean said many years later: 'Why rehearse in the studio when I can rehearse on the golf course? I did more rehearsing than anyone else in the show.'

Sometimes Dean himself didn't know who that singing partner would be until he arrived at the NBC studios on the day the show was to be taped. He never knew who his other guests were going to be. That wasn't because he was playing some kind of Russian roulette or because he would be stimulated by surprise. He just didn't think it was necessary for him to find out.

Star and producer had their differences. Garrison wanted Dean to enter via a spiral staircase. 'Hell, I get nose bleeds that far up,' he said – and then added for good measure: 'This is my show. No one tells me what to do.'

Before long, they compromised on a routine that became part and parcel of *The Dean Martin Show*. Dean came into what was supposed to be his living-room at home, sliding down a fireman's pole.

The first thing he did every time on arrival was to go through with the musical director the songs he had learned on cassette. That would take him up to about 12.45 – when he would go into his dressing-room. There was a monitor TV in the room on which he could watch Greg Garrison going through the Dean Martin lines with the guests he was always surprised to see turning up for his show. When there were bits of business he had to learn, or particular props he had to get to know, Garrison would call the dressing-room and suggest that Dean go through them himself. The whole routine was geared towards the mix that both Dean and Garrison had decided the public wanted to see, without putting the slightest suggestion of a strain on the star.

At four o'clock, there would be a run-through, in which Dean would be expected to read his cards, pick up his props and sing his songs. By five o'clock, there would be an audience in position and the show would be taped in front of it – with Dean stumbling through lines from cards he hadn't read properly, or picking up the props that were supposed to be used by his guests. Each time he did something wrong, he made it seem like another funny part of the show. No one else would dare do things that way, but with Dean it worked – partly because that was what people expected to happen. Between six and seven, there would be a break and at seven o'clock, the show would be taped a second time – with Dean leaving the building at eight.

The first 'performance' was in some ways a dress rehearsal for the second, although before long what went out was a compilation of the two, with about fifty per cent of the first taping being used in the final programme. As Garrison observed: 'Compare that to the average variety show which, if it was taped on Friday, they would go in on Tuesday and people would work on it over and over again. It would be technically a marvel but the performances would be maybe a little lacking.'

Dean's way of working didn't always commend itself to the other people on his show. More than one of his guests, who were supposed to be thrilled at the thought of being the butt of a Martin routine, wound up in near panic when they realised what was going on in the studio. 'But by the time we got around to taping the second show, they were all surprisingly relaxed,' said Garrison.

Wilfrid Hyde White had a reunion with his old *Ada* colleague on the series, playing a detective who thought Dean was really a wanted criminal dressed up as a woman. 'It was a crazy thing. Made no sense at all. But Orson Welles, who was in the same show, thought it was very funny,' he told me.

Orson Welles? He took to *The Dean Martin Show* better than most things he had done since *The Lady From Shanghai*. The downhill journey that began on the heights of Citizen Kane and had gone through *The Third Man*, the traumas of *Othello* and ended up with a series of TV commercials, developed a few happy stops when he went on Dean's show. He was delighted to be fooling around, saying lines he would have spat at other people. He even did the odd time step with his host and, by all accounts, the audiences were pleased, too.

To see Dean and Welles in the same programme was like watching Laurence Olivier on *The Morecambe and Wise Show*. They didn't seem to fit together, yet it was a question of a square peg slotting very nicely into a square hole. Dean would occasionally use the same line in more than one programme. With Orson, the line went like this – or variations of the same: 'You got any pictures of your wife, naked?' 'No.' 'OK, you wanna buy some?'

That it all went so well had a great deal to do with Greg Garrison, a close friend of Orson's. The most unconventional of actors found rehearsing with Garrison, deputising for the star, a thoroughly enjoyable experience. To have survived that kind of rehearsal and still look good on screen was something of an achievement.

About the lack of rehearsal, he said: 'I'd rather he hadn't have done it, because it could get quite unnerving. But then he's such a nice man, it didn't matter. And, in truth, I'm a bit like that myself when it comes to rehearsing. The only trouble was, we never played the same character twice, so we just had to hope we had the right cue cards.'

Anthony Quinn was one of those who liked the show the way Dean did it. 'All of us,' he said in 1966, 'seemed to be plagued by responsibility, hemmed in by convention. Dean is the symbol of the guy who can go on, get drunk, have no responsibilities.'

The story is that Lucille Ball – who told Dean: 'You make cooked spaghetti look tense' – loved the show because it was the only programme on which she could take a nap before going on the air. But it was a back-handed compliment. When Dean went back on her show – that was one convention he was unable to overturn – he had to rehearse four times as long for the twenty-minute spot than he ever did for his whole show.

Danny Thomas, himself no mean TV performer in his day, actually registered a formal complaint about what he called Dean's 'slovenly' work habits. And he added: 'You're making it harder for the rest of us. I had Martha Raye on my show complaining about rehearsals. She said that she didn't have to do them on *The Dean Martin Show*.'

Everything about it worked – providing you were really not looking for polish or for something theatrically brilliant – and apparently people were not. The *Los Angeles Times* said: 'No one works harder trying to preserve his devil-may-care image than Dean Martin. Compared with Dean, Bing Crosby is in an advanced state of St Vitus Dance.'

Other performers who tried to take advantage of the fact that they had rehearsed their material before – and perhaps sneak in some business to Dean's disadvantage – were not invited back.

Practically every top name in show business was a Dean Martin guest – with the notable exception of Jerry Lewis, who had his own show being taped along the corridor at NBC, despite his earlier flops there. Sometimes they would meet and shake hands between shows. 'We're all very friendly with our across-the-hall neighbours,' Garrison said at the time.

To Dean, of course, the complaints from his guest stars – serious or light-hearted – helped boost the way he liked people to think of him. Not for nothing would he turn to one of the cast in the course of a show and say: 'How long have I been on?'

Jonathan Winters was a regular and so was Bob Newhart. Dean and Newhart got on like a studio on fire – as the monologuist did TV versions of his famous LP routines, like that of the driving instructor ('No madam, when I said turn left, I didn't mean in the middle of the freeway') or of Walter Raleigh returning to England to report on his discovery of tobacco ('What's that, Walt? You roll it up and set it on fire?'), Dino laughed as though he were hearing them for the first time.

Sometimes he wished that the first time would also be the last. Like the time Linda Ronstadt came on the show and was shielded by a team of hangers-on who wouldn't allow anyone to talk to her. That was even more unnerving than an unrehearsed star.

The most dangerous time was when Sinatra came on the show. NBC planted its own tame censor in a booth, just in case things got too raunchy, but none of that scared away the people who weren't on *The Dean Martin Show* to be funny, like Ella Fitzgerald or the man whom Dean considered the best singer in the business, Gordon MacRae. (What Sinatra thought of that judgement isn't on record.)

Either way, there was always Dean's insistence on doing his parodies – and the audience didn't object.

He would do a little dance when the occasion called for it. The little time step was hardly of Fred Astaire standard, but then little was. Real dancers took a little convincing. Gene Kelly, a total perfectionist, didn't relish the way the show's host worked. 'When it came to that moment and we were scheduled to dance with Dean,' he recalled, 'well, we dancers knew there would be no rehearsal. More than anything, Dean knew it. So what did we do? We winged it. There were times when he preferred to just sit and sing and let someone else do the work.'

Clearly, Dean and most of his guests got on very well. In some cases, there were whispers that he got on with them a little too well. It seemed, for instance, that when Petula Clark (the British star who had made France her home at the time) appeared on the show, their friendship was pretty deep. Rumours of a romance ran through Hollywood, but there were no apparent repeat performances.

It was a formula that plainly worked. In February 1967, the Nielsen ratings showed *The Dean Martin Show* to be number one on American television – although the critics seemed to think that Dean's appeal was mainly to middle-aged women. Not so, said his office. Surveys conducted by the Los Angeles *Herald Examiner* confirmed this view. They said he was equally popular with 'teeny-boppers, the grandmas and a surprising number of males [even though] men traditionally shy away from variety shows'.

It was just as well liked by the live audiences. People were having to wait for up to three years before their application for seats at the show could be met. What they wanted was to see Dean, the show girls, Dean, his guests, and Dean telling his crazy quips – like the time he told one of the girls: 'Don't bite your nails. Remember what happened to the Venus de Milo.'

Hal Humphrey wrote in the *Los Angeles Times*: 'Live TV is dead, but Dean Martin comes as close to exhuming the corpse as anyone.' It was a theme to which others would constantly return.

Time magazine in March 1966 described Martin as a 'slightly blue rhinestone-in-the-rough, fortunately set in an after-hours time slot (10–11 p.m., Eastern Standard Time) when the youngsters are in bed, and need play nobody but himself . . . The I-don't-care, be-yourself air helps make the programme an even more sought-after showcase for visiting stars than the "guest villain" spot on *Batman*.'

Life magazine wrote about 'Dino's breezy way to easy money'. While others in show business liked to think of themselves as being cool, 'true cool comes only on Thursday evenings (NBC) when *The Dean Martin Show* freshens the stale ether with a spontaneous, slapdash air. Near the end of a second season and comfortably near the top of the ratings charts, Martin succeeds by ignoring the fact that live TV has been mummified by being put on tape. While other performers erase their errors, Dean Martin saves his for the public, having learned that professionals can tape a show without embalming it.'

The magazine, however, couldn't avoid mentioning another aspect of Dean's image. 'Although the Martin mystique is carefully preserved in alcohol, only his bartender knows for sure how much Dino drinks.'

The shows were to get to the top of the ratings year after year in the United States. But they did not travel well. In England, where Perry Como and, later, Andy Williams had devoted followings with their smoother than smooth approach, audiences were not easily able to appreciate the school of: 'Well, hello Buddy. Let's see if this works, and if it doesn't we'll have some laughs out of it.' One exception was Italy, where they apparently thought it a gesture to their heritage to honour Dino Crocetti by a series on their national network. The show appeared with all voices, including Dean's, dubbed into Italian.

He didn't sound too bad. But when Frank Sinatra appeared on the show, he was like Mussolini in full flow.

On one occasion, Dean began the warm-up himself: 'Good evening ladies and gentlemen, this is not *The Andy Williams Show* with milk and cookies. This is a show about booze and broads.' And he even rubbed it in on another occasion: 'I got up at eleven this morning and had a bowl of Bourbon and crackers . . . but this is my first drink.'

The sketches in which Dean took part were usually terrible – like the time he avoided his nagging wife by travelling continents, swimming oceans, catching shark – always to return to the same woman sitting in the same chair, continuing the same boring conversation. (Later, Marty Feldman would repeat almost the same sketch on the show.) All the props looked as if they were made of cardboard, and the worst quality cardboard at that.

Mostly the guests did like appearing on the show, simply because they enjoyed the total lack of pressure in being able to take part in something that everybody knew was so awful. Week in, week out, Kay Metford played his mother. Joey Bishop once asked her: 'This is the worst sketch I've ever read in my life. How can you do it?'

She said: 'Believe it. Then I have no trouble with it.'

As Bishop told me: 'The sketches were terrible but Dean didn't mind, simply because he knew he could have fun with it.' Every week, Dean would go over to the piano and then climb on top – singing one time:

> In your Easter Bonnet
> With all the frills upon it
> You'd look a bit peculiar in the
> Men's room my dear.

(Irving Berlin probably hated it; he used to have a notice printed on the covers of all his sheet music prohibiting parodies.) Or it could be:

ALL IN A NIGHT'S WORK

Our love affair
Is a wond'rous thing
Because your husband
Doesn't suspect a thing.

Dean made mistakes constantly. But his real art was in making all of them look like carefully prepared business. When Dean crashed into a piano, one was made specially for him on a future programme, out of balsa wood, which meant that no one would get hurt when the collision occurred. It was also cheaper than a Steinway. He laughed as he rubbed his bottom. So did the audience.

'He'd get a laugh reading *my* lines from the cue card,' Joey Bishop remembered.

In fact, Dean was funny in a way that Sinatra and the rest of the Pack were not. Each of them would say things on stage that no scriptwriter would have dared put in a script, although the really funny lines were scripted for them by the writers. Dean was the exception. You couldn't write for a man who would say he would only fall on the floor when he was sure he could hold on.

In one of their best shows, the Pack played at the Villa Venice (pronounced Veneese) near Al Capone's home town of Cicero, Illinois. There was an ecstatic response, from both the audiences and the gangsters (mainly Sam Giancano) who still ran the place. Frank said he wanted to sing 'I've Got Rhythm'. 'I can't,' replied Dean, 'I'm Catholic.'

They kidded around wherever they were. When they went into the studio to record 'Don't Be A Do-Badder', neither Dean nor Frank could get it right. Sinatra was always very fussy about his recordings – he could ruin a movie take and do nothing about it, but not when making records. He had once interrupted a session, protesting, 'You're trying to cheat the notes. You can't cheat the notes.' When recording 'Do-Badder', it was Dino who was making the mistakes and overriding the bells that were sounded to indicate that recording was about to begin. 'I said the wrong words,' said Dino. 'I said, "Don't take it from me . . ."' To which Sinatra responded: 'You're not paying attention.' Dean wouldn't stand for that. He told the conductor, the omnipresent Nelson Riddle: 'I think your bells are flat.'

When Dean guested for other artists, Garrison would frequently produce his sketches for him – using the same tired but highly successful formula. In one show, in which Dean appeared with Angie Dickinson, a duck was supposed to come flying in through the window. It was a stuffed prop on a seemingly invisible wire. But it kept getting caught up in the window frame. Every mistake appeared in the final show because Garrison and the studio audience thought it hilarious. That can't happen with most artists. 'He just lay back and waited for something to happen,' Garrison told me. 'Like a fighter waiting to give the counter punch.'

And always there was the glass of apple juice which everyone thought was something stronger, and always the glazed look in the eyes that convinced audiences Dean wasn't appearing direct from the bar, but was actually being filmed under it. There was always a miniature bar on the set. Not that it was always just apple juice. 'Sometimes it did contain *a little* booze, too,' Garrison confessed. 'But then there's no one who can handle his booze better than Dean could.'

More than once, celebrities went back to Dean's dressing-room after a show expecting to meet a paralytic drunk but instead being offered a cup of coffee and a slice of cake. 'You son of a bitch,' one of them told him. 'You're stone-cold sober!' Dean virtually collapsed when he heard that. He took it as a compliment on his acting ability.

He never doubted the reason for his success – and getting up to forty million viewers every time was success by anyone's standards. 'Wanna know why this show's a hit?' he once asked *Good Housekeeping* magazine. 'The reason is that it's me up there on that screen. It ain't nothin' phony; that's really me. You take everybody else on TV – they're puttin' on an act, playin' something they aren't. But when people tune me in, they know they're getting Dean Martin.'

It was clever, because to establish a style that is so closely identified with you is a sign of stardom indeed. He would even sometimes go out on a stage pushing a barrow loaded with liquor bottles and not really need to do anything else for the next forty minutes. Once, he did so while appearing on the same bill as Frank Sinatra. For the forty minutes that Dean was on stage, the audience were hardly aware that they had already seen Sinatra. That was not just a singer or even a comedian at work. It was an Entertainer – the reputation Dean made for himself on that TV screen that he had aspired to hate so much for so long.

How (Not) To Save A Marriage 14

There were thirty Dean Martin shows a year and twelve of them were repeated – which meant that he was on the air for forty-two weeks of the year, excluding his guest appearances on other people's programmes and his own 'specials' which could amount to another seven annual shows. And he also continued in the other departments of the career named Dean Martin.

As the Sixties moved on, there were record hits like 'King of the Road', 'Born To Lose' and 'Welcome To My World'. And then there was one that his accompanist Ken Lane had written fifteen years before. It wasn't merely another best-seller from which Dean could afford to buy another ranch with another Cadillac in the garage. It was 'Everybody Loves Somebody Sometime' – which Dean himself loved so much it became his signature tune for ever after. It sold two million copies in its first month and was hailed by the American music industry as the answer they had been seeking for more than a year to the sound that was coming from across the Atlantic in Liverpool. 'Everybody Loves Somebody Some Time' was dubbed by Tin Pan Alley 'the Beatle Buster'.

The amazing thing was that Dean had been able to do what even Frank Sinatra – 'He's a much better singer than I am,' he once told me – had failed to do. When the song was first written, Sinatra had recorded the number and it flopped miserably. Dean, after his own success, sent his old friend a telegram saying: 'YOU JUST DIDN'T KNOW HOW TO DO IT.'

On the TV show, however, he was content to offer less philosophical statements, such as 'It's June in January – 'cause I'm in Australia.'

In 1965, his record sales were all of fifty-five places ahead of those of Sinatra, and he was said the following year to be the biggest-selling crooner in America, as far as singles were concerned. His income was in the region of one million dollars a year – precisely the same figure as that claimed for Sinatra.

Ask Dino who his own favourite singers were and he'd list Sinatra, Como (well, of course, they were Italians, weren't they?) and, surprisingly perhaps, the Mills Brothers. 'That's what you call music,' he said to me. 'Just listen to the way they do it all so smoothly. When you can sing like that and don't need an orchestra, that's art, brother.' But he had no need to look to anyone else's style.

By May 1967, *Variety* was saying that a combination of the TV show, record royalties, club dates and the money from his movies had multiplied that one million figure five times.

He was becoming big in other business, too. In 1969, the Riviera Hotel in Las Vegas awarded him ten 'points' – which meant that he would receive ten per cent of the profits for his trouble in appearing there. He had a share – with Herb Alpert of the Tijuana Brass – of the Los Angeles Rams ball team, for which he was paid $19 million.

Most significant of all, Dean signed a new three-year contract for $34 million with NBC in 1967 giving the network no further options at all. (Not all of that went to him, of course. It was the sum they paid for the complete shows, but every one of those dollars had the name Dean Martin stamped across it just as much as the head of George Washington.)

It was the kind of figure no one in entertainment had ever played with before, outside of that Monopoly board. 'God, I'm not worth it,' he said when the lawyers gave him the paper to sign.

People don't automatically think of Dino the businessman, but his earnings proved that he was clever enough to take advice, if not to think of everything himself. When he sold his show to NBC, he took the money half in cash and half in NBC stock – which made him if not the largest stockholder in the network, then pretty close to it.

'This Man Earns More Money In A Year Than Anyone In the History of Show Business,' said TV Guide, heading an interview with the unlikely picture of Dean drinking a cup of coffee. Dick Hobson reported in the piece that Dean's business manager had said there was bad news. 'We're making too much money again this year.' To which Dean nimbly quipped: 'It's hard for me to believe that the Government and I are worth that much!'

The magazine reported his saying: 'I only left the house four times last year and made a million dollars.'

Jeanne might have been pleased had that been true. The money was an understatement by a fifth and she couldn't quarrel with that, since every whim of hers and of the children was assiduously taken care of. But she still thought he shut his front door behind him much too often.

Nevertheless, The Clan teased him unmercifully about what they believed to be his unswerving loyalty to the 'little woman'. 'Goin' home like a good boy to your wife?' they asked him on a number of occasions when they were about to do the town.

But those in the know had to assume that any activity had to take second place to his golf. And not just the golf. This was an athlete, a swimmer who could beat the best of them when it came to diving: seemingly, he was able to defy gravity and stop in mid-air. He also played tennis as if he were competing at Wimbledon.

His golf, however, was always the big mystery, the big one about him, which his friends found difficult to unlock. Ask them when they were never to phone him – and phoning was always a problem, since he hated answering the damned thing – and the answer was usually in the morning. That was when he was out with the clubs at the club. Really close friends thought that he was at his best when playing at

Las Vegas, up till really late on stage, sleeping until the early afternoon and then going off to play golf. Actually, he was always up early and out playing – whatever time he had gone to bed.

Dean owned apartment houses as investments and homes in which he and the rest of the Martin clan lived in Palm Springs and Beverly Hills. He had enough securities to cause a mini-Wall Street crash any time he threatened to sell. He had become a major landowner in California's Ventura County when for more than two million dollars he bought 989 acres in the kind of investment attempt for which you only needed the money to start with in order to make a great deal more. Some of it was being spent on a Spanish house to be built on his ranch at Hidden Valley. It would have its own stables and heliport. Just a place to live,' he insisted. And not merely a place to get away from his public. 'Gettin' away from the smog.'

He said that all his success was due to 'just being myself'. There was also the power to influence others. In 1965, his daughter Deana signed a contract with Columbia Records, although with none of the success that Sinatra's daughter Nancy later achieved, let alone even a smudge of her father's triumph, originally with Capitol and most recently with Sinatra's label Reprise.

Friends said they detected much more self-confidence in Dean, although there was to be sufficient evidence to contradict that assumption from time to time. They also noted that he was becoming more complicated. As his friend Shirley MacLaine said: 'I sense a great deal churning up inside him.' But what was churning up most was more and more success. And Dean's film career was blossoming, too. There was another semi-reunion of The Clan, with the addition of several new members, in *Robin and the Seven Hoods*, which spoofed the Sherwood Forest story in a Chicago setting – a convenient site for the Jimmy van Heusen-Sammy Cahn hit 'My Kind of Town', which won an Academy Award nomination. Dean, Sinatra and Sammy Davis Jnr were joined by Bing Crosby, Peter Falk, Barbara Rush and, in a cameo role, Edward G Robinson. One of the best songs in the film was 'Style' which Dean, Frank, Sammy and Bing sang together.

Kiss Me Stupid had Dean playing a sexually highly active, drinking pop singer in a movie that was to have co-starred Peter Sellers had he not been flayed by a heart attack. The Sellers role was ultimately taken by Ray Walston, and both played opposite a delicious-looking Kim Novak. The most interesting part of the film should have been a trunk-load of songs by George and Ira Gershwin that had never been heard before – except that there were very good reasons why they had never been heard before.

It was written (with I A L Diamond), produced and directed by Billy Wilder who told me he had no happy memories of the movie at all. He wished he had never made it.

The Sons of Katie Elder had Dean back in cowboy clothes playing another of his straight roles – along, once more, with John Wayne, Michael Anderson and Martha Hyer. It was not a memorable movie.

But the director Henry Hathaway, a Hollywood Western veteran if ever there was one, was ecstatic. He said that the *Katie Elder* location 'probes the depths of a man's soul. It is tough and rugged, everybody has to sacrifice more than a little bit. Those who can stand up under it and still smile and think of the other fellow's problems are the real giants.' The reason things went well was in no small way due to Dean. 'It wasn't merely that he's a pro and does his job well without complaining. It was his attitude – matter of fact, philosophical, humorous and witty. His spirit spread through the entire company and made him, in that sense, the most valuable member of the team.'

Dean was now constantly being asked to analyse his view of acting. That he responded may indicate more his latent insecurity than his conviction that he really had something worth while to say. 'Work?' he said at the time. 'What work? Man, this ain't work. Just like stealing candy from a kid, making your living this way . . . I prefer golf. Except they don't pay me for that. For this, they do. So I guess you'd just call this business, if you stretched a point.'

All things being equal, golf *was* the most important thing in his life. He played early in the morning, in all weathers –even when it was so foggy he could hardly see the ball. But it was all worth it to him – and justified the expense to which he put himself in building a practice range at home. At Encino he became the local champion. 'You know,' he said, 'it's not how you play the game. It's who wins.' There were a number of Olympic athletes who in their hearts felt the same way. Another time, he said: 'I like doing comedies best, but you've got to do the serious stuff to play golf. And to feed my kids.'

His nightclub work continued apace, too. If there were any problems with that, it was that his audience had long memories. Frequently, someone would call out: 'How's Jerry?' It was the one question that, legend had it, riled the laid-back, unflappable Dino. 'I don't know where he is,' he always replied in a riposte he had by now perfected. 'But wherever he is he must be doing just fine, because he has bundles of talent and he's a wonderful guy.'

Now not even his PR man would suggest that Dean meant every syllable of that comment. But it always brought a hefty round of applause and an opportunity for Dean to say something rude to the questioner like: 'How do you feel now, you jerk?' Not even Dean Martin could ever resist the opportunity to barrack a heckler. But then he wasn't working very hard at that either. When Dean did two shows a night at Las Vegas in August 1968, he even took a pill between performances so that he would fall asleep as soon as he locked himself in his suite. He was, however, increasing his drink intake – and on stage, too. A number of people were now saying what others had suggested all along. The apple juice in the JV whisky bottle was not always apple juice. Before taking the between-shows sleeping pill, he would go off for his favourite Italian dinner, which usually included a bottle of wine. After the show, he would have up to five more drinks. 'Millions of guys drink more than I do,' he said. 'Hundreds of thousands are more smashed all the time.'

But as Jeanne was able to testify, when he wasn't working in Vegas, he was in bed by ten o'clock and took so much care of his body that he had a practice rowing boat installed in his bathroom. He did two hundred strokes a day. That was his story.

In truth, his lifestyle *was* having its effect on his physical condition. For the first time, he was suffering seriously from an ulcer that would before long severely incapacitate him. He even cancelled a show with Sinatra because of it. His telegram was read to the audience and the private affliction became public property.

On the other hand, there were times when the compliment was returned. Frank called Dean once and said: 'My throat's giving trouble.' Dean promised: 'I'll be right down' and substituted for Old Blue Eyes (Dean himself was being called Old Red Eyes now, and not without reason). He did two of the Sinatra shows and flew home again. Three days later, there was another call: 'My throat's gone once more.' He did two more performances in Frank's stead and the audiences seemed very pleased. He sang and told his usual jokes like: 'My drinking buddy Joe always says you're not drunk if you can lie on the floor without holding on.'

Most people wanted to know all they could about his relationship with Sinatra. He had an answer for them, too, that sounded like the opening lines of the constitution of a mutual-admiration society. 'I just love and adore Frank. We talk baseball and football or about some gag we're going to pull. That other Dago is the most.'

To which Sinatra would reply: 'It's rather like a brother thing with Dino and me. We're not together all the time, but Dean calls and says, "What's the matter? Your phone out of order or something?" and we're off again.'

Contrary to previous allegations, now it seemed that he was a great family man. When his eldest son Craig had married in 1963, Dean joked that he hadn't lost his boy, he simply had an eighth mouth to feed. He also looked forward to grandfatherhood – 'in nine months, maybe earlier. They're young. They don't know how long it takes.' In the event, it was to take a little longer.

Once a year, he organised a benefit concert for an Italian women's group that his mother ran. Frank Sinatra and the rest of The Clan usually took part.

But Dean was still happier alone most of the time. He was the loner personified. Jeanne was no more pleased about that now than she was earlier. The tensions were getting stronger and there were rumours that a break couldn't be far away. For the moment, however, they were putting on a front of being happily married.

Once, a visitor was pointed in the direction of a sleeping figure on the living-room couch. 'Look at him,' said Jeanne, not laughing as much inside as she was externally, 'the big ball of fire. America's life of the party!' Jeanne knew, though, that he was really happy only when he was getting the laughs. Or when he was on the golf course. After his one really big meal of the day – a breakfast of pancakes, sausages, eggs and coffee – he was as before, on the links while the grass was still covered in dew.

He was one of the original members of the Beverly Hills Country Club which was just a golfball's throw from his back garden. He specified, at the time, that the club would be strictly unrestricted, which didn't necessarily mean that he insisted it would be open to singers with a drink problem. It resulted, he said, from an incident at another club when he had been chided for bringing a Jewish friend along on two successive days. His answer at the time was to throw his bag of clubs through the window. 'You can sell my membership – and these clubs,' he said and huffed out of the clubhouse never to return.

For months, he would take friends to an observation point on the top of Summit Ridge Drive in Beverly Hills and point to where the club would be built. Dean was fronting a group of anonymous backers and was immediately appointed President. Membership – for a lucky six hundred – was to cost $25,000 a time. Facilities were to include health clubs for both men and women, tennis courts, card rooms, swimming pools, dining and banquet halls – all with a Spanish motif – and the most luxurious locker rooms known to any man who had ever hauled a bag of golf clubs.

What surprised a great many people was the way that Dean Martin, the easy-going boy from the steel town of Steubenville, could do more than just sing, more than just come out with the funny witty lines. No one was happier on a horse and few were as accomplished a rider. That was why he was so outstandingly good in *Texas Across the River* in 1966. It featured his Pack pal Joey Bishop.

He was always so happy whenever his agent offered him a Western. He could sing a country song better than any other nice-'n'-easy performer. Get him to warble 'Houston' and you were listening to a man from the West, if not from the area of it that was wild. As his daughter Gail has said: 'He was a Marlboro Man.' That was him.

It was Dean's picture all the way – which isn't necessarily a compliment. Leslie Halliwell said that it had jokes added 'when someone realised it wasn't good enough to be taken seriously'.

They had to make up their own Indian dialect – with Bishop resorting in the end to a string of Italian singers' names when it came to reporting that the local schoolhouse had burnt down. 'Como – Sinatra – Damone – Martino,' said Joey. 'What the hell did you say?' asked Dean on camera. It didn't matter then any more than it did when he himself loused up a scene on his TV show.

The director, Michael Gordon, sometimes demanded more, however. Dean soon put him right. 'Come here, I want to talk to you,' he told him. 'We're performers, not actors. The best shot you're going to get from us is number one. Perhaps number two.' As Joey Bishop told me: 'After that, there was never any question of us doing a third take.'

But Gordon wasn't exactly pleased. 'Dean doesn't like acting, really,' he said. 'We set scenes up so that he only has to work in short spurts. Rock Hudson, Gregory Peck – those guys like to work. The more takes you do, the better they get. With Dean, it's all instinct. He just does.'

Dean put it somewhat less delicately at the time: 'Motivation is a lotta crap. Acting is reacting. You jes' gotta be yourself, right baby?' Rosemary Forsyth, his leading lady, smiled appreciatively.

And yet his own lines had been rehearsed to perfection. 'He not only knew his lines, but he knew everyone else's, too,' Bishop recalled. The lines that were in the script, that is. But Bishop told me: 'Dean enjoyed himself as though he were a member of the audience.'

The interesting thing about his attitude to films was his insistence that he didn't want to be the principal star, without anyone else to share the burden with him. He usually wanted the female lead to have the bigger role. That, too, could have been part of the ever lingering Martin insecurity.

It changed in 1966 with *The Silencers*, which had Dean playing opposite the Israeli actress Dahlia Lavi and Cyd Charisse, who told me she thought that Dean was a 'very lovable man' on the set – perhaps because neither of them this time had Marilyn Monroe to worry about. What was significant about the movie was that it was the first of a series, based on Donald Hamilton's pot-boiling secret agent Matt Helm. It established a theme which seemed to succeed well enough in the early years of the James Bond era. There was violence and lots of sex, or at least as much sex as was permitted in the last years before Hollywood discovered the full frontal. One Matt Helm movie begat another, as might have seemed appropriate considering all the hopping in and out of bed that occurred.

The same year as *The Silencers* there was *Murderers Row*, which provoked another of the periodic rows that appear to be close to a serious sport with the film community. Dean complained that he was owed a lot of money for the film. Columbia countered by saying that he still owed them cash. As always, it was settled – with the lawyers being the main beneficiaries.

In 1967, Helm was the central figure in *The Ambushers* but he died out with *The Wrecking Crew* the following year. Sharon Tate, shortly to fall victim to the Charles Manson murders, was one of Dean's co-performers. Another was Tina Louise, a beauty in the true Hollywood sense who loved being with Dean. 'Oh, he was *so* charming,' she told me. 'It was a real kidding-around film. He gives you his undivided attention.' With Tina Louise, it wasn't surprising.

'I think Dean likes to be with beautiful women and he didn't mind giving them centre stage.'

She had previously done a TV spot with him, the only girl among three men, and he treated her like a princess. Elke Sommer was in the film, too. For once, here was a woman less than ecstatic about working with him. 'He was not really the kind of man whose company I enjoyed,' she told me. 'He made no effort to be nice to me. I know there were a lot of girls he cast eyes on, but he wasn't my type at all.' But she did also add: 'Of course, we were all young, just there to look pretty, and he had other interests that were not ours. He was much more serious than I expected, but he was a helpful colleague.'

The film, originally called *House of Seven Joys*, was not without its problems. In one scene, Dean had to handle a trick camera that was supposed to emit smoke. It did more than that. It caught fire and Dean was slightly burnt.

In truth, Dean's movie career, while helping his bank balance and disciplining him to do the things he was taking very much for granted on TV, was hitting something of a slough. The man who had been tipped for an Oscar after *Some Came Running* and *The Young Lions* was wading his way through the kind of rubbish his image seemed to demand.

While the Matt Helm series was in progress, he also made *Rough Night in Jericho* – another Western, this time with George Peppard and Jean Simmons. Then came *Bandelero!* which would have been equally uninspiring had it not had James Stewart providing his usual dash of polish and a young Raquel Welch breathing in all the right places. Nevertheless, Dean was hardly worrying. He was said to be worth $30 million, give or take a million, and every time he was short of a buck or two he only had to indicate to the Riviera Hotel or some similar sort of establishment and they were delighted to allow him on their stage to sing 'Every time it rains, it rains bourbon from heaven.'

Five Card Stud in 1968 brought Dean back to work once more with Hal Wallis, and with Henry Hathaway directing. It was about the gradual seeking out and eventual murder of every member of a lynching party. There were people who said that that should have been the fate of the men responsible for the movie, although one critic did say it was 'so mediocre, you can't get mad with it'.

But there were people who got mad with Dean, like one of his fellow actors in the film, John Anderson. Not that he didn't like the man, but because he suspected him of a fault that others recalled from the Jerry Lewis days – the charge of not having sufficient concern for other people's problems. Dean turned out to be a better professional actor than Anderson imagined he would be, but that was not the fact that stays in his mind.

Hathaway had a fight with at least four of the players in the film – winning hands down, by all accounts. The fifth one to be at the receiving end of the director's somewhat caustic tongue was Anderson. 'I did the unforgivable,' he told me. 'I took a break while the scene was being relit. I took a cup of coffee and a cigar.

'His standard rule is no coffee anywhere near the cameras, which he regarded as a symbol of a slovenly lack of professionalism. He went into a rage. He shut the cameras down when I said I needed the coffee for energy and made some cutting remarks to the rest of the crew. He didn't speak to me again for the remaining three weeks.

'I sort of faulted Dean – and Robert Mitchum, who was in the picture, too – for not answering back to Hathaway. They have the power to say, "Come on Henry. Let it go." But neither of them did. They got their close-ups and left. I knew Dean was a compassionate warm guy. I wondered then and I wonder now why he didn't say anything.'

Before long, however, Dean found that Hathaway was a cross that he himself had to bear, too.

The film was shot in Durango, Mexico – where Dean, on a day off, decided to hold a party. Mitchum was there with Inger Stevens, Roddy McDowall and Anderson. 'He sat and sang and drank all day long. I must say that Dean's drinking powers were prodigious. You'd never know what he put away.'

By the evening, Dean was – to use Anderson's phrase – 'a little mellow, a little crazy, but not drunk'.

'Hathaway resented this. He said, "Haven't you anything better to do than get drunk?" Later on location, he called for Dean. But that isn't what he said. Instead, he demanded: 'Where's the drunk?'

When Dean heard about it, he was less than happy. 'He didn't say anything, but he was very quiet,' Anderson told me.

But he got his own back. He refused to attend the press conference that the director had called. Yet Anderson said he was still more concerned about the star's failure to go to his aid. 'I've thought about it a lot and you wonder why a guy is unwilling to be protective of people who need to be protected.'

He didn't always stay quiet – like the time there was a fight in a Beverly Hills restaurant in which Frank Sinatra was involved with Dean. It was Martin's birthday. A man at an adjoining booth took exception to the conversation he overheard coming from their party – other people were with them, too – as a result of which the man was struck and ended up in hospital. The story at the time was that it was not Dean who hit the man. But he left California when Beverly Hills police started making inquiries and he made himself unavailable for any investigation that followed.

Years later, he admitted in an interview that he had heard the man say, 'There go the two loud Dagos.' As he explained: 'Well, Frank got there one split second ahead of me and hit one guy. I hit the other, picked 'em up and threw 'em against the wall. The cops came. We said we didn't know who did it. But we did . . . yeh.' It materialises that Sinatra had picked up a telephone and smashed it into the head of the man who had complained of the noise from their table. For twenty-four hours he lay in intensive care, between life and death. Sinatra spent the entire day and night by his bedside.

About this time, *TV Guide* noted how difficult it was to get an interview with Dean because he was constantly surrounded by an ever growing retinue. 'Today,' said the magazine, 'reaching Dean Martin is more difficult than getting an audience with the Pope.' It took ten months, two weeks and three days to arrange an interview in which Dean was asked if this was his third or fourth TV season. 'Boy,' he replied, 'that's a tough question.'

Mack Gray's brother, Joe, was on the lot of *Five Card Stud*. He was Dean's stand-in and general factotum. 'He was never invited to Dean's table with Mack and the others,' John Anderson remembers. 'That worried me a bit. But he'd always be around and with a three iron in his hand just in case Dean had time to practise pit shots or whatever.

'But I found Dean a warm guy and easy to get to know. He was very funny.'

Word got around that the actors were in the location area. Women from the district came to see the stars have their seven o'clock breakfast in the open air. He met them and signed autographs. When people complained about his not always being as affable as that, he told them that was his make-up. Jeanne liked sailing, he hated it. 'Where am I going to go on a boat? Fish? I don't like to fish. Sail? I don't like to sail. Everybody says the bow, the stern, let's go to the Pointed End. I don't know what that is. Others like politics. Like Frank. I don't. I stay out. I might do a show 'cause Frank asks me . . . but I stay out. All these actors who go into politics. I do a gag on the stage when I say: "I only would become governor if all the drunks vote for me."'

When Ronald Reagan was Governor of California, he told him: 'I know you're the Governor, but if you want a small little part, just playin' an Indian, in my next picture, just call me.'

He told writer Oriana Fallaci that he and Bobby Kennedy were friends. 'Sometimes he stops here and we go down to his sister's house at the beach and there we would sing. Man, how bad he sings. Old college songs, that's all he knows. With that voice, the worst voice in the whole world.' He also felt sorry for President Johnson for all the stick he was taking in Vietnam. 1968 was election year, and Frank Sinatra – partly through his devoted friendship with the Vice-Presidential candidate Spiro Agnew – had converted to the

Republicans and was now Nixon's man. Dean, though more right-wing and Conservative than any other member of The Clan, stayed away. He was going through one of his periods of 'absent friends' as far as Sinatra was concerned. 'He wasn't around when we all went to the desert for the campaign,' remembered Ruta Lee. 'I was always conscious of missing Dean.'

But he was mostly just interested in his next film. One of the most indifferent was *How To Save a Marriage and Ruin Your Life* in 1968, a title which Dean might have taken closer to heart. It was meant to be funny and sexy and wasn't really either, even though Dean could have competently dealt with a few humorous lines and Stella Stevens was able to bring the man out in most males. (Actually, she brought *him* out in the plot. It was the first time in his forty-odd film career that Dean had ever played a married man. Jeanne might have said he hadn't had enough experience.)

There came a time during the making of the film when it seemed that the problem would be more saving the movie than anyone's marriage. Dean took umbrage at once more being asked to over-rehearse. Fielder Cook, the director, wanted not just rehearsals but up to fifteen takes of every shot. Dean gave a similar answer to the one he had employed in *Texas Across the River*. When the director still insisted, Dean used his influence, and the head of Columbia Pictures, Mike Frankovich, moved in and instructed his director to shoot the picture 'Dean's way'.

If anything could save Dean's marriage, he was convinced it was his children – whom he tried to persuade to go to college, although none of them lasted more than a couple of years through their courses. Jeanne always thought that the blond, blue-eyed Dean Paul was 'special' to the older Dino. But maybe that is what one should expect of a dark-haired Italian who started life as Dino Crocetti.

It was always Jeanne who administered punishments – the favourites were denial of TV for the younger kids, of the use of family cars for the older ones. She spent weeks teaching them how to shake hands and the best of table manners – only to see Dean himself treating the dinner table like a baseball ground. When the youngsters started getting married, Dean tried to slow down on the jokes and increase his role as parent and guide.

Gail Martin, writing in *Coronet* magazine in May 1967, said that her father was such a family man that he never ate a meal without one of them being present when he was at home. 'Our dining-room resembles the mess hall at a junior college but that's the way he likes it,' she wrote. As for his drinking, 'Frank Sinatra spills more than Dad drinks.'

Four of Dean's children appeared on his TV show. Craig – who gave his father his first two grandchildren – served as programme coordinator and Gail, Deana and Dino were all on it as guests.

On 17 June 1969, the Martins gave a reception at their home for two of their offspring. That afternoon, Deana had been married to writer Terence Guerin at the Church of the Good Shepherd, Beverly Hills. Ten days earlier, Claudia was said by her father to have 'kinda eloped' with Keil Martin (no relation) at Santa Monica. She and her husband were equal guests of honour.

But there were less cheerful events in the Martin family life. Mr and Mrs Crocetti died within months of each other, soon after Bill's death. And at home in Beverly Hills, it appeared that Dean had only taken to heart the second part of the title of the movie *How To Save a Marriage and Ruin Your Life*. By the time the film was playing in the neighbourhood theatres, Jeanne was seeing her lawyers and announcing: 'My husband has fallen in love with someone else. I will comply with his wishes.'

His wishes were that they get a divorce. It was not a happy way to end the decade.

You're Never Too Young 15

Everybody loves somebody some time. The trouble as far as Jeanne was concerned was that Dean was loving too many. Deep down, she thought that he still loved her. But, less deep down, a statement she had made not long before seemed to ring true. She said: 'The truth is, I bore the hell out of Dean. I always loved him. Most women do. He's not a ladies' man. He's a man's man. I like that about him.'

Nevertheless, she knew he was in the midst of what she would tell Barbra Paskin was his 'silly midlife crisis'. He was not a womaniser, she would again and again protest. Arthur Marx – son of Groucho and a biographer of the Dean and Jerry partnership – on the other hand, maintains that that was precisely what Dean had been in his younger days. 'I was in New York,' he told me, 'in the offices of Dean's old agent, Lou Perry. He showed me a pile of letters, perhaps a hundred of them, all in longhand, written by girls from way back, from the time he lived in Steubenville, all of whom he had made pregnant. But that was when he was growing up. I guess he might have been more careful later on.'

The problem now was that there *was* a lady whose man he had seemed to have become. Gail Renshaw was twenty-two – four years younger than Dean's eldest son – as pretty as anyone appealing to Dean Martin might have been expected to be, and she was the 'other woman'. She was also a Miss USA – her measurements were

39-26-36 – and when they first met, she called him Mr Wonderful. He was bowled over like a Boy Scout who had had a kiss on the cheek from the girl to whom he had just given an apple. The girl from Arlington, Virginia, with a Southern accent to match her complexion, was perhaps no more a threat to Dean's marriage than some of the other things that had happened in the past few years, but this time when he said he was smitten, Jeanne decided to cut her losses and press for an alimony settlement that would bite deep into the new contract that her husband was about to sign with NBC.

Dean was inwardly as surprised about the prospective break-up as was his wife – surprised, that is, that it had reached that stage. Only a short while before, he was telling reporters how much he loved Jeanne.

Of course, Jeanne had been expecting it for a long time. She had established a life for herself going out while he was working away from home or sleeping when actually in it. Now she knew the break had to come. 'I haven't met her,' she told reporters. 'But evidently all the children have. All I know is that he asked for a divorce – which surprised me – but I wouldn't want to live with a man who's not happy with me. I've had twenty marvellous years with him. I'm in good health and I have no financial problems. He's been very good to me. Now he's free, which is good. Now he can hide – which is what he does best.'

Where he was actually hiding was in a suite he had taken at the Beverly Hills Hotel. While the news was in the papers, Dean had a choice as to whether he wanted to brazen it out or ignore the interest in his marital state. He chose to exploit it in his routine. Once on stage at Las Vegas, he said: 'I didn't have much trouble finding my luggage. It was all out on the sidewalk.' Another time, when Jeanne said she was going to claim the new ranch, he said he didn't mind at all. 'I could never find the place anyway.'

If anyone doubted that this was serious, they only had to read the newspapers. Gail had resigned as Miss USA so that she could devote her time to her fiancé. Or so it seemed. The romance continued for about four months – and then fizzled out before any marriage plans could be announced or any divorce finalised. But Jeanne, herself still the right side of forty and still curvy enough to model for a *Playboy* centre spread if she ever felt she needed the money – which was unlikely – was determined at last to go through with it. Dean had someone else in view now anyway. But Jeanne wouldn't have been willing to put a great deal of cash on the likelihood that her husband would ever be the ideal love mate. Just two years before, she had said: 'I don't know him. The important thing to say about my husband is that I don't understand him. Nobody can. There is something in him that is unreachable. You might find occasions when you think that he's reachable, but the procedure is so painful that you get tired of trying and give up.'

Jeanne was emphasising to all who would listen that she was dreadfully unhappy that matters had now reached this pass. 'It is painfully difficult for me to make this statement,' she told reporters. 'My deepest concern at the present is for our children. It is my hope that all concerned will make every effort to see that their lives are kept within as normal a pattern as the situation will permit. The children have always felt great love and respect for their father and I fully intend it to remain so.'

But the truth of the matter was that he had seemed to have proved another of her earlier theories: 'He's a cold calculating impersonal man. He's cold and completely withdrawn.' Only fourteen months earlier, she had told another writer: 'The marvel is that I still love him. But I would have to love him because he loves me. I would almost love anyone who loved me. That's the way I am.'

The Clan were the first to range themselves around their fellow member (most of them had been through the experience on a number of occasions). Sammy Davis Jnr was surprised that anyone would think it unusual: 'Man,' he told one reporter, 'are you talking about Dino or are you talking about a saint?'

Nevertheless, there was reason to pity Jeanne who, in the midst of an outwardly happy marriage, had felt compelled to spell out all her disappointments to *Look* magazine in December 1967. She loved him as much as ever, she said. 'It has been tough. There have been battles. At times, I've tried to skip from him, but only to find out that I am happiest with him, that I love him as the first day. He is one hundred per cent man. I am not supposed to be an authority on men, I am an amateur student, yet I adore all men between eight and eighty years old and Dean Martin covers the range between eight and eighty-year-old men.'

One of his problems, she said, was his aloofness. Even then, eighteen years after they were first married, he was intimidating her. 'I can't be my best with him. I can't shine.'

Barbara Rush, who had acted with Dean, told a similar story. 'I think Dean hasn't much to say to a woman,' she was quoted as saying in the *Look* piece. 'I think a woman to him is something soft and cuddly and pink and he hasn't much time to waste on them.'

He was, however, now wasting his time on a cuddly and pink thing called Kathy Hawn, who worked as a beauty parlour receptionist. She, too, fulfilled most of Dean's criteria in women. And this time, he stuck to her – filing for divorce himself to try to speed things up – while his family wondered whether he had been struck by the male menopause. As he was serenading Kathy, his own daughters Claudia and Gail were again about to make him a grandfather. And Dino Jnr had announced he was going to marry Olivia Hussey who three years before had starred as Juliet in the Dino de Laurentiis version of *Romeo and Juliet*. After his divorce, he married the Olympic gold medallist, Dorothy Hamill.

One writer, at least, understood what all the fuss was about. An article in *Coronet* magazine declared: 'Dean Martin is healthy, wealthy and very, very sexy. At the age when most men are resignedly thinking of laying down their arms, Dino at fifty-three has his biceps up and around some curvy chick. He makes no passes. He sounds no mating call. He just stands by, half smiles, with an air of availability around him.'

The divorce action was there to prove that available was the one thing he was not. Kathy was determined to get him. But it didn't work out quite as simply as that. Jeanne thought the rumours she heard about the money Dean was spending on the woman who hadn't yet usurped her title of Mrs Martin were threatening what she believed she was herself entitled to.

It took until February 1973 for the divorce to be finalised, and Kathy to be ready to say 'I do'. She was also not afraid of making public her feelings about her fiancé. 'Do you know how hard it is to love someone?' she asked rhetorically of one writer. 'After a while, it just didn't make sense to me. Maybe I lost myself, maybe I acted crazy, but that night I asked Dean, "Do you still want to marry me or not?"'

Dean promised that it wasn't just a giant stalling operation and put matters in hand to guarantee Jeanne not just a living but what would become the biggest alimony settlement of all time. It amounted to $6.5 million. She got the homes in Beverly Hills and Palm Springs with all the contents – including antiques, works of art and recording equipment and projection rooms. There were two cars and part of Dean's portfolio of stocks and shares. She was also expected to receive a share of the proceeds of the lemons on the Martin family ranch. Dean decided that the most sensible thing was to sell the ranch, to help pay the cash that Jeanne was also awarded by the divorce court judge.

Once it was all tied up, Dean agreed to look to his own future. He was still infatuated by Kathy and the question had been popped long before. All that was left was to settle the date. It would be in April 1973. He had all his plans for the ceremony and Kathy knew exactly the dress she would wear and what her bridesmaids would have on their pretty backs. But it didn't happen so easily. Dean was rushed to hospital for an emergency operation for his stomach ulcers – which could not have been helped by the worry of the previous few years. People were surprised that Dean had chosen Kathy to marry. She was very different from the previous Mrs Martin; very little about her was like Jeanne.

As things turned out, Dean made the wedding – and in style. Jeanne indicated that she wouldn't be there. 'I'm getting out of town,' she said. 'I don't want to hear that wedding march. I'm so close to them now I can see the cars lining up.'

Jeanne also confided to friends that she was finding things very tough, despite all the money coming her way. She couldn't get a date. 'People around these parts won't stop thinking of me as Mrs Dean Martin – despite Dean's carrying on.'

The carrying on was about to be legalised. When he heard that Kathy was planning on having eight hundred guests, he said there wouldn't be room for more than eighty cars. For once, he was almost the winner. Kathy's total was cut by 695.

The ceremony was held at the Beverly Hills Hotel, with a room converted into the closest thing to a Catholic church that a Hollywood studio designer could manage. Not that that was meant to have any great significance. Before he became engaged to Kathy, Dean specified that she could have anything money could buy – just providing it wasn't of any religious significance. The man who took a St Christopher's medal wherever he went and who said his prayers night and morning, still didn't want to be dominated by the Church. But, on the day of the wedding, church was the way the new Mrs Martin and her six-year-old daughter, Sacha, who was chief bridesmaid, wanted it.

The bill for flowers alone came to $70,000. The lilies and tulips were flown in from Paris. Frank Sinatra was best man. All the guests, including Sinatra – who as everyone knows had everything – got a present from the bridegroom worth about twenty dollars.

Ross Hunter, who had just made a new and highly unsuccessful version of *Lost Horizon*, looked around him and said: 'Everyone must have his Shangri-la.'

The menu was a Beverly Hills gourmet's delight, with caviar flown from Iran. If any guest dared to walk around the room with his glass half empty, the hovering waiters – one, it seemed, to each invitee – were instructed to fill it to the brim again.

Before meeting Dean, Kathy had been earning little more than eighty dollars a week. Now, suddenly, she was mistress to a fortune. She set about proving it the day the deeds of the Bel Air house he bought for her were finally signed and sealed.

She brought in Phyllis Morris, who had the reputation of being not just one of the most artistic interior decorators but the most costly, too, to redesign the rooms. Kathy decided that the old Spanish style of California suited her tastes most, and Dean, as sanguine about this as practically anything else at home, agreed. His children – to say nothing of Jeanne – thought he had had a very expensive brain storm.

Dean tried to make sure that his home life and his professional work didn't clash. Gail would be the only one who would come on the programme more than once, occasionally, but that was about all.

If Dean really liked someone and if he were in the midst of one of those rare occasions when he actually engaged in conversation, he would talk of himself in the third person. When he loved his companion, as when his daughter Gail would sing with him on his TV show, he would say, 'point the Italian'.

The family fun, however, seemed to disappear when he married Kathy – with a new regime plainly in operation. She not only would come on the set, she would give instructions to technicians and directors. 'I remember that happening when I went to see the show,' said Walter Scharf. 'It was a terrible experience.' So was, he said, hearing the rows between them. Before Kathy appeared on the scene, the only sounds coming from Dean's dressing-room – apart from his snores, that is – were the sound of a TV set being switched on or off, or of a golfball being putted from one end of the room to the other. When Kathy was around, however, the noise could be heard throughout the lot, by all accounts. 'It was,' says Scharf, 'like a scene from *Who's Afraid of Virginia Woolf?*' But this was just the first act. There would be other scenes.

Showdown 16

All the time that the Dean Martin love affairs and his subsequent divorce and remarriage were eating up the Los Angeles newsprint and providing tittle-tattle all the way from the Polo Lounge at the Beverly Hills Hotel to Nate 'n' Al's delicatessen on Beverly Drive, he was maintaining his work schedule – continuing the TV series, playing assorted club dates in Las Vegas and Lake Tahoe and making the now only occasional movie.

Few films, however, were as big as *Airport*, based on the Arthur Hailey novel and the forerunner for a whole series of *Airport* movies, most of which simply had a date tagged on to the end to distinguish one from the other.

The 1969 *Airport* film was the best. Helen Hayes won an Oscar for her role as an old lady who single-handed had managed a season-ticket to swindling the airlines of the world. Dean didn't get an Academy Award himself, but he was more convincing as the pilot facing the twin catastrophes of a broken marriage and a broken-down airplane than he had been in any other picture for years. When the film was shown in 1970, most critics were excited about it. In the London *Evening Standard*, Alexander Walker wrote: 'For sheer contentment there is nothing to beat the sight of constant catastrophe happening to other people.'

Time was less enthusiastic. It was as if 'somehow they carted *The VIPs* from the *Grand Hotel* out to the *Airport* to make one of those old-fashioned Hollywood movies they don't make any more.' What the magazine's critic didn't know was that after this, they would go on and on and on and on making more of them, creating the new disaster film cult. 'The movie,' said the magazine's reviewer, 'spends two hours proving what every seasoned traveller already knows; waiting around airports can be a drag.'

The London *Sunday Telegraph* said that the picture was 'really an exciting tribute to the special effects department. The people come second . . .' And that included, besides Dean and Miss Hayes, Burt Lancaster as the airport manager, George Kennedy as the chief engineer (who appeared in most of the other *Airport* films) and Jacqueline Bisset as the air hostess.

Dean himself was very pleased with the film. 'It isn't like the Matt Helm pictures which make a fortune at the box office and which need . . . a heap of gimmicks to get by. This one has a lot of depth and a lot of emotion. It's the most interesting film I've done in years.'

Not that he was pretentious about it. After all, Mr Martin was a man skilled in the culture of the theatre, and he had to admit yet again: 'It ain't *Hamlet*, but could you see me doing *Hamlet* anyway?'

Dean was now fifty-three and the thought had occurred to him to start addressing himself to issues that have been known to cross the minds of others in his position and at his age. 'Five years, five more years that's all. Then, I'm gonna stop and go off somewhere and spend all the goddamn money I got!' It was the sort of prediction that people like to remember. He should have been more careful.

Barbara Hale, an actress who was best known at the time as Della Street, the sidekick of Raymond Burr in the *Perry Mason* TV series, played Dean's deserted wife in *Airport*. She remembers him being 'a wonderfully funny, lovely man' working on the set.

He was usually disciplined but one day he arrived late. The scene they were shooting that day was in a car. He rushed into his place and Barbara asked him why he had been delayed. 'Well,' he said as though playing before a live audience after deciding he couldn't read the cue cards, 'listen Barbara. I got a little hungry. Went into the kitchen, opened up the icebox and when the lights went on, I did the best performance I've done in years. And once that happens, you can't get off.'

As Barbara Hale added: 'You wouldn't believe the number of little girls who were chasing after him. They had to be roped off. He was great fun. It was like watching him on stage. He makes a ploy that it's all easy come, easy go. But it wasn't. He worked very hard at being very serious. He was also terribly shy.'

The film was shot in a real airport, with real snow clogging the runways. It was certainly more real than most of the movies that followed. If only for the money Dean claimed after it was made. Three years later came another law suit. He demanded at least one million dollars because he said his contract provided that he received ten per cent of all gross proceeds exceeding 'breaking point'. The debate was over when that stage had been reached. Once again, the matter was settled privately.

There was a chance in 1970 that Dean would become a Disney voice, which by then had become one of the most prestigious things that a top star could do. It could have been regarded as easy money – all he would have to do would be to record a song or two, just as if he were making a new 45.

He might well have wondered about that. Part of the excitement of a Dean Martin performance on film was watching the way he manipulated the camera angles, to give the women in the audience the excitement of seeing his profile and those strange faces that he would make and send them into a swoon.

The film they wanted him for was *The Aristocats*. Maurice Chevalier sang the title song. Phil Harris, who had begun to make a new career for himself as a Disney voice, was in it, too – and wanted Dino to join him. They were golfing partners and he brought the idea up during one of their better games. He later told me that he said: '"Say, Dean, you've got all the old ladies, now why not pick up the kids?" Dean said: "Well, you'll have to see my manager."' That was not the usual Dino response.

Harris thought that Dean would be ideal and he knew he'd say yes to the offer for *The Aristocats*. 'He would belch to give a guy a hand. He couldn't belch after a Hungarian dinner.

'I said to Dean, "If I were to tell you that on *Jungle Book* alone, we had nine principals." I thought that would be enough to persuade him.' Unfortunately, Dino kept saying he was busy, so it never happened.

Harris was surprised, 'Because Dean's not just the most beautiful guy you ever met in your life, he's also on fire.' When he 'kept going to Dean', Dino replied again: 'I'm busy, I'm busy.' It was a shame that many a Disney fan might have regretted. To this day, long after their deaths, Harris and Chevalier are heard every time *The Aristocats* appears on television and on video, each time with a brand-new audience for their talents. Even Peter Ustinov has gone down in a kind of posterity thanks to the cartoon version of *Robin Hood* in which he voiced Prince John.

Something Big in 1971 was anything but. It was a Western that went West. Shown on one theatre run, turning up occasionally on television, it has since then gone the way of all indifferent celluloid. The movie was shot in Mexico. Albert Salmi, who was one of the supporting players, told me how surprised he was that Dean didn't socialise while it was being shot. 'He just disappeared after the day's filming.'

What Salmi admired was the fact that in fight scenes in which he was supposed to give Dean a heavy beating, the star asked him not to pull his punches. 'I must have grabbed him violently a dozen times, really hurting him, but he never said a word.'

In 1973, the year of the Showdown with Jeanne, Dean made *Showdown*. It was another Western, this time with Rock Hudson sharing the honours, such as they were. In fact, Dean walked off the set because he didn't like the way things were going on a picture for which he had been guaranteed $25,000 a week for twelve weeks. Before long, that, too, was patched up and Dean finished the movie with no great credit to anyone.

The Seventies were not Dean's decade, no matter how charitable one might like to be. He still joked with his friends when he met them – like telling Joey Bishop to leave the room every time he arrived at a party at the Martin Bel Air home – but he didn't see them that often. Kathy was jealous of her husband's time and was less willing than Jeanne to let him spend it away from her.

He was also in great pain. His ulcer problem hadn't been completely eradicated by his operation and there was more surgery to come. He was suffering increasingly from arthritis and was on a number of drugs that were making his face all puffy – the face that for so long had been so exciting to women. When doctors put him on Percadon, it was clear before long that he needed to keep taking it.

It was Mack Gray who had first mentioned Percadon to him. Gray suffered from migraines and it seemed to help his problem considerably. To Dean, it just gave more worry. But for a time no one thought it was more than the usual Martin feigned inebriation. When he appeared on stage at Las Vegas or on his TV series, he slurred his words and that seemed like just part of the act.

At the beginning of the Seventies the appeal of the series began to pall, but still the old routine continued and for much of the time, the audience accepted gratefully – if not ecstatically – what it was being offered.

Every week, there was the same pattern. The scene was in Dean's home den. He would go to the grand piano and sing his parodies – like 'Hello young lovers – you're under arrest'. Some of the new lyrics were written for him specially by Sammy Cahn. Like:

> When you're drinking
> When you're drinking
> The show looks good to you
> When you're drinking
> You get stinking
> It helps your point of view.

And then there was:

> What a day this has been
> I've had Bourbon, Scotch and gin
> Why it's almost like bein' at home.

Once, the Prince of Wales came to see a show. He wasn't yet married at that time. So Dean, courtesy of Sammy Cahn, had a special ditty for him:

> I'd say this evening is more than just great
> It's quite an honour that we celebrate
> Prince Charles is here and he needs a date
> But still the gentleman is a champ!
>
> Despite the fact we live different lives
> His Highness calls soon as he arrives
> He wants to date all my ex-wives
> But still the gentleman is a champ.

After the parodies, Dean was ready to get back to the show. On one occasion, he took a look at the spiral staircase that had at last been provided, and muttered, 'Prefer 'em straight.'

Once finished, he would go to the couch and sing a straight song. On the way to the couch, he always passed a door. There was a knock – and a celebrity guest would appear. 'He never, never, ever knew who that guest was,' recalled Greg Garrison. The guest would appear on camera for fifteen seconds at the most. Just so that there was no risk that Dean would dry up embarrassingly, a cue card was held over the guest's shoulder with the mystery personality's name. Anybody could forget a person's name. With Dean it was a highly likely professional hazard.

'After about twelve weeks,' recalled Garrison, 'we thought we'd spruce things up a bit. Dean went to the door as usual, opened it – and there was a girl back there. Totally naked. But nobody in the audience could see it. Only three people knew it was happening. The girl herself, the wardrobe mistress and me – and then Dean.' Not only could the audience not see it, the cameramen couldn't either. The cue card over the girl's shapely white shoulders said 'Bing Crosby' – to which Dean knew he had to respond, 'Ah, Bing – with two pink cherries.'

Dean just stood there, gave the girl a big hug and a kiss and walked out, doubled up, to his dressing-room. He then came back and sang his song, still no one any the wiser. As Dean was in full throat in the middle of the romantic ditty he had learned for the occasion, the girl found her way back to the set and stood behind the camera. She was wearing a pretty dressing gown. Just as Dean got to the finale of the number, she casually opened the gown and stood in front of him, totally and utterly nude.

'Dean,' said Garrison, 'without missing a note just said, "Oh yeh!" and kept right on with the song.'

The girl was beautiful. But Dean wasn't interested, once the joke was over, to carry it over. He just gave her a kiss and said thanks for being such a sport.

He might have felt the same about the people buying his albums. He would still record half a dozen titles at a single session as easily as his reputation had him lining up and consuming glasses of booze. And they were selling better than those of his competitors. What he didn't claim was that he was better than they were. For as he once told me: 'There's nothing to write home about. It's all right. I'm no Sinatra or Tony Bennett. I have more gold albums than they do. But my voice isn't as good as they are. And they can't understand why I sell so many records.' But then he hated rock music (he was convinced that rock singers 'ate' their microphones, they put them so close to their mouths) and thought his own secret, as far as the record-buying public was concerned, was: 'I sing songs that they understand.'

By 1974, both Greg and Dean knew that audiences were being good sports watching *The Dean Martin Show* every week. It had been remarkably successful. Not only was it, at eighteen years in continuing production, the longest-running programme on television, no other show had achieved anything like the ratings that it knocked up. As no mean sidebar to that, the very rich man Dean Martin became even richer. He still owned fifty per cent of the show himself, although he eventually sold to Greg Garrison, the real creator of the whole enterprise. Without him, it would never have happened. Garrison told me when I interviewed him in the Eighties: 'It was a wonderful arrangement for us both.' How much he made out of the show, Dean would say he never knew. It was probably true. As long as he had enough money for the essentials in his life – his home, his golf and, above all, to give his family sufficient to enjoy a very comfortable lifestyle (including the hefty alimony payments he was having to pay Betty and Jeanne) – he was happy. Ask him how much he had in the bank and in his investments, and he wouldn't have known the answer to that either. But even *The Dean Martin Show* couldn't last for ever. Garrison might claim it was the last vestige of live television, but as an *Esquire* writer commented, that was a fraud since much of the time Dean looked half dead.

Of course, there was always the chance that he would be completely dead – if he didn't please those gentlemen from the Mafia. The Mob, who had undoubtedly helped Dino get started, were always around and he continued to work with them.

If Dean liked it to be known that his days with these unsavoury characters were at an end, the FBI were not going to let it happen, although they kept a discreet distance from him most of the time. Certain things, however, were inescapable. Phones were tapped and the Federal agents discovered things that Mr Martin might have hoped would be kept between himself and the gentlemen with long overcoats and twisted noses. When the phone of Mafia don Sam Giancano was listened to, a conversation with Johnny Formosa, another gangland boss, was more than Dino might have wished to be known. Plainly, he wasn't all that happy with the alleged association, but there would never be much he could do about it.

Giancano told Formosa: 'You go and see Dean Martin. You tell him I want ten days out of him.'

'Ten days? What if he says he's booked?'

'Find out when he ain't booked.'

'OK. I'll tell him this is a must. Tell him you said it. Tell him, "Hey Dean, this is a must. Sam says he wants you for ten days."'

'Just put it to him for a couple of weeks.'

'Right. Well, I'd better go West then.'

'Don't make a special trip. Call him.'

'Call? You can't call him. I'll have to go out there to lay the law down so that he knows I mean business.'

'It seems that they don't believe us. Just give him a little headache?'

'Maybe they'll come to their senses.'

The *Chicago Tribune*, which had reported the activities of Al Capone in all their glories, was well aware of the connection. When Dino appeared with Sinatra, it was more interested in the audience than the show itself. The cast of characters – a stream of names that Damon Runyon might have found it difficult to justify – were not the usual constituents of a telephone directory: 'A host of gangsters were on hand for [the] first night. Among them were Sam Giancano, Willie 'Potatoes' Dadano, Marshal Caifano, Jimmy 'The Monk' Alegretti and Felix Alderiso . . . The Fischettis were there from Miami and a delegation of Wisconsin gangsters occupied a ringside table.'

In 1974, Garrison told me when we met a decade later, one of the mobsters rang and asked for a favour. He wanted Dean to do a concert at a place they ran at Westbury, Long Island. He did it, appearing on stage for a scheduled thirty minutes and then adding another fifteen after that. He didn't charge, although the show made millions.

Dino told his producer: 'It was my way of saying thank you.' He was referring to the help that the Mob had given him when he needed that boost, a step up from small-time vaudeville and cabaret to superstardom. As Garrison said years later: 'If a bomb went off, organised crime would have been over for fifteen years, because they were all there.' But then, in addition to every name in the 'Who's Who in American Crime', there were also a few dozen henchmen positioned outside, each with his own sidearm that he promised not to use unless provoked by someone from outside the family.

Returning favours, particularly with the Mob, was a given now that he was on top; Dean had to remember the ones who had helped him when he wasn't. As Greg Garrison told Barbra Paskin: 'You have to pay back in this world.' He would get a call from a member of the Fischetti family asking for a favour – they wanted a spot on Dean's show for a 'broad' at a New York club. The answer was always 'Sure'.

Dean's determination to recognise when he had to say thanks applied to those outside the Mob, too. Like to the comic Gene Baylis, who appeared for rehearsals one day – much to Greg Garrison's surprise. When Greg asked how Dean knew him, Baylis said that at one time he'd given Dean 'milk money'. Dean had been broke with a wife and three children to feed, and Baylis had been the one who had given him enough money to buy milk. Now Dean was having him regularly on the show. 'Dean had a big smile on his face,' said Garrison. That, too, was a way of saying 'thank you'.

It was time for a new formula. Garrison found one, based on an old idea he had seen at the Friars Club in New York, the hangout of practically everyone who was ever anyone in American show business. This was the 'roast' – in which celebrities were subjected to such indignities that they lined up to be included in the insults. The most offensive thing to a Broadway 'name' was not to be insulted by your contemporaries on a 'roasting' platform. A half-hour roast was included in the last thirty Dean Martin TV shows. When the contract for the weekly shows ended, it was agreed that there were would be twenty-five hour-long roasts in their place.

Jack Benny was an early victim guest. Dean himself was a subject – with Don Rickles taking Martin's usual chair.

What happened in front of a huge portrait of the very willing victim was that at least six people, mostly men, would be invited by

Dean, the chairman, to be as rude as possible to the celebrity of the week – who would later be invited to answer back in his or her usual style. But none of them wrote their own words. Only Don Rickles was allowed to do that. 'Because Don is, like Dean, the total counter-puncher, reacting to every piece of business going on on that stage. He was the perfect guest on a roast to take shots at everyone else,' said Garrison.

None of the other guests was permitted to do that. They were sent their own material a week before taping – but were never allowed to see what anyone else was going to say. That way, it would sound funny to them, too – and there was a chance that when they were filmed pounding the desk in front of them, they meant it – even when there were special 'reaction' shots. They were not allowed to use their own writers either – each was given material considered to be in their style.

'It became an assembly-line operation. We knew how long to shoot. We had about twelve writers on the staff.'

One guest said of George Burns, for instance: 'George has to be very careful these days. Every time he passes his house, his pacemaker opens up his garage door.' Every Jack Benny line was an insulting reference to the stickiness of his hands when it came to dollar bills.

One writer commented on the quality of the material – 'particularly the jokes, the cue card jokes, the mammary gland jokes. The men all wore black ties and heavy leers, the women consisted of legs and navels.'

The roasts were the really big thing in Dean's life now. They were an unusual means of celebrating a mutual-admiration society. Stars queued up to be 'victims' of the best insults in the world. If you were denigrated on a Dean Martin roast, you had not only arrived, you had been there for a long time. Greg Garrison wanted to invite Jerry Lewis into the hot seat. Dean vetoed the idea, which was a fairly unusual thing for him. His reasoning was a lot kinder than might have been thought: Dean was a much bigger success now than his old sparring partner. He wouldn't want it to seem as though he were showing off.

Nobody would escape the insults when they got on to a Dean roast – which is precisely why they stood in line to be roasted. Before Ronald Reagan became the most important man in the world, he went into the oven and loved every moment as the heat was turned up. As 'the Gipper' banged the table and laughed, Dean told the other gathered roasters (and a few million in the live and TV audiences): 'When you talk about all the bad things about a person . . . how he could be a governor when he was such a bad actor . . .' the rest of the sentence was lost in the roasters' laughter. After the future President had been on, other government figures wrote to Dean asking to be roasted, too.

There were also times when Dean appeared at other people's roasts, particularly at the place where the whole concept originated, the celebrated Hollywood Friars' Club. Here, the host was George Jessel, the one-time Broadway actor and movie producer who now revelled in the title of America's Toastmaster General. Jessel, who loved to make speeches and appeared to need to do so as much as he needed to eat, introduced Dino to the guests at a Friars' tribute to Gary Cooper.

'After the break-up (of Dean and Jerry),' he declared, 'people said it would never work. One wants to do too much. One wants to drink too much. These opinions were decidedly wrong. One is a prominent member of the Hollywood Clan. With all due deference to their thinking, he is the most charming of the entire group.'

Dean clearly liked that and sang a song: 'I don't know why the Friars are honouring Gary Cooper,' he sang in Sammy Cahn's new lyric:

> I've never seen him in the club . . .
> I even saw old Bing who never shows up anywhere
> But him, he's never been at the club.
> He don't even walk on Rodeo Drive.

That was just the stuff from the singer who could also provide (care of Sammy Cahn again) his own version of 'The Lady Is a Tramp'. He sang, 'That's Why The Gentleman's a Tramp':

> I like the free fresh booze that you get
> So I'm in debt
> I'm flat, take that.

The only thing that riled Dean was the constant suggestion of his overdrinking. Once he got so angry that he put it all into his idea of perspective: 'Suppose,' he told a man who suggested that he really did like the bottle too much, 'just suppose you owned a TV station. Would you put up five or six million dollars for a drunk to do a show?' No. It was much nicer for him to joke about other people, even when the jokes themselves seemed very serious.

But he could joke about himself. There were, of course, times when he did conform to the stereotypes. He could stop a friend in the midst of a conversation in the middle of the day and offer a drink. When he did so, he had a familiar riposte for any protestations about the hour. 'It's dark in there. Your insides don't know the time.' Over the years, several people told me the same story. He had that one sentence to answer all those people who queried why he did so much drinking. Walter Scharf said it was his principal weapon against all those who worried about the excesses of his alcohol intake.

Dean worried more than most people imagined about the Dean Martin legends – the ones that said he was drunk and lazy. 'I think down deep they know I'm not a lazy guy,' he said once. 'Whenever there's a benefit and somebody calls me, Frank and I are always there [and so is] Sammy Davis. They think I'm lazy but they know I work. Could I be where I am today if I were lazy and was a boozer?'

It was a theme to which he constantly returned. On one occasion, a woman in the audience stood up and suggested he might consider attending Alcoholics Anonymous meetings. 'My dear young lady,' he snapped, 'I do about three major feature pictures a year, make a lot of records. I play at Vegas and do these 39 TV shows and make a lot of money. Do you think they'd pay that kind of money?' The woman apologised and resumed her seat.

In truth, the question of Dean and his drinking would be linked to him in people's minds as if it were a well-known phrase – like gin and tonic or whisky and soda. Yet you never saw him suffering the effects of intoxication. Greg Garrison and others who worked with him on the TV show still insist that rarely did he take more than apple juice when working. Sinatra was the real drinker in the Pack, which explains why he was buried with a bottle of Jack Daniel's close by in a lead coffin. Nevertheless, Dean, the man who only drank moderately and kept that case of Moderately in his dressing-room, knew it was good for business. Later, he told me: 'Oh, I cultivate that [being a boozer]. I drink but I'm not an alcoholic or anything like that. People like to see I'm a regular guy and that I drink.'

So what was the truth of the drink-for-real stories? 'I drink,' he said in 1983. 'I don't drink like I used to in the Rat Pack days. We didn't even open the bottles. We went right through the label.' Even so, if this were a court hearing, there would be plenty of people around to testify that he drank more than was admitted by that rare group who could claim to be close to him. Mel Shavelson told me: 'I had the feeling that the bottle was a big problem for him.'

So, assuming that this 'regular guy' did drink, what was his favourite tipple? Oh, it was easy to answer that one, he said: 'Scotch and soda, beer, margarita, a Martini, I'll drink anything, yeah.'

Sometimes, Dean's jokes really appeared to bite. But always the victim had to look as though he were enjoying it more than anyone else – and knowing that it was much worse not to be sitting there at all. When Dean introduced Milton Berle, he said: 'Here's Milton Berle, a man of a thousand jokes. All belonging to other people.'

In his *Esquire* piece, Jean Vallely reported Dean as saying – after fluffing a series of lines – 'I'm so sick of these flicking roasts.' But he went on. There was a contract that said he continued to host the

Dean Martin Celebrity Roast and the ratings were saying that people sitting at home by their television sets were glad that he did.

He sang to Jack L Warner, boss of Warner Bros. Studios:

> Jack L Warner
> That Jack L Warner
> He don't know nothin'
> He just keeps yackin'
> Keeps on yackin' along.

Once, he told Tony Randall: 'My handkerchief is funnier than he is.' He said that Glen Campbell was a country boy. How else, when he went out with him, did both of them end up with pigs? The team was even rude to the audience. 'You got in for nothing,' snapped Milton Berle, 'because you're good for nothing.' Don Rickles paid tribute to James Stewart – but said he wondered how long he would stay awake. Dean topped it. 'When Jimmy's in a romantic mood, his wife can hear him snoring.'

Joey Bishop didn't spare Dean when the star was his own victim. 'We're gathered here today,' said Bishop, 'to pay homage to someone who can't see us or hear us.' That was all he said about Dean. Instead, he turned to Frank Sinatra and berated him for not answering a phone call. 'I ignored Dean completely,' he told me. 'He liked that. He was hysterical.'

It was all a question of attitude. As Bishop told me: 'Did you realise that you can't wait to hear what Dean's going to say? It fitted beautifully into the Roast pattern. The most brilliant comedians may have been on, but the one you wanted to hear most was Dean. Dean is that best of comedians. You're not hearing him, you're overhearing him. He says it and you think that maybe the guy next to him didn't hear it as well as you did.'

The shows were filmed from the stage of the MGM Grand Hotel in Las Vegas before 900-strong audiences. Later, the scene was recreated in the studio, with the same portrait and the same fake props – so that the subsidiary shots could be taken. In the end, they simply ran out of names. 'We almost got to one point,' Garrison remembered, 'when we shut our eyes in embarrassment at some of the names we were thinking about and using. I would say, "Now there's a greengrocer who could be interesting . . . !"'

Another problem was that they were practically restricted to veteran performers. That was Garrison's judgement. 'The young people were not experienced as stand-up performers. They were either singers, who couldn't do anything more than stand in front of a microphone while a dozen engineers figured out how many tracks to use, or people who came out of situation comedies and hadn't learned their trade yet. The additional problem was that older performers didn't want to knock the young ones.'

In fact, the only 'young one' that Dean was at that time happy to knock – only figuratively – was Kathy, who seemed to be regarding her husband as a one-man Bank of America, which in many ways he still was (without the payments to Betty and Jeanne he might have qualified more in the Fort Knox league).

He had more gold and platinum LPs, mostly from country and western numbers, and his song 'Gentle On My Mind' was a hit on two continents. But that did little more than help the cash flow.

Kathy was welcomed along the smartest shopping streets in Beverly Hills as though she were visiting royalty. In the beauty parlour where she once worked, she was the number one favourite customer. But there was nothing particularly new in that.

She was equally warmly welcomed in the boutiques of Beverly Hills where she spent prodigiously – although she complained that Dean left her to it. 'He hates shopping,' she explained. 'He just sits there on the couch and carries on a conversation that has nothing to do with what is being bought.'

One shopkeeper told me of the time he sold her thirty T-shirts at one go. But that was just casual wear. Formal clothes she would choose at first sight and then order according to her taste. Jewellers also admired her self-assurance.

At first, Dean humoured her. He told friends it was because she was still young. So young, he used to apologise to audiences: 'I have to go home to burp my wife.' But he seemed loving enough. He called her young daughter Sacha, 'my baby'.

Kathy would have liked people to believe it was all a necessary substitute for the kind of love so many married women still crave. Once she told TV host Mery Griffin: 'I know you think that material things matter to me. But they don't. What I really want is Dean. I used to see him more before we were married than I do now. I thought he would settle down. But he runs off to Palm Springs and other places. If I don't feel like packing a suitcase in an hour, I stay at home alone.' She said she thought he was happier with a couple of drunks than with her. She told him that her husband still noticed her 'when he's sober'. More often than not, she spent her evenings sitting in front of the television set – wearing a $1,000 dress that no one else was ever going to see. As for having friends over, Kathy said she was afraid that Dean would turn up in a bad mood 'and kick them out'.

What she really wanted was another child. But that was no longer possible with Dean. She was not charging that her husband had lost his virility. It was simply that the man who more than once confessed to a pathological fear of hospitals, was doing the most fashionable thing imaginable in the mid Seventies. He had a vasectomy.

Dean tried his best to patch things up – the non-medical ones, that is. 'We are human beings,' he began in one of the speeches of apology Jeanne had got to know so well. 'We have our misunderstandings. But that doesn't say we don't also have a deep love and respect for each other. Kathy is a fine lady and she has made life for me extremely beautiful.'

She, however, was going about doing the opposite to her own life. When her $65,000 Statz Blackhawk car crashed into a tree in Beverly Hills, everyone thought she had been seriously injured, yet she escaped with minor damage. But she didn't really think that was the case with her relationship with her husband.

What A Way To Go 17

It was another watershed in Dean's life. He still had plenty of money – but as a friend said, with Kathy carting things home in a front-loading truck it was disappearing fast. Until, after three years, it was not possible to see the marriage continuing.

Eventually, it did come to an end in July 1976 and Dean found himself a sympathetic judge. Kathy didn't walk away with anything like the sort of settlements the previous Mrs Martins had gained. For three years, she would receive $1,250 a month – which would hardly have kept her in silky underwear – although most of their property was divided in half. Dean also promised to pay $250 a month to Sacha until she was either eighteen or got married. He would pay, too, her school fees and any medical or dental bills, and meet any costs should she need to see a psychiatrist. (In Hollywood nobody could be sure).

Dean's reaction was to find himself another woman. And when he found her, he looked for someone else. In 1974, he wasn't ready to settle down again. Nor was he in much of a mood to look for work. The roasts kept him busy on television, he still worked in Vegas or Lake Tahoe, but he wasn't ready for the hard slog of making movies and playing actors again. That was too much. It was a philosophy he would adopt for at least two years.

But in the meantime, people were wondering. The Los Angeles *Herald Examiner* had the courage to pose the question out loud:

'What has happened to Dean Martin? It seems that . . . he has faded out of the picture.'

He wasn't any happier with his family than he was with his film career. Dino Jnr was arrested on a firearms charge – until it was realised he was a registered gun collector – and at the same time his wife Olivia Hussey filed for a legal separation. Dean was really worried about that, and perhaps more so because it was a battle he was having to fight alone. 'No matter what difficulties I or my family might encounter,' he said, 'we will come through them together.'

'Running away is not the way we solve our problems. I respect my son. He's a fine young man. And I'm with him all the way. He knows it.'

Dean did make another film in 1974, although it would be another year before it would be released by MGM. This was *Mr Ricco*, another straight role about a defence counsel fighting a lone battle to save his black client. It was finished ahead of schedule, which should have worried the backers, but delighted Douglas Netter, the producer. 'Everyone will say that we brought this in so fast because Dean won't rehearse,' he said pre-empting the expected flak. 'But that is not true. He has rehearsed so long and as often as we needed him. Even the weather has gone right for us.' And he was backed by his director Paul Bogart: 'You better believe it. There's no drinking, smoking or wise-cracking about *Ricco*.'

No, privately, Dean didn't feel as if he had a great deal to wisecrack about. When he was funny, it was in his nightclub act. As always, he rejoiced in the presence of the people he regarded as greats or near greats. His old Hollywood buddy Ronald Reagan was one of them. When Reagan and Nancy, soon after giving up the Governor's mansion in Sacramento, came to see one show, Dean gave them a special introduction from the stage: 'We're the only club in town that validates hangovers,' he told them. And then insisted privately that it had been years since he had one himself. That did not mean that Ol' Red Eyes was in the pink of condition. His arthritic back was giving him a lot of agony and his ulcers were more painful than he could remember them. His forced dependence on Percodan was beyond a joke. Whenever he felt under the unavoidable weather, he would take a tablet. By the mid Seventies he was hooked – and his bloated face gave every indication that that was so.

He was living alone in the big house in Bel Air – on the letter box of which was a sign making it crystal clear that guests wouldn't be welcome without invitations. If one did get into the house – and not collide with his car that bore the word DRUNKY instead of a number plate (a sure warning for any traffic cops who might take him too much at his word) – there would be gasps of astonishment. Hardly any of the rooms were furnished. Kathy had taken most of the luxurious fittings and Dean as he reached the end of his fifties wasn't in any mood to buy more furniture. For quite a time he moved in with his business manager-cum-agent Mort Viner – a partner in the Citron-Chasen agency formed when they left MCA. In mid 1976, soon after the divorce from Kathy became final, Dean took a gun from a shelf in Viner's house – and ended up with twenty stitches in his hand after the automatic went off accidentally.

George 'Bullets' Durgan told me: 'Everywhere I'd go, into a bar or a restaurant, I'd see Dean sitting there with Mort Viner by his side. They seemed to be playing a waiting game. What they were waiting for I'll never know.'

It wasn't Jerry Lewis. However, they did get together that year – thanks to Frank Sinatra. Quite unaware that the other would be there, they were both invited on to the Frank Sinatra TV show. They arrived simultaneously from opposite ends of the stage – and embraced. 'I thought it was about time,' said Frank. Jerry looked thrilled and embarrassed and buried his head in his old partner's shoulder like a prodigal son returning to tell his deserted old father how much he really loved him. Dean just looked embarrassed. But he clasped him in his arms (although Peter Bogdanovich, the film director, afterwards said that he thought he did it a little too patronisingly).

Frank was the happiest of all. The smile on his face seemed to stretch all the way from California to his old home in Hoboken – as indeed did the assembled smiles of the people watching at home.

Jerry was reported to be chewing his lower lip. Dean . . . still looked embarrassed. And was saying silently (although there were lip-readers around who identified the sentence) 'You son of a bitch!'

Both were handed mikes but said little. All Jerry could say in Dean's direction was: 'You working?' For once, Dean, he of the ready quip and biting put-down, had nothing to say. As Bogdanovich commented, Dean was the straight man again. Jerry walked off at Sinatra's behest. He was being seen off like a visiting emperor, but Jerry felt like the poor boy who had been given a hug from Santa Claus in the orphanage.

Meanwhile, Dean had to prove that he *was* still working. Instead of, as planned, continuing a straight duet with Frank, he turned it into a Dean Martin comedy routine, altering the lyrics, telling jokes and showing how very bright he was.

It was soon after George Burns and Walter Matthau had teamed up in *The Sunshine Boys*, about an old vaudeville act – who in real life hated each other – getting back to work again. Once more, just as with Jerry, there were many who watched that Sinatra show who thought they were watching the Sunshine Boys come true. Except that there was not a glimmer of sunshine left in the relationship.

A few years earlier, *Esquire* had tried to feature just such a reunion on a Christmas cover. Jerry had said he was willing. Dean refused. The cover would have been captioned: 'Peace on Earth'.

When it was all over with Kathy, Dean was dating again. One of his companions was the luscious Angie Dickinson, who found him 'always adorable' even if he 'didn't talk a lot'.

Many people were now talking about Dean the loner. 'When you saw him in a restaurant,' George Durgan told me, 'he'd be alone very often, but he'd want you to join him. However, if you ever phoned him, there was the distinct impression that he was sorry you called. Maybe because when most people phoned, they were wanting something.'

Dean himself had wanted something very badly – to rid himself of his claustrophobia. As he told me himself, he was getting tired of walking up the stairs of skyscrapers because he was frightened of elevators. 'My dentist was on the ninth floor. By the time I'd walked all that way up, I really needed gas!' So, opening at the MGM Grand Hotel in Las Vegas, he struck up an idea. 'I got into a back elevator and went up and down for three hours,' he told me. 'That sure cured my claustrophobia. Never scared of elevators since then.'

Dean in 1977 was sixty years old, the kind of age when people want to sit at your feet and seep up some of your wisdom. Who, he was asked in that year, was his favourite character in American history. 'Eli Whitney,' he replied. 'Anyone who can make gin from cotton is OK in my book,' he said. There was no answer to that.

He seemed to be most interested – even more interested than in golf a lot of the time – in just sitting down and watching television. 'He'll never open up,' said his son Dean Jnr.

The only way you heard Dean was by sitting in the audience at Las Vegas – it was easier to get tickets for his shows now than a few years before. The MGM Grand was paying him $200,000 a week for an eight-week season there. His humour was much the same, as the *Esquire* writer reported. Jokes like: 'I got hungry last night and went across the street to the store. "Got any dates?" I asked. The guy says no. "Got any nuts?" Still the answer was no, except that the man in the store added: "If I had nuts, I'd have dates."'

The jokes got better: 'Don't believe it when they say carrots are good for your eyes. I stuck one in mine last night and it hurt.'

It was Sinatra's friendship that Dean valued most, almost as though he still needed the approval of the man who was Chairman of the Board. In September 1980, he and Sinatra played baseball – at three o'clock in the morning after having finished a benefit concert in Atlantic City which, since the relaxation of the gaming laws, had become the Las Vegas of the East coast. Ol' Blue Eyes talked Ol' Red Eyes into the event which would, he said, be from 'dew to daylight'. Dean himself played on what he said he was sure was 'one of those moving fields. I ran to first base and it was gone'.

It was described as a game of Dom Perignon-fuelled softball. Sinatra said the teams were made up of 'unemployed bartenders and those who failed the Alcoholics Anonymous physical exam'. Two thousand people watched and donated money after the seven innings. The score was 18–18. But a local blind rehabilitation centre benefited by a similar degree as that to which the two stars – joined halfway through by Sammy Davis Jnr – had fun.

In 1980, Dean was offering support to another old friend. Together with Sinatra – 'a nice lovable tough guy . . . there's nothing phony about him, my dearest and best friend' – Dean went on the campaign trail. Ronald Reagan, with the taste of power as California's Governor behind him and so close to getting the Republican nomination for the Presidency four years before, was trying again. This time he made it. Dean and Frank stomped the country during the primaries and, after he became the official Republican candidate, in the election itself. When Reagan became President, few people were more pleased than his friend Dino. 'I like him. He's my friend,' said Dean three years later. 'I like what he stands for. Frank and I helped him. We travelled around with him a little while.' I call him Ronnie and he calls me Deanie. He speaks short words. Not long ones you can't figure out.'

But he had no political ambitions himself. 'I campaigned for him for six weeks. Compared with what he has to do, show business is . . . nothing.'

However, there seemed to be clouds hovering on the Martin horizon just the same.

It was Dean's health that seemed to be the primary consideration. Like his other problems, he didn't hold back from mentioning them on the stage. He said that his doctor told him the only cure for his love problems was to run ten miles a day. After two weeks, the doctor asked him how his love life was. 'I don't know,' said Dean. 'I'm halfway to Las Vegas.'

He was becoming so much of an enigma now that there were people who were delighted to know that he was halfway to anywhere. His love life, at least, didn't seem to be too much of a problem. In 1980 he was seriously dating a Vegas show girl named Phyllis Davis. 'All the family's singing the chorus of "That's Amore",' he said. If they were, they changed the lines when the romance went sour. It could have had something to do with the way he looked. In 1981, Dean was interviewed on a TV programme intended to detail the great moments in his career. All it succeeded in doing was showing a series of 'Before' and 'After' shots. Before he had been attacked by illness and his drug dependence, he was the handsome-looking Italian with the smooth voice that may have sounded a lot like Bing Crosby's but was really very much his own. In *The Best of Dean Martin*, he wasn't so much a shadow of his former self, as a cloud. His features were so puffy as to be distorted almost beyond the point of recognition. His voice was even more slurred than usual.

In February that year, he and Sinatra had what was reported as their first row together, when Dean did not appear on Frank's TV show. All sorts of allegations were made, and then quoted as reasons, but it was sorted out before long. The show was put on to celebrate Reagan's inauguration. Dean saw the show from the front row of the audience.

There was a reason for Dean's behaviour, which he didn't want to talk about. He was feeling ill. He was also deeply disturbed by the death of Mack Gray which had just occurred. It was like the end of another of Dean's marriages, so close had their relationship been. Sinatra was the first to realise the problem and quite shortly they were friends once more.

Dean wasn't doing much work now. He received a million dollars for a TV commercial for AT & T and he rejoiced when his daughter Gina designed a black belt buckle which was widely displayed at

Beverly Hills's most chic boutique, Georgios. But the things for which he himself had been famous seemed like old history. For two years, he did virtually nothing. Worse, when he did open in August 1981 at the MGM Grand at Las Vegas, he – to use that unfortunate American showbiz terminology again – bombed.

One of the critics who charged that Dean wasn't as good as he had formerly been said that it was 'a rip-off to charge customers thirty dollars to see Martin swagger and sing a few songs'. He had had nicer things said about him in Steubenville.

It was the night that the hotel reopened after its disastrous fire. A celebrity audience were in the main hall to see him and, said Joe Cross in the Los Angeles *Herald Examiner*, must have been 'in awe – to the point they didn't remember to applaud very often and loud'.

Gregory Peck was in the crowd. Cary Grant made the customary introduction of Dean having come 'direct from the bar'. Dean told the assembled company not to worry about the risk of another fire. 'This,' he said, 'is the safest place in the world. I ordered smoked salmon for breakfast and the sprinklers went off.'

Cross wasn't in a totally complaining mood. 'Dino's voice is as mellow and as good as it has ever been – for the little bit of singing he did. While most entertainers usually sing, if not all, at least a goodly number of their hits, Martin sang about six of his – then spent the rest of the evening playing (ho-hum) the slow-talking drunk.' Dean said afterwards that he knew he was a 'little slow and didn't know where I'm at'.

The police were advising him on similar lines – when Dean was seen wearing a gun holster as he got into his car outside a Hollywood restaurant. He insisted that it was only a water pistol given to him as a joke by his son Ricci. But the story was that, following the murder of John Lennon, there were scores of show-business people doing the same thing. The police told him to get rid of it – because if he didn't, no hold-up man would risk finding out first if the gun was real or a plaything. Nevertheless, he kept hold of it. 'Every time you stop at a red light a kid can come at you with a gun,' he was to say. 'I fired mine in the air a couple of times and the word was: 'Keep away from that Dean Martin, he's crazy.'

Before long, he was in hospital again. Once more, he had ulcer surgery. The visit was kept strictly secret, Hollywood style. When his manager's office felt compelled to issue some statement or other, they said he was suffering from a bad case of gastroenteritis. But it convinced nobody. There were rumours that he had suffered complete kidney failure. Others even that he had died. Dean was forced to say himself that he was alive and well. The first part of the statement was true, the second wasn't. What really got tongues wagging was a visitor seen going into the Cedars Sinai building near Beverly Hills . . . Jeanne. She came to say that she still cared for him and knew how he was feeling – Dean's old fear of hospitals had not yet left him. By the time he was well enough to leave hospital, Jeanne felt close enough to him to want to continue the relationship.

She was by his side after he came out of hospital and went to court – charged with unlawful possession of firearms. He hadn't taken the policeman's warning to heart and was arrested for carrying the gun in his car, DRUNKY. There were no charges made for drunken driving. He pleaded not guilty – 'You really need something when you go out at night' – but made no pretence about its being merely a water pistol now. In the end, he was fined $192 and placed on probation for a year. The gun was taken away from him.

Then, he said, he had a better weapon at home – a number-seven iron. He had a stronger one than that. He and Jeanne seemed set for a new life together. As he was to tell me soon afterwards, they had lived on the same street and 'kept bumping into each other'.

Everybody Loves Somebody Sometime

18

The big question for anyone interested in the up-down life of Dean Martin was whether he was going to marry Jeanne again. She wasn't saying much herself – except that she was seeing a lot more of her former husband now than she had during most of the years of their marriage. She hadn't exactly been nursing him, but it was plain to see that he was a lot better having her worrying over him.

She still looked pretty, still had an attractive figure, and when, at Christmas, she gave a party for some of Hollywood's loveliest ladies, she stood out among them like a lighted tree. It was clear that she was much better for a man of sixty-five than the young girls he had been dating so regularly before, as if in the belief that they provided him with some kind of rejuvenation process.

Dean didn't look young. But he looked fitter. And certainly happier. He was ready to make a new film with his old Clan partner Sammy Davis Jnr, *Cannonball Run*. It was no great artistic triumph, but the film, in which he played a priest, was a sufficient success – his first since 1978 when he made a TV movie called *Angels in Vegas* – for him to sign up for a sequel, *Cannonball Two*.

Ask him why he was doing better, and he would say it was all because of Jeanne. Seeing them together in a booth at Chasens or some other Beverly Hills nitery, it was a convincing reason and the affection seemed mutual.

He admitted that he found the need to 'get a grip on myself. I told myself I was getting older and resolved to make myself try a little harder and to sing a little better. To do a better show.' When he said that in February 1983, it really seemed to be so.

He was telling people again that he was happy – words which close friends had not been sure they would ever hear from him again. It was like, he said, getting a second wind. 'I really like performing more than I ever did before. I love to sing. I love to have fun. If you're not having fun doing something, there's no reason to do it.'

Frank Sinatra and he were as close as ever. Once, he and Frank were stopped by a suspicious policeman who thought they might have a fraction too much alcohol in their systems. When he saw who the men were, he told them to sit in the back – and drove them home himself. On another occasion, a policeman asked Dean where he thought he was driving. 'I was going to a party,' said Dean. 'But it must be over. Everyone's coming back.'

Dean was happy legally, too. A long-festering row with Warner Bros. Records was settled. He asked for three million dollars because the label failed, he said, to provide him with the 'creative' subjects to which he felt he was entitled. That was settled privately, too.

His relationship with Jeanne was such now that he was once more a member of her family. He even gave a birthday party for his former mother-in-law – and invited his old friend Sammy Cahn to supply him with the lyrics. The two of them had more fun that evening than they had done for years.

When they did 'Gallagher and Shean', it wasn't all that polite – either to Mrs Peggy Beigger or to Jerry Lewis.

Cahn:
  Oh Mr Martin! Oh Mr Martin!
  Do you have the slightest notion why you're here?

Martin:
  I have not the slightest clue
  They said Peggy, I said Who?

Cahn:

You're not serious

Martin:

I'm utterly sincere

Cahn:

Oh Mr Martin! Oh Mr Martin!
Are you saying you would like to disappear?

Martin:

The only Peggy I know at all
Is a call girl that I ball

Cahn:

On the level Mr Martin?

Martin:

On the bias Mr Cahn.

In the middle of the familiar tune was what the trade calls a vamp.
Jerry wouldn't have liked it at all.

Sammy:

How do you like working with a partner again?

Dean:

I didn't like that other Jew either.

(Had it been written by anyone else, that would have had the B'nai
B'rith Anti Defamation League in uproar. By a leading supporter of
all Zionist and Jewish causes like East Side-born Sammy Cahn, it was
OK). But it didn't mean a very great friendship between Dean and the
songwriter. 'It's very difficult to be friendly with Dean Martin,' he
told me shortly before he died. 'He's still a very insecure man.'

In June 1983, Dean decided to try his fortune at the one place he could never say was kind to him – London. True, his record albums and singles always did well in Britain, but his TV shows still flopped every time they were shown – sometimes very late at night, simply because they had been bought as part of some package deal, and the ratings they received were derisory. And behind it all was the memory of thirty years before at the London Palladium. He and Jerry had been the only American top stars – Mickey Rooney apart – to leave the Palladium feeling that they were smaller personalities than when they arrived. Now, on the advice of Mort Viner, Greg Garrison and the ticket box office at the Apollo Victoria Theatre, near London's Victoria Station, he was trying again.

To say he was surprised at the outcome was an understatement. He figured that he was now well enough established not to bother about nerves, and Jeanne was going to accompany him to London, so if nothing else it could be a second honeymoon. When he and she were both asked if they would marry again in London, neither denied the possibility. Jeanne came and she seemed deliriously happy. He was near to it.

Not only had every seat been sold for the week-long run, but the show was being extended by three more days. It was due to open on 9 June – which also happened to be Britain's general election day, but that didn't seem to be nearly as important to the people who welcomed him to London in the kind of greeting he hadn't experienced since the crowds lined up outside New York's Paramount.

In some ways, it was more ecstatic. Two days before the opening, he was celebrating his sixty-sixth birthday – having lunch with the Queen's daughter Princess Anne. The Princess was guest of honour at a lunch given for Dean at the London Hilton Hotel by the Variety Club of Great Britain. For once, he wasn't too afraid of his table manners – except there was one *faux pas*. He sat down before the Princess did.

But he only had one drink, a glass of white wine. As he told a press conference afterwards: 'If I drank as much as they said I did, I would have been dead thirty years ago.'

When the Variety Club's Chief Barker, Jarvis Astaire, read a couple of telegrams, Dean was everybody's idea of the perfect birthday boy. One was from Frank Sinatra that said: 'I WOULD HAVE BEEN THERE FOR YOUR LUNCHEON DEAN BUT I WAS AFRAID YOU'D GET DRUNK AND EMBARRASS ME.'

The other, from Washington, DC, said: 'NANCY AND I OFFER OUR CONGRATULATIONS ON YOUR BIRTHDAY AND THE TRIBUTE YOU ARE RECEIVING FROM THE VARIETY CLUB OF GREAT BRITAIN STOP WE WISH YOU CONTINUED HEALTH AND GOOD FORTUNE HAPPY BIRTHDAY AND GOD BLESS YOU RONALD REAGAN.'

The sixty-sixth birthday party was an opportunity for Dino to demonstrate two distinct strata of his personality: his humour and his laid-back 'don't-let's-give-the-impression-that-I'm-working' character.

Ron Moody, then at the peak of his form so soon after his triumphs playing Fagin in both the stage and movie versions of *Oliver!*, introduced the guest of honour, who throughout gave the impression that he couldn't have been more amazed had he discovered that Jeanne was giving him a surprise party in his living-room. He had nothing prepared, he said, and regretted it. On the other hand, it turned out to be a wonderful demonstration of just how the Martin wit could rise to any occasion, particularly when he was at the end of the toasting line.

As he said in his impromptu speech, he didn't know the tribute was being planned until three months before, so he hadn't had anything prepared for the occasion – enough to raise a laugh in itself. If only someone had told him earlier. 'After listening to these wonderful gentlemen,' he said of Ron Moody and the Chief Barker, producer and businessman Jarvis Astaire, 'I wouldn't give this spot to a leopard . . . I don't have anything to say, nothing at all. I would like to make a toast to the men – may our wives and sweethearts never meet. That's about it.'

Ron Moody said of the guest of honour: 'He loves life. And we love him for it. And in paying tribute to a gentleman who has done all the things we wanted to do and didn't: he still looks better than we do – with hair. I say with respect and affection, Happy Birthday, Dino.'

The lunchers shouted out: 'Don't say anything. Just cut the cake.' Then a chorus demanded: 'Sing! Sing!' He agreed to perform 'That's Amore'. When the pianist asked, 'What key?' 'What key?' he repeated. 'I'm lucky I know the words.'

He may have been having fun, but his face was that of a man much older than his sixty-six years. When he spoke, the voice seemed muffled. When on stage or on television, and he sang numbers like 'Let It Snow', there was little about the performance that sounded like the creator of 'Volare' – or 'That's Amore'.

The lunch was broadcast on British television that night. And succeeded only in a further bombardment of the box office at the Apollo Victoria. The show's reviews were adequate, but the papers were mostly swamped by election news. Mrs Margaret Thatcher returning to Number Ten Downing Street for a second term was more important than Dean Martin returning to a London stage. But for Dean it did the trick. So did the enormous success of a new Dean Martin country album. He had gone to Nashville and been offered thirty new tunes. He selected ten of them. There was no more talk of retiring. 'When you quit working,' he said, 'that's when you start dying.'

He was now sounding very much like the old Dean. He was looking forward to *Cannonball Two* with Burt Reynolds and Sammy Davis Jnr. It would be his fifty-second movie.

When he was asked about modern music, he wasn't terribly complimentary. 'I don't enjoy rock,' he said. 'I don't understand it. Don't want to understand it. That's for the teenagers.' And his fans? 'They're the Deanagers,' he told me.

Dean had few pretensions about himself. 'I'd like people to think of me as a good entertainer. Not fantastic, brilliant, because I'm not.'

He was full of advice for other people – like New York's Mayor Koch whom he thought he could help with his water-pollution problem. By diluting the water with alcohol.

As for himself, he told the press conference: 'People like to see you're a regular guy.'

Dean continued to be a regular guy on the golf course, too, playing in about eight tournaments a year with stars of the links like Arnold Palmer and Jack Nicklaus. But he was still a loner. Musician Walter Scharf, a fellow member of the Riviera Country Club, told me that he never saw Dean practising with anyone. 'Always by himself. He's still an introvert.'

Off the course he kissed and hugged Jeanne. 'We've had a lot of fun living away from each other. Now we've decided to have a lot of fun together again,' he told me. When they left London, they were still very good friends. In mid 1984, that remained their status. But Dean Martin seemed happy enough. People still wanted to know about his relationship with Jerry Lewis, but he was reconciled to the fact that that would follow him till the day his obituary notice appeared in *Variety*. He wasn't going back to Jerry and that was that. But if things worked out right, he would go back to Jeanne.

King Of The Road 19

If Dean once sang 'I'm Sitting on Top of the World', that was precisely his position in the early 1980s.

His voice may not have been what it was, but the odd stage appearance, the occasional TV variety show and the *Dean Martin Celebrity Roast* kept his name before his adoring public. And those records were still achieving amazing sales. His name on a record sleeve – and the photograph that perhaps was just a *few* years old that went with it – was enough to ensure sales that his competitors in the singing business would have envied.

The days of the Rat Pack, or The Clan as some still liked to call it, were basically over – although there were always attempts at reviving the gatherings.

People who imagined that the Rat Pack in private was always a bundle of womanising, drinking riots would be disappointed by Dino's participation in these proceedings. As Jeanne now recalls, the relationship between Dean and Frank was one of two 'scoundrels . . . two Italian rakes'. But there would be a stopping point. 'They would have fun together for just a little while and then Dean would have had it. You see, Dean didn't drink. Frank did.'

The difference would become really apparent when the drink got less and less diluted in Sinatra's bloodstream in the course of an evening. Pretty soon during the proceedings, Frank would get angry and go off looking for a 'broad', while Dean just wanted to get home and go to bed – with Jeanne.

Nevertheless, while there was still a chance to put his golf clubs to use, he was a happy guy.

What really made him happy, however, was living with Jeanne. When he first went back to her, it could have been seen as just another symptom of what she described as 'his silly midlife crisis'. But then, clearly, it seemed to be much more. When they came to London together, the question was not *if* they would marry again, but *when*.

And yet neither had any intention of doing that; though neither did Dean plan to leave the home they shared and go off with someone else. It was the most unusual romantic story in the world of show business. Before long, it became obvious that Dean and Jeanne really were married again – except they were not going to have any new ceremony. There was no need for it. They didn't want any more papers. As far as both were concerned – and certainly as far as Jeanne believed – they were merely carrying on where they had left off. This wasn't a second marriage – it was the same one. The wedding to Kathy could be forgotten as if it had never happened.

When he had Jeanne next to him and his children around, Dean was a happy man indeed. As they grew older, Dean remained proud of his children and happiest when he was with them. Dean Paul was the apple of his eye, but he showed no preferences to any of them. When Gail, the one Martin child who sang for a living, opened for him at The Sands in Las Vegas – taking time off from her own performance at the rival Caesar's Palace – he was the proudest fellow on the block.

On the whole, though, no more than he had before, Dean didn't need people outside of his family. As Gail would say: 'It is an Italian thing.' Having all those children living with him and Jeanne, and considering the amount of time he spent with them at home, you have to realise that this was indeed a family man. As he said: 'Families do come first. I don't have fun all the time. I work and the reason I work is to provide for my family and when I work, it's serious work. And the serious work that I do, I try to have a little fun with it. I must work and I love the work.'

Dean knew that was right. 'We're having a lot of fun,' he said. 'Now the fun is starting with all the children, a different kind of fun than I had with Frank. It's being with the children and grandchildren. I'm older but I don't feel ill. They came for me a couple of times but I said, "I'm not ready yet. Go get somebody else. Don't come near me because I'm not ready to go."' Sadly, there would soon be signs that he was all too ready. But for the moment at least, everything was great. He wasn't about to alter. 'I wouldn't change one thing, one thing. You retire: you die. You've got to get up to something. You can't get out of bed to do nothing. You've got to get up for something. I'll never retire.' That, too, would be a decision soon to be taken out of his hands.

Gail would always say that Dean had had a wonderful life – 'a beautiful life' – and had done all that he had wanted to do. She remembers Jeanne and her father being a 'wonderful couple'. They never talked politics – in fact, they rarely talked at all. Dean really did love to have his family around. He would even agree to go to church, which for a nominally Catholic family was very often the clincher in togetherness. But, Gail remembered, Dean was happy to tell his children that if they felt a little off-colour, he wouldn't at all mind taking them home before the service ended.

Jeanne said she was never worried about competition from other women, either in the shows or in the audience. He was not like Frank Sinatra or the image of the Rat Pack. In her 'heart of hearts' she knew there was a deep love between herself and the man she considered to be her husband. As she told Barbra Paskin: 'Unless you approach it in that way, you are in a great deal of trouble. We were separated for ten years. Then he was back. I was the only girl he ever loved.'

Had they never divorced, they would have celebrated their fortieth wedding anniversary in 1988. But they were not the kind of couple who invited guests along for ruby wedding festivities. Like the idea of actually going to the altar again, it was all unnecessary.

None of that meant that Dean was totally safe from female approaches. One day, Shirley MacLaine came to call. Jeanne remembered thinking that she had come simply for a meeting with Dean, a business meeting. The business on her mind was, though, something very different: she came to declare her love. Dean, his ex-wife remembered, didn't seem interested in an entanglement with her. When he did get involved, it was in an attempt to save her life! Shirley had started to choke. He and Jeanne picked her up, turned her upside-down – a view of Shirley MacLaine not usually seen – while Jeanne pumped her back. It was an embarrassing end to what could have been an embarrassing occasion. Jeanne thought that, had Dean been alone at that moment, he would have ignored Shirley altogether and gone off to watch one of the five television sets he had in the same room.

Despite Dean's reluctance to be sociable – in most people's definition of the term – Jeanne was the best hostess in town and, as far as the guests were concerned, any tune played on the family hi-fi could have been 'The Anniversary Song'.

Certainly, Dean hadn't changed the way he related to people; very few actually fazed him. He wasn't impressed by big entertainers unless he particularly liked them as people. The story was that Milton Berle came to the house one day while Dean was upstairs watching television. He refused to come down to see him.

You didn't ask Dino to a party and expect him to be the life and soul of the event. He was still a man who wouldn't merely 'chat', a fellow to whom the idea of giving an interview was like being told he'd never be granted the privilege of seeing another bottle of whisky, let alone drinking one. Yet he would write long, long letters to Jeanne expressing his love and his feelings. When he was abroad on tour, a six-page letter was a matter of course. It was his best, his only, way of communicating.

Dino left his work behind when he got home, that was clear. But he took that determination to separate work from his private life to an incredible degree. He wouldn't even sing when he was at home. On the rare occasions that he did, it would usually be a tune from an era long before his, like the Twenties.

You didn't disturb him in the studio either. The comedian Shecky Green would say that he was 'like royalty'. You couldn't just go up to his dressing-room and expect to be allowed an audience.

Frank Sinatra would never have been turned away, however. Certainly, Dean and Sinatra were still close friends, and both went on record saying that they were brothers. On the other hand, it was brotherly love of the strange kind that Sinatra had demonstrated so many times before. When his close Rat Pack pal Sammy Davis Jnr had the audacity to sing 'My Way' and add 'Eat Your Heart Out, Frankie', they didn't speak again for six years.

Before long, Dino, too, would receive the Sinatra cold shoulder. Dean himself remained loyal, and in good times he would recall that brotherly affection. 'We keep in touch with each other,' he told me. 'Families are together. We're brothers. We don't like each other, we love each other … he's just a nice, tough guy. Nothing phony about Frank Sinatra. He's my dearest and best friend. And also we would go on the road together, Frank and I. We'd go out on the road, five or six weeks at a time. We'd do funny things with a little bar we brought out.'

But, contrary to most people's ideas of the way Dino lived his life, he couldn't stand the Sinatra lifestyle. The womanising wasn't for Mr Martin. According to Jeanne, he couldn't put up with Sinatra banging on his door while they were on this final tour. All Dino wanted to do was sleep. As Jeanne said: 'He just couldn't put up with Frank's . . . nonsense any more. Frank was hearty and drinking, Sammy was drinking . . . and they're both drinking and smoking and playing all night. Frank never went to bed. He would come pounding on Dean's door. Dean just couldn't take it.'

In turn, there were those who wondered why Sinatra would dare give Deputy Chairman of the Board status to another singer. But Sinatra didn't see Dean as competition; to him Dean was a comedian.

And according to a professional practitioner of that art, Shecky Green, 'Sinatra was not as good a comedian as Dino. Sinatra would have given anything in the world to have what Dean had, but he didn't have that.'

While Jeanne is now happy to stress the differences between Ol' Blue Eyes and the Deputy Chairman, Gail on the other hand will say that her 'Uncle Frank' was 'so dear', a man who would ring up to ask if anyone was 'bothering her'. Her father would have the same relationship with Sinatra's children.

There had been a few blips on the Martin horizon over the past few years. Dean's health could have been better. The arthritis, the ulcer and the creeping effects of emphysema were causing problems.

To his mind, though, the worst thing in his life was the relationship with Dean Paul. Dino Jnr had never understood the reasons for his parents breaking up. Most of all, he hated the thought that his father had married another woman. The fact that Dean and Jeanne were together again wasn't enough. Father and son hardly spoke.

And then on 20 March 1987, everything was put into a terrible new kind of perspective. There was a phone call from the March Air Force Base, where Dean Paul, a member of the Air Force National Guard, was stationed. The call came from Major Steve Mensik of the 163rd Tactical Fighter Group. Jeanne took the phone call. She burst into a flood of tears. When Dean heard her screams, he wept, too – so much that it seemed he would never stop.

Dean Paul had been flying an F4-C Phantom jet, and it had disappeared off the radar. The officer was optimistic. Dean Paul was one of the best pilots they had and he had a considerable amount of survival gear with him. They had sent out search parties, but they couldn't yet find him. Jeanne knew immediately with a mother's instinct that her son was dead. Dean refused to believe it. A psychic was sent out to try to locate him. His body was not found for five days. It was Jeanne's birthday when the news was finally confirmed. The plane had crashed into the side of a mountain; Dean Paul had been killed.

Dean was distraught – and would remain so for the rest of his life.

The family funeral was a ceremony that few who were there could ever forget – the grief of a Hollywood superstar was too great.

The family knew that Sinatra – 'Uncle Frank' to the Martin children – was sitting in a pew behind them. They didn't know until they got home that Jerry had been there, too, although not in the church itself. He hadn't been easy to see, yet there were a few who recognised the figure hiding from any public gaze – and in particular, hiding from journalists who would have dearly loved the colour of a Martin and Lewis reunion. No reporters saw Jerry hiding behind a tree.

No outsiders either were privy to the phone call that Lewis made that night. When I saw Jerry years later at London's Adelphi Theatre, he told me: 'It was the most heart-rending experience of my life. I was trying to offer condolences to my brother and he was showering love on me. It was what I was giving him.' It was a moment that, to Jerry at least, confirmed that they were together again. No one ever talked of their working together again, but if there had been animosity, it was now over.

The whole of Hollywood and California society came to offer their condolences. The Reagans, President Ronnie and Nancy, were among the first on the phone.

Dean, never the most gregarious of people, was now a virtual recluse. His pal Frank Sinatra tried to entice him back to do a new Rat Pack tour – just the two of them and Sammy. It was 1988. The wound of Dean Paul's death was still raw. He still regretted that they hadn't ever made up their quarrel.

A new tour might just bring Dean back to life – not that that was Sinatra's motive in it all. Sinatra said he wanted to boost the income of Sammy Davis Jnr, who was broke.

Sammy Davis Jnr wasn't aware of Sinatra's thinking. 'It was Frank's idea,' he remembered. 'He wanted to do it. He did it for two reasons. First of all, there was the great affection and love we all have for each other. He said, "This will probably be the last time when we'll have such fun. Let's do a whistle-stop in America and let's go while it's still fun to do." I said to my wife, "I hope it's not just pleasant warm talk." Three months later, he had it ready to go. He had his people come in and said, "Here are the dates. Is this all right, Sam?" I said, "Are you joking?" And Frank looked at Dean, and Dean said, "You tell me when to be there."'

But the good will was not enough. The whistle-stop began at the Oakland Coliseum Arena, just across the bay from San Francisco. The place was packed. After just a few days, Dean said he had to go home. He wasn't well. In truth, he couldn't just throw off his grief and pretend to be happy again.

Sinatra, unlike Sammy, couldn't take it. To him, it was crass disloyalty. He didn't speak to Dean for another two years, Greg Garrison told Barbra Paskin. He maintains that Dean knew he wouldn't be able to go through with the show 'five minutes' after he said yes, let alone after the opening in Oakland. Dean's part in the show was taken by Liza Minnelli.

From that moment on, Dean Martin was never seen in public again, unless you knew which restaurant an elderly man would go to, the one where he would sit in a dark corner, sipping an assortment of drinks that were no good for his ulcer – and sometimes with his teeth lying on the table in front of him.

Sometimes he was at the Hamburger Hamlet in Beverly Hills, not a fashionable place, but one where agents and show people would gather for quiet business lunches. They knew better than to disturb him. In the evenings, it would usually be Matteo's, an Italian eatery where he could get a digestible dish of veal, at which he would pick, knowing he was never going to enjoy anything ever again. If people approached him, he would be polite, but most of the diners, aided by the advice of the proprietor and the waiters, knew better than to disturb him.

This was a sad, broken Dean Martin, hardly a shadow of the man who had suffered Jerry Lewis's slapstick, who had been the Rat Pack's wit, or the funster who had happily insulted the great and the good in one of his roasts. He was now the centrepiece of a drama for which he could never possibly have rehearsed.

His emphysema had taken its toll, to the extent that he could hardly breathe. His doctor wanted to operate on his stomach and his kidneys. He refused. It seemed like a death wish. If it was, it was granted on Christmas Day, 1995. He died in Jeanne's arms, telling her that she was the only woman he had ever loved.

That's amore.

Index